BOWING TOWARD BABYLON

BOWING TOWARD BABYLON

*The Nationalistic Subversion
of Christian Worship
in America*

Craig M. Watts

Foreword by Michael Kinnamon

CASCADE Books • Eugene, Oregon

BOWING TOWARD BABYLON
The Nationalistic Subversion of Christian Worship in America

Copyright © 2017 Craig M. Watts. All rights reserved. Except for brief quotations in critical publications or reviews, no part of this book may be reproduced in any manner without prior written permission from the publisher. Write: Permissions, Wipf and Stock Publishers, 199 W. 8th Ave., Suite 3, Eugene, OR 97401.

Cascade Books
An Imprint of Wipf and Stock Publishers
199 W. 8th Ave., Suite 3
Eugene, OR 97401

www.wipfandstock.com

PAPERBACK ISBN: 978-1-4982-9185-9
HARDCOVER ISBN: 978-1-5326-1174-2
EBOOK ISBN: 978-1-5326-1173-5

Cataloguing-in-Publication data:

Watts, Craig M.
Bowing toward Babylon : the nationalistic subversion of Christian worship in America
Eugene, OR: Cascade Books, 2017 | Includes bibliographical references and index.
ISBN 978-1-4982-9185-9 (paperback) | ISBN 978-1-5326-1174-2 (hardcover) | ISBN 978-1-5326-1173-5 (ebook)

1. Nationalism—United States. 2. Nationalism—History—United States. 3. Public worship—Christianity—United States. I. Title.

JC311 .W36 2017 (paperback) | JC311 .W36 2017 (ebook)

Manufactured in the U.S.A.   03/03/17

Contents

Foreword by Michael Kinnamon | vii
Acknowledgments | xi

Introduction | 1
   A "Worship War" Worth Fighting | 3
   Personal Patriotism | 5
   Nationalism and Claims of Loyalty | 7
   Uniting Citizens, Dividing Christians | 9
   An Overview | 11

Chapter 1
Nationalistic Idolatry in the Church of Babylon | 13
   Living in Babylon | 14
   Babylons Beyond Babylon | 16
   Political Idolatry and the People of God | 19
   Adoration Any American Can Offer | 25
   Weak Justifications | 28

Chapter 2
Who God Is, Who We Are | 32
   Confusing Our Identity | 33
   Identity in Community | 36
   True Greatness | 37
   Credible Christian Worship | 40
   Liturgy of Nationalism | 45

Chapter 3
Where Are We Worshiping? | 49
   American Israel | 50
   Chosen Nations | 55

    America As Babylon | 60
    Local Worship | 63

Chapter 4
What Time Is It? Holidays or Holy Days? | 68
    We Are What We Celebrate | 68
    Telling Time in Church | 71
    Wrong Calendar, Wrong Story | 75
    Independence Day: The Myth of "Our" Origin | 77
    Memorial Day: Rightful Remembering? | 80
    Thanksgiving Day: Being Grateful for Us | 84

Chapter 5
Displaying the Banner of Babylon | 88
    How the American Flag Got into the Church | 89
    Enforcing Flag Honor | 96
    Flag Idolatry in the Church Today | 104

Chapter 6
Pledging to Babylon's Banner | 110
    The Pledge's Backstory | 111
    Passion for the Pledge | 118
    Adding God to the Pledge | 124
    Creed Not Pledge | 127

Chapter 7
Singing the Songs of Babylon | 131
    The Place of Singing and the Problem of Nationalism | 133
    Affection and Connection | 134
    Singing for the Wrong Ends | 137
    Are Patriotic "Hymns" Really Hymns? | 140

Chapter 8
Born into a Larger Family and Eating at a Bigger Table Than Babylon | 147
    Dead in the Water | 148
    Baptism and Barriers | 150
    Beyond the Baptized | 154
    Lord's Supper: Rightly Remembering | 158
    Christian Unity and the Eucharistic Imagination | 162
    The Lord's Table and the Messianic Banquet | 165

Bibliography | 169
Index | 177

Foreword

"You can safely assume you've created God in your own image," Anne Lamont has famously written, "when it turns out that God hates all the same people you do." Let me suggest an addition: We can safely assume we have created God in our image when God is said to bless our nation above all others. And we can be sure that the church has become idolatrous when its worship includes celebration of God's special love for us and our country—as if our devotion to the Creator of all that is goes hand in hand with devotion to America.

Bowing Toward Babylon is not simply another book about civil religion. Its author—the pastor-scholar, Craig Watts—takes us beyond by now familiar discussions of the vague deity invoked in American public life to explore what happens when this Americanized god is given a place in the life of the church. This blending of religious devotion to America with the faith of the church he calls "Christian nationalism."

Watts powerfully argues that Christian nationalism undermines the identity of the church by emphasizing our bonds to other Americans rather than our intimate connection to Christians, of whatever nation, in the one body of Christ. It undermines Christian worship by insinuating into it a "competing liturgy," complete with sacred hymns ("God Bless America"), holy days (Memorial Day, the Fourth of July), symbols (the flag in the sanctuary), and a mythic narrative that speaks of America's divine appointment to be a "light to the nations." Christian nationalism undermines the church's mission, especially its mission of reconciliation, by blessing this country's use of violence as righteous, even redemptive. It undermines discipleship—with its radical demand to love neighbors, strangers, enemies—by confusing it with citizenship. It undermines Christian faith by usurping a loyalty that belongs to God alone. As someone has said, "No one can serve two masters."

Church leaders wring their hands when surveys show an increase in the number of "nones"—persons who are indifferent to organized religion. Watts insists that the real threat to Christianity is not so much secularization as idolatry. In Luther's famous phrase, "that to which your heart clings and entrusts itself is really your God." For many Americans, it is the nation that provides security, identity, and meaning—and, thus, deserves their pledge of allegiance. And since many of these people fill their pews, churches frequently acquiesce in this idolatry.

One response to the challenge posed by Christian nationalism, a response historically favored by parts of the Anabaptist wing of the church, is to withdraw from regular engagement with the culture and participation in the state. Watts, by contrast, believes that Christians should live in the tension between withdrawal and assimilation—in the world but not of it. The New Testament scholar, Robin Scroggs, has offered this summary of Paul's theology: "The church is not prohibited from entering the world; the world is excluded from entering the church."[1] Watts would agree.

Where do we learn to live in this tension? Where are we shaped as people who give thanks for a divine love that recognizes no national boundaries? Where do we gain an understanding of the world that is often at odds with the dominant culture? The answer set forth in *Bowing Toward Babylon* is clear and compelling: in worship. As a result, much of this book deals with worship as the place where Christians discover and express their true identity—and where Christian nationalism poses its biggest threat. "There are," Watts contends, "'worship wars' that are worth fighting"—because the identity of the church and the faith it confesses are at stake.

This focus on what the church is in worship, rather than on what it does, means that this is not a book about specific political issues. Watts's argument is more fundamental: if worship is doing its job of glorifying God, then it is inherently "political." To praise the living God is to challenge the human-centeredness of every political system. To confess belief in God as creator, redeemer, and sustainer of life is to undercut the pretensions of every dominant ideology. To live in obedience to God, made known in Jesus Christ, relativizes the assumptions of every nation—including the USA.

---

1. Scroggs, *Paul for a New Day* (Philadelphia: Fortress, 1977), 52.

Foreword

As this suggests, the danger of Christian nationalism is not peculiar to the United States. The title of the book reminds us that "Babylon" has become a biblically grounded metaphor for any empire or nation which insists that it is a proper object of ultimate devotion. The Roman Empire, according to the great missionary leader Lesslie Newbigin, easily embraced various cults aimed at promoting the personal salvation of their members. What it couldn't tolerate was a community called into existence by the good news that God, incarnate in Jesus Christ, is Lord of all creation, the One to whom alone ultimate allegiance is due.[2] "Hitler had no objections to Christians who confessed that Jesus is Lord," Arthur Cochrane points out in his excellent study of the German Church Struggle, "but he was enraged when they confessed that Jesus is Lord and Hitler is not."[3] It is instructive to recall that, in the Third Reich, the majority of German Protestants identified themselves with the "German Christian Movement" whose leaders expressed a desire to be "an evangelical Church that is rooted in our nationhood" and repudiated "the spirit of a Christian world-citizenship."[4] Old newsreels show altars draped with the swastika and nationalistic songs being sung in worship.

Even as I write this, however, I can hear Watts protesting that Rome and Hitler's Germany are misleading comparisons. America's idolatry is more subtle, and, thus, harder to recognize and oppose. "What's wrong with thanking God for the blessing of being an American?" "Haven't people around the world seen this as the Promised Land, the guarantor of freedom?" "Hasn't God made this nation powerful to be a bulwark against evil?" In the absence of idolatry as blatant as that practiced under Nazism, Christians in America are like the frog in ever-heating water, unable or unwilling to name our sometimes distorted worship for what it is.

A book such as this is bound to raise numerous questions, even from those sympathetic to its basic argument. For example, does Watts's strong emphasis on Christian identity, as part of the transnational body of Christ, exacerbate the risk of pitting Christianity against other religions? He maintains that Christian solidarity need not, should not, undermine the willingness of Christians to stand with others on behalf of the poor or

2. Newbigin, *The Other Side of 1984* (Geneva: World Council of Churches, 1983), 32ff.

3. Cochrane, *The Church's Confession Under Hitler* (Philadelphia: Westminster, 1962), 211.

4. This is from the "Guiding Principles of the Faith Movement of German Christians," published in 1932. See ibid., 222–23

the environment or peace; but a stress on global Christian identity will still strike some as, ironically, provincial. Can it be that nations have a necessary, religiously significant role in promoting harmony among diverse faith communities?

This book may also raise questions for those who underscore the importance of local particularity in the worship life of the church. Watts affirms that the church shows its catholicity by its capacity to adapt to diverse contexts. Worship in India or Ecuador will and should differ from that in Kenya or the United States. But Watts insists that not all accommodations to local culture are equally legitimate, and this is not always an easy line to draw. Being a Christian in America can be positive; being an American Christian can be problematic.

I have known Craig Watts for many years as a friend and colleague in the ministry of our denomination, the Christian Church (Disciples of Christ). His prophetic witness, especially with regard to the church's peacemaking vocation, has long been highly valued by many Disciples. My hope is that this book will introduce his work to a far wider audience.

One role of a prophet, writes Walter Brueggemann, is to remind the people that they are in exile. It is easy to become so comfortable in Babylon that we forget our true home. And so a second role of a prophet—as we see, for example, in the later chapters of Isaiah—is to provide images of who we are and where we truly belong.[5] Watts reminds Christians in America that our home is the church where God, and God alone, is worshipped. Such a reminder is, indeed, prophetic.

Michael Kinnamon
Former General Secretary,
National Council of the Churches of Christ in the USA

---

5. See, e.g., Brueggemann, *The Prophetic Imagination* (Philadelphia: Fortress, 1978).

Acknowledgments

Numerous experiences, conversations, and readings contributed to the formation of this book. It is impossible for me to acknowledge all who helped in one fashion or another to form the thinking that went into these pages.

I am particularly thankful to the congregation of Royal Palm Christian Church for offering me their encouragement and the time necessary to bring this book into completion. I am tremendously grateful for the privilege of serving such a warm, faithful, and supportive community of faith. Further, without the help of the church's office staff, Alice Price and Alyssa Sikora, this book would not have gotten into publishable form. I deeply appreciate their proofreading that caught numerous blunders I made and their work in the tedious formatting of the manuscript.

Several people took the time to read parts or all of the manuscript as I was working on it. I thank Dr. Joe Jones, former president of Phillips University and past dean of Christian Theological Seminary; Jan Linn, former professor of the practice of ministry at Lexington Theological Seminary; Bob Cornwall, minister at Central Woodward Christian Church and editor of *Sharing the Practice* for the Academy of Parish Clergy; Justin Bronson Barringer, editor of *A Faith Not Worth Fighting For*; Jim Higginbotham, associate professor of pastoral care at Earlham School of Religion; and Michael Kinnamon, the immediate past general secretary of the National Council of Churches, who also graciously wrote the foreword to this volume.

Finally, I thank my wife Cindi for putting up with me while I was preoccupied reading and writing as this book took form.

Introduction

With a bundle of enthusiasm and a small, tightly packed moving van a recently ordained graduate of divinity school headed off to serve his first church. Like most young ministers, he was passionate about his calling and eager to prove himself. During the months that followed he worked hard to serve the people of his congregation and to encourage them in the good work they shared in the name of God. Not surprisingly there were minor bumps along the way. But largely the people of the church seemed to appreciate his ministry.

About a year after he had arrived, while he was away at a workshop, the worship committee met. This was not unusual, given that the church had a history of strong lay leadership. It so happened that on that particular year July 4th fell on a Sunday. The members of the worship committee thought it appropriate to plan a special Independence Day service. The service would be complete with patriotic music, a color guard to process into the sanctuary with the American flag, and the congregation would recite the Pledge of Allegiance. For them this was an unremarkable thing to do. Of course the committee assumed the minister would preach an appropriately uplifting patriotic sermon in keeping with the occasion.

When the pastor got back to the church and heard a report about the plans of the worship committee, it was like someone clobbered him in the stomach. He felt a deep ache because he knew, contrary to their assumptions, he couldn't lead the kind of service they intended.

With a sense of responsibility weighing down upon him, he called the worship committee to reconvene. Before the meeting the young minister spent much time in prayer, reflection, and study. He hoped to explain as clearly and persuasively as possible why he could not lead the service they planned for Independence Day. As he sat with the committee members, he spoke of his love for them and his hesitancy to go against their desires. But he continued by explaining that the worship service they wanted him to lead was at odds with what he believed about the nature of the church, the purpose of worship, and the character of God.

He spoke of the need to celebrate the God revealed in Christ and to come together in worship united in a faith that transcends the often hostile differences that plague humankind. The young minister questioned the practice of using worship to honor one nation and its flag to the neglect of others. He reminded them that the commitment that rightfully draws them together in worship is the commitment shared by Christians throughout the world, not narrower loyalties incidental to faith. As to pledging allegiance to the flag, he insisted that especially in a service of worship God should be the exclusive focus of allegiance.

The responses of those on the worship committee ranged from surprise tinged with pity to full-fledged outrage. "Oh, you seem to be misunderstanding what we want to do. We are simply giving thanks to God for America and all the blessings we have here," said one woman. Another offered, "Surely, we all agree that this is a Christian country. We praise God when we honor the country." One of the men, face red with anger, thundered, "Clearly, you don't love America! You insult the troops who fought and died for the flag! Where do you get off saying we shouldn't sing patriotic songs and pledge allegiance to the flag in worship?! What kind of pastor are you? You sound like some crazy Jehovah's Witness!"

In the end, the committee agreed to back off from some of their ideas for the Fourth of July worship service. But word of the minister's refusal to lead the patriotic service quickly spread throughout the congregation. At the next church board meeting there was a motion made to fire him. Though the vote failed—barely—he knew that his ministry with that congregation was over.

Prior to the painful board meeting, however, the young pastor had gone to the regional executive minister of his denomination for counsel. Paternalistically smiling, the older man told him, "This shouldn't be a difficult problem to resolve. Just go back to the worship committee of your church and tell them now that you've thought about the matter some more you realize it was just a misunderstanding on your part. Go ahead and lead the service." The young minister was dismayed at the advice. It appeared he was being urged to save his ministry with that congregation by abdicating

Introduction

his obligation to lead the church theologically toward greater integrity of worship. The young minister was gravely disappointed at what he saw as the theologically impoverished pragmatism of the regional executive.

The weeks that followed were filled with self-castigation on the part of the young cleric. He continually agonized over the conflict. Though he had tried his best to be responsible and faithful in his work and though he attempted to be sensitive and tactful in dealing with the matter, still he couldn't help but feel that he had miserably failed. Repeatedly he asked himself, "What did I do wrong?"

A "WORSHIP WAR" WORTH FIGHTING

In fact the turmoil resulting from his refusal to support the Independence Day worship service was most definitely *not* a result of what he had done wrong. It was the consequence of what he had done *right*. Resisting a deeply entrenched practice that uses worship for something at odds with the rightful focus and purpose of Christian worship is not an aspect of ministry that should be ignored by those given the responsibility to lead congregations.

The events of the above story actually happened. I know because this is my story. As the often quoted words of minister/novelist Frederick Buechner put it, "All theology, like all fiction, is at its heart autobiography."[1] But while the above is my story, it is not mine alone. It is the story of many ministers who have tried to faithfully urge the church to be itself, particularly in worship, and not to use the liturgy to promote values and loyalties unworthy of the whole *ecclesia*, that body called to be in the world but not of it. To resist worship practices congregations value is not an easy task. Nevertheless, what takes place in worship should always be for the glory of God and the clear witness of the church. There are "worship wars" that are worth fighting. Opposing nationalism in church is among them.

Those in the early church in the Roman Empire, the superpower of the age, saw themselves as a people living in exile from their spiritual home. They viewed Rome as the Babylon of their time, a place of captivity, and they understood the need to be wary of the political/military power of the empire and resistant to the spirituality that lent support to Rome.

Many churches in America lack a similar awareness. This is evidenced by the expressions of nationalism have been given an important place in the worship of many of them. Though this may not happen on a weekly

---

1. Buechner, *The Sacred Journey*, 1.

basis, it does occur with regularity. The legitimacy of bestowing upon the United States special honor when the congregation gathers for praise near national holidays seems self-evident to many Christians in this country. Consequently, the ministers or members who dare to oppose singing patriotic songs in worship, displaying the flag, giving special recognition to members of the military, or reciting the Pledge of Allegiance often find themselves at the center of very uncomfortable controversy.

Not surprisingly, many ministers have concluded that it is not worth the trouble to take a stand against nationalism in worship. Though a considerable number of clergy personally are opposed to it, many of them end up saying, "You have to choose your battles." And they choose not to engage in this particular one because, after all, it is an emotional minefield. They may say to themselves, "Are the stakes genuinely high enough to justify the possible conflict and pain?"

Of course some ministers—and very many lay leaders—don't see a problem at all with displaying the American flag and celebrating national holidays with songs, gestures, and symbols. In fact they would insist that it is a good thing to do. So rather than discourage the practice, some ministers actually encourage it. Some seek to make the nationalistic displays as elaborate as possible. There are churches that not only focus on the flag, recite the pledge, and sing nation-centered songs, they also spotlight members of each branch of the armed services and even manage to have some sort of fireworks display. They broadly publicize these special "patriotic" services in hope of drawing in people who otherwise might not attend church. They imagine the nation-saturated service is not only an acceptable approach to worship but a suitable form of evangelism.

"What is wrong with such practices?" some may ask. "What harm is there in them?" But better questions would be, "What do the symbols, rituals, and songs of the nation say about the character of God? What do they suggest about the purpose of worship? What do they say about the identity and loyalty of the church? What does it say about the unity of the church that transcends race, class, or nationality? How welcoming is nation-celebrating worship to people who love Jesus but have no attachment to America either because they are disenchanted with the nation or because they are not American? Does worship that celebrates the nation and national identity foster genuine discipleship or does it refashion discipleship into a religious version of pride-filled citizenship?"

Introduction

The legitimacy of nationalistic practices in the life of the church should not go unquestioned. It is not at all clear how the church is being true to itself or faithful in its representation of God when it gathers to "celebrate America." How can the church be true to its God-given character, message, and mission when it emphasizes national identity and pride in the context of worship? Christian worship has but one overriding purpose: to praise the God revealed in Jesus Christ.

PERSONAL PATRIOTISM

It needs to be made clear that personal patriotism is not the issue being discussed in this book nor is what is written here intended to disparage patriotism in itself. There are forms of patriotism that are natural and not at all incompatible with the faithful devotion of *the individual Christian.*

New Testament scholar and master preacher Fred Craddock tells of being on an airplane flight during which he visited with a woman who was returning from vacation. She had been to Switzerland, that small country of breathtaking mountainous beauty. She spoke of her marvelous experience and the delightful things she had seen. But time had come for her to return home to western Oklahoma. Once the terrain of the state became visible, she peered out the window intently and lovingly, craning her neck as she gazed down. Though she had just left a land that was fabulously lovelier than her own state by just about any measure, it lacked one attraction Oklahoma had for this woman: the beauty of home.[2]

That perception of beauty is the essence of patriotism at its best. This sort of patriotism doesn't swagger with pride or in any way seek to diminish anyone else's home. It is noncompetitive. If it moves us to say, "My land is the greatest in the world," this claim is not to be mistaken for an objective truth. It is a truth of the heart, much like saying, "My mom is the best in the world." It is not as though I have actually had an opportunity to compare her qualities to those of every other mother.

The statement is a hyperbole of love. There is no serious expectation that others will agree or even should agree. Healthy patriotism is like that. It grows from being nurtured by a particular people in a particular place. Intimate familiarity and the affection that accompanies it are at the heart of patriotism. It is the simple attachment to and love for home. I can find nothing in it that conflicts with Christian devotion.

2. Craddock, *Craddock Stories*, 84f.

Bowing Toward Babylon

The sentiment of this kind of patriotism is expressed in the words of the hymn, "A Song of Peace," often sung to "Finlandia" by Jean Sibelius. The words of the first two verses are by Lloyd Stone, the third by Georgia Harkness.

> This is my song, O God of all the nations,
> a song of peace for lands afar and mine;
> this is my home, the country where my heart is;
> here are my hopes, my dreams, my holy shrine:
> but other hearts in other lands are beating
> with hopes and dreams as true and high as mine.
>
> My country's skies are bluer than the ocean,
> and sunlight beams on cloverleaf and pine;
> but other lands have sunlight too, and clover,
> and skies are everywhere as blue as mine:
> O hear my song, thou God of all the nations,
> a song of peace for their land and for mine.
>
> This is my song, O God of all the nations,
> a prayer that peace transcends in every place;
> and yet I pray for my beloved country—
> the reassurance of continued grace:
> Lord, help us find our oneness in the Savior,
> in spite of differences of age and race.

While patriotism can be affirmed, this does not mean it is never problematic. When a national crisis occurs, natural feelings can become exaggerated and misshapen. An excessive focus on pursuing the interests of "one's own" can turn a natural love into a pathological passion. This is certainly true of patriotism. "It is characteristic of patriotism in war time that the group personality becomes temporarily deranged," wrote Louis Snyder in his study *The Meaning of Nationalism*. "Every social institution is brought into line and every objection to national policy is stifled as anathema . . . no longer a benign love of county, patriotism becomes epidemic."[3]

Certainly it is a natural desire on the part of a Christian citizen to want the blessings of God upon his or her nation. It is equally appropriate for the individual Christian to want God to bless his or her family. I certainly pray that God bless the Watts family. But my personal focus is not a legitimate theme for *the church at worship*. The church must maintain a view to the blessings of much more than my family or even the country I love as home.

---

3. Snyder, *The Meaning of Nationalism*, 158.

Introduction

The nature of the church is not defined by either my family identity or my nationality. And Christian worship must not offer special attention and praise to either my family or to the nation where I reside that is not equally offered on behalf of others. The Christian message is that "God so loved *the world* that he sent his only begotten son" (John 3:16).

NATIONALISM AND CLAIMS OF LOYALTY

Certainly not all forms of nationalism are identical. There is a vast difference between the nationalism promoted by Gandhi from that advanced by Hitler. Experts in the area differ in their definitions of nationalism. They don't uniformly agree whether it is a strictly modern phenomenon or not. For the purposes of this book it is unnecessary to settle many of the questions about nationalism pondered by academics. However, a working definition is needed. An adequate one is found in the study of religious nationalism by Atalia Omar and Jason A. Springs who suggest that "nationalism refers to a group identity defined in terms of political, ethnic, or cultural identities, associations and attachments."[4] This identity is conveyed through stories that inspire pride and essentially say, "This is who we are." An identity is forged as a shared narrative is internalized and group rituals are enacted by members of the nation.

One of the great theologians of the twentieth century, Emil Brunner, wrote, "The State and the Church are the two sole forms of community which make a claim to universal loyalty; therefore the relation between Church and State is the greatest subject in the history of the West."[5] Not every nation has a state but nationalism is the strongest when a nation of people and state, a territory with a sovereign government, are joined. As we engage in faithful worship we are formed into a certain kind people: a people capable of saying "Yes!" to God and "No!" to all other powers that seek our sweeping loyalty and honor. But malformation is inevitable when worship incorporates expressions of honor for the nation. At that point, what Brunner called "two forms of community" blend into one. Consequently, loyalty to God loses its distinctiveness and the "Yes!" to God becomes difficult to separate from the "Yes!" demanded by the nation.

Philosophers Robert McKim and Jeff McMahan insist, "It is a defining feature of nationalism that it demands that the members of a nation be

---

4. Omar and Springs, *Religious Nationalism*, 3.
5. Brunner, *The Divine Imperative*, 552.

loyal both to the nation and to one another, which involves their giving priority to the national interests or each other's interests over the interests of others . . . [because] they are related to one another in ways that give them special moral reasons to favor one another."[6] Notice, nationalism doesn't entail merely loyalty but a *preferential* loyalty that *supersedes* all other attachments. Other attachments are permissible, but they must remain subservient.

Religion can either help or hinder the aims of nationalism. Knowing this, leaders of nations emphasize the importance of the identity of people as citizens with the goal that this role "will take precedence over a host of other poles of identity, such as family, class, gender, even (*perhaps especially*) religion."[7] This is most effectively done when religious leaders help by blurring the distinction between religious identity and national identity. The loyalty to nation is presented as inseparable from loyalty to God and therefore a sacred duty that should not be compromised by any other obligation. Christian nationalism is the project that adopts and alters the Christian story found in the Bible so it can be used to underwrite a particular version of American national identity and lend support to national unity. Religious faith can be put in the service of nationalism only if God and nation are never seen as alternatives between which a choice must be made.

This merging of religious faith and nationalism shows up in a variety of ways. I pulled up at a stop light behind a car with a bumper sticker that speaks to the problem found in so many churches. The sticker contained the often repeated words, "Jesus Saves" . . . but with a twist. On this particular red, white, and blue bumper sticker the two words were pushed together and the three center letters were enlarged and emboldened: JesUSAves. Who saves? Is it Jesus or the United States of America? Two thoughts, two affirmations, two commitments were so blended as to become indistinguishable. It was not clear where the one ends and the other starts because they are part of each other. Celebrating America in the minds of many Christians in the United States is a perfectly appropriate aspect of worshiping and serving God because the distinction of the one from the other has been largely lost.

The ill-defined god found in the Declaration of Independence, the national motto, the Pledge of Allegiance, and other such official sources is a god largely empty of content other than that of having a special interest

---

6. McKim and McMahan, "Introduction," 5.
7. Taylor, "Nationalism and Modernity," 40. Emphasis mine.

in America. This god-talk has frequently been categorized as civil religion. It is often employed by politicians. But the vagueness of this civil religious god gains content by being blended with the faith of the church. So when the Americanized god is given a place in the life of the church, rather than calling this civil religion, I believe it would best be labeled Christian nationalism. The religious dimension of America is given a structure for articulation and affirmation by being institutionalized in the worship and life of the church. Unlike civil religion, it does not exists "alongside of and rather clearly differentiated from the churches," to use the words of sociologist Robert Bellah's classic essay on the subject, but as an aspect of the conviction and practice of many American churches.[8]

All great geopolitical powers have a religious dimension, some more overt than others. America is not exceptional in this matter. Still there have been sustained efforts on the part of both preachers and politicians throughout the nation's history to associate God with America. In one way or another, numerous voices have asserted that the special providential work of God has been playing out in the founding and subsequent history of the nation. Because of this, the God worshiped in many churches has become notably American. Consequently, celebrating America in worship seems natural.

UNITING CITIZENS, DIVIDING CHRISTIANS

Religion has the potential both to unite and to divide peoples. When successfully recruited to serve the nationalistic project, religion can be a powerful tool to deepen national identity, pride, and unity. However, for that to happen the bonds that bind together people of different nations to the same faith must be loosened. Nationalistic worship helps loosen the global unity of Christians. The unity that is reinforced in worship that blends God and nation is the unity of citizens with one another at the expense of the unity of Christians to each other as members of the body of Christ. Nationalism in worship undercuts the unity of Christians given in Jesus Christ through the Holy Spirit.

On the other hand, the unity that faith produces is a challenge to every other form of unity. "Christianity produces divisions within the state body precisely because it has pretensions to be a body which transcends state

---

8. Bellah, "Civil Religion in America," 21.

boundaries," William T. Cavanaugh has noted.[9] When worship is used as a means of support for the unity of the nation ecumenical unity is damaged.

The church comes together in worship as an eschatological gathering. We gather in anticipation of the kingdom of God fully come. Walls of hostility fall. The divisions and distinctions that put peoples at odds with one another give way for the sake of the oneness in Christ brought about through the Holy Spirit. Christ is the center and none other. Members of the church gather as citizens of heaven in anticipation of the worship with the angelic host, who declare in praise, "You are worthy . . . for you were slaughtered and by your blood you ransomed for God saints from every tribe and language and people and nation" (Rev 5:9). The church cannot faithfully echo the spirit and truth of the clear-sighted angelic worshipers while paying honor or offering special recognition to a single tribe, language, people, or nation.

The church created by the power of the Spirit transcends the lines, barriers, and boundaries defined by powers and loyalties not of God. If these are not transcended but reinforced in worship then Christians will not learn to see to whom they are joined by faith. To cite Cavanaugh once again, "To recognize Christ in our brothers and sisters in other lands, the El Salvadors, Panamas, and Iraqs of the contemporary scene, is to begin to break the idolatry of the state, and to make visible the Body of Christ in the world."[10] So long as the church uses its worship to strengthen national identity and foster national unity the church will fail to be itself, a sign of the God-promised future.

Congregations in many churches throughout America sing the words of this hymn:

> In Christ there is no East or West,
> In Him no South or North;
> But one great fellowship of love
> Throughout the whole wide earth.

Yet even as the words resound in the sanctuaries, the worshipers face an America flag very presence of which serves to limit the impact and qualify the meaning of the lyrics. The flag and use of songs and rituals of nationalistic significance remind the congregations of affections and loyalties that in practice supersede Christian solidarity. As Michael L. Budde has written,

---

9. Cavanaugh, *Theopolitical Imagination*, 38–39.
10. Ibid., 90.

Introduction

"The fallout from the existing subordination of Christianity to other allegiances, loyalties, and identities is widespread, scandalous, and lethal.... How can Christians be good news in the world, in what ways can they presume to be a foretaste of the peaceful recuperation of creation promised by God, when their slaughter of one another is so routine as to be beneath comment?"[11] The way we worship impacts the way we stand together or fall apart as Christians in times of war and shapes our willingness or unwillingness to kill Christians in nations in conflict with America.

This emphasis upon Christian identity and unity does not imply that we have no obligation of love toward others. In no way does Christian solidarity lessen the necessity to stand with the poor and oppressed where ever and whoever they are. Nor does it suggest that Christians should not join in pragmatic and provisional unity with others for good causes. Rather the peaceable unity based on a common identity in Christ is for the good of the world we have been called to serve and it is a foretaste of the unity of all humankind.

AN OVERVIEW

In the following chapters I will explore in more detail why honoring and celebrating America in worship in incompatible with faithfully worshiping the God revealed in Jesus Christ. Rather than being innocuous practices, expressions of nationalism in worship constitute manifestations of misdirected worship that lead to the spiritual malformation of worshipers. In titling this book *Bowing Toward Babylon*, I draw from an important biblical archetype. Babylon is the name of an ancient power than conquered the southern kingdom of Israel in the sixth century BC and took into captivity a large portion of the citizenship where they faced the challenge of resisting assimilation in an idolatrous foreign land while endeavoring to live in a positive and product way.

But Babylon is also a metaphor for any empire or nation where people of God live and endure the temptation to succumb to the gods adored and embrace practices celebrated by the majority that are at odds with the truth as manifested in Christ. Christians in the first century recognized that the Roman Empire was the Babylon in which they were required to live (1 Pet 1:1, 5–13; Rev 14:8, 17:5, 18:10). Babylons have continued to arise in post-biblical times, each with distinctive seductions and peculiar

11. Budde, *The Borders of Baptism*, 4–5.

forms of idolatry but all of them ultimately drawing glory away from God while directing it to itself, the chief object of idolatry. This is not always done through the efforts of government leaders. Often it is accomplished through the willing aid of religious leaders and institutions.

The Babylon in the title of this book is obviously America. Every Babylon is unique, despite similarities they share. In the following chapters I will examine why so many Christians and churches in the United States enthusiastically incorporate American nationalism into worship, thereby *bowing toward Babylon*. And I will discuss why it needs to stop. As Peter Leithart observed, "American churches have too long discipled Christians in Americanism, and that makes Christian involvement in American polity far smoother than it ought to be. Churches must repent of our Americanism and begin to cultivate martyrs."[12]

In the first chapter I further explore the background of Babylon as a metaphor and archetype applicable to America. I also discuss the idolatry embedded in every Babylon-like culture by looking at some characteristics of idolatry in the Bible. From there I will explore the idolatrous nature of nationalism. This will be followed by two chapters—asking where we are and who we are—that offer an overview of the religious interpretations of America and American identity that have provided churches with justifications for bringing nationalism into worship.

Subsequent chapters will look at specific expressions of nationalism that are frequently found in churches in the United States, pointing out ways these are at odds with faithful Christian worship. These expressions of nationalism include the celebration of nationalistic holidays in worship, singing patriotic hymns and songs, displaying the American flag, and reciting the Pledge of Allegiance to the Flag. The final chapter will focus on baptism and what we variously call the Lord's Supper, or Holy Communion, or the Eucharist. These rituals are, I believe, the least marred by nationalism. I will argue that in baptism we are born into a holy nation and granted a heavenly citizenship that must always be distinguished from and never collapsed into American citizenship. Further, I'll discuss why participation at the Lord's Table demands that nationalism be eliminated from the church so there can be an unimpeded invitation to all who desire to sup with Jesus in sacred unity and thankful praise as we look forward to the gathering of people from every nation at Messianic Banquet in the kingdom of God.

---

12. Leithart, *Between Babel and Beast*, xiii.

CHAPTER I

Nationalistic Idolatry in the Church of Babylon

Only those deeply shaped by the practice of bowing toward Babylon could have designed or displayed the image I faced as I walked into the sanctuary of a church. On the wall was a large banner. At first glance it appeared to be a depiction of the Angus Dei, the Lamb of God. But this was a revised version. It had been strikingly altered and Americanized. Instead of the Lamb having a foreleg hooked around a cross or around a staff with a banner of a cross, as would be seen in the traditional iconography, this Lamb bore a flag pole from which hung an *American flag*.

I was appalled.

Can anyone honestly imagine that removing the cross and giving the Lamb of God a national flag does not deeply distort the meaning of the familiar and beloved symbol? Can anyone seriously claim that the message conveyed by the nationalized Lamb of God is the same message communicated for centuries by the traditional symbol? The banner glorified the American flag and idolized the nation at the expense of the centuries-old meaning of the Christian symbol.

The traditional Angus Dei symbol conveys a conviction universally confessed by the church. The Lamb of God is the Christ who was sacrificed. The cross or banner of the cross borne by the Lamb is a symbol of resurrection triumph, the victory of the crucified one over sin and death. This is not the message conveyed by the co-opted, nationalized Lamb. At the very least, an American flag-toting Lamb of God demonstrates a special attachment toward the US. The purpose of the Lamb is intertwined with the purpose of America.

The apparent message of the banner was that honor due to the Lamb is likewise due to America. In fact the universal relevance and cosmic significance of the Lamb of God who takes away the sin of the world is lost in the Americanized version. The Savior and the savior-nation become one. If the Lord who is the Lamb flies the flag, how can followers of Jesus do otherwise than worship what our Lord himself elevates?

Christian worship has but one overriding purpose: to praise the God revealed in Jesus Christ. How can worship foster the praise of the God revealed in Christ when it promotes nationalism?

In responding to the nationalistic idolatry that was infecting the Church in Germany in the 1930s, the Barmen Declaration stated, "We reject the false doctrine, as though the church could and would have to acknowledge as a source of its proclamation, apart from and besides this one Word of God, still other events and powers, figures and truths, as God's revelation."[1] Babylon in its various forms and through its many friends—often religious leaders—continues to tempt the church to bend its knee and lift up praise in the name of God to that which is not God.

LIVING IN BABYLON

The Babylonian Empire is long gone, falling to the Persians over 500 years before the birth of Jesus. The city of Babylon, once a great center of power and culture, was largely abandoned by the time the church was born. But the memory of Babylon and its impact on the chosen people of Israel had not faded in either the synagogue or the church at the time the New Testament was being written. The spiritual significance of Babylon remained relevant in the first century and I believe it continues to be so today. Whenever the name of God or trapping of religion are used by the state or church to imprint national identity, reinforce national unity, foster national loyalty, or mask national failings the interests of Babylon are being served.

The Babylonians had conquered Judah, the southern kingdom of Israel, in 587 BC. Their forces entered the walls of Jerusalem and completely destroyed the city. The most skilled and educated of the population were

---

1. Cochrane, *The Mystery of Peace*, 163.

taken as captives to Babylon. In Babylon the people of God faced the tremendous challenge of clinging to their own identity and loyalty to God in the midst of a culture that was superior their own by all obvious external measures. To live in Babylon faithfully the people were required to resist assimilation. They were not to lose their identity by being absorbed into Babylonian society. They were not to share in Babylonian pride. Above all, they needed to distance themselves from the Babylonian idolatry that played a prominent role in the culture. This was not an easy thing to do because the idolatrous religion of Babylon united the population and it was believed to confer divine blessings, confirming the greatness of the empire over against other nations.

This idolatrous worship lent support to the king and cemented loyalty to him and to the empire that was an extension of him. In the ancient Near East the king was regarded as the earthly representative of the gods. As such the image of the god was a symbol of the legitimacy of the earthly king.[2] Idolatrous worship served both religious and political ends. Indeed, those ends were nearly impossible to separate because where the one ended and other started was not easy to discern. For this reason the people of Israel needed to vigilantly remember their status as outsiders who must remain loyal to their God. Though they found the affluence, knowledge, and power of Babylon impressive, they were not to give their hearts to Babylon. Even in captivity they were to remember the God who led them from slavery in Egypt. They were to continue being a distinctive people who were defined by their experiences with God.

The imperative to resist the nation-building and unifying role of religion in Babylon can be seen in the stories found in the book of Daniel. In order to serve the nation official religion had to exclude competing loyalties and objects of adoration. At the same time, the authority of the king was undergirded and enhanced through worship. Transcendent power and earthly power were aligned. To oppose one was to oppose the other. To support the one was to support the other. The captive people of Israel were in the difficult situation of seeking to live at peace in a foreign land while withholding themselves from the spirituality that permeated that place.

But, on the other hand, they were not to simply distance themselves from the society in which they found themselves. They were called upon to care about the well-being of Babylon. The prophet Jeremiah told them to trust and obey God while continuing to be a distinctive, set-apart people.

2. Hendel, "Social Origins of the Aniconic Tradition," 381.

He instructed the displaced, captive people of Israel to live among the Babylonians peacefully, productively, prayerfully. They were to accept responsibility for its society, albeit in a limited way.

Like the other inhabitants of the ancient superpower nation they were to have families, raise their children and work fruitfully for good. God's word to them through the prophet Jeremiah was this: "Seek the welfare of the city where I have sent you into exile, and pray to the LORD on its behalf, for in its welfare you will find your welfare" (Jer 29:27). The captive people were to live in Babylon but they were to refuse to allow the spirit of Babylon to live in them.

BABYLONS BEYOND BABYLON

Long after the remnant returned to their homeland, Babylon continued to be an archetype and metaphor for the great geopolitical powers that trampled over the land of the Jews. The Babylonian threat was successively embodied in the power of the Persians, Greeks, and Romans. In each case the people of Israel had a God-given responsibility to cling to their faith and the peculiar identity bestowed on them by their relationship with the God who led them from slavery, gave them the law, and made promises to them.

Early Christians, too, saw Babylon as a metaphor important for understanding their own experience. The ancient leaders viewed the church as a community of exiles. Out of their experience living in the mightiest empire of their time, they could speak of themselves as the "church in Babylon" (1 Pet 1:1, 5:13). The glorious and sprawling power of Rome whose tentacles touched all the world they knew was Babylon for them. As the power, wealth, and culture of Babylon lured and enticed the captive Israelites, so, too did Rome seductively draw the church away from its true love (Rev 2:4). Only if faithful people continually resisted the glories of Babylon/Rome could the church glorify the Lord with integrity.

No one was exempt from being marked in some fashion by Babylon/Rome. The empire defined the world, subduing resistance, demanding submission, always claiming that in so doing it was creating peace, even when it left behind devastation. Yet this great power was tolerant, after a fashion. But there were definite limits. Babylon/Rome was filled with gods. So long as a religion did not subvert loyalty to the empire, it was allowed to practice without harassment. Only if adherents disdained the imperial theology and viewed the authority and power it undergirded as secondary to their cult would the tolerance of Babylon/Rome to be stretched to the breaking point. This presented a problem for the church as it proclaimed, "Jesus is Lord!" clearly repudiating Caesar as Lord.

Babylon, in whatever form she takes, is sustained by blood. In the book of Revelation the personification of Babylon/Rome—"the Great Whore"—is depicted as holding a golden cup in a posture of blessing but the cup is filled with "abominations and unclean things" (Rev 17:4). We are told she was drunk with "the blood of the saints and with the blood of the witnesses of Jesus" (17:6) but also more generally "of all who have been slaughtered on earth" (Reve 18:24). New Testament scholars Wes Howard-Brook and Anthony Gwyther have observed, "This image of Babylon holding the cup of blood is a powerful indictment of empire. It indicates, in a graphic and lurid way, that empire blesses its people with the blood of its victims and those loyal to empire share in this cup as a sign of their acceptance of empire's control over their lives . . . . Empire routinely engages in killing, yet claims to be a benign actor in the world."[3]

Those aligned with Babylon/Rome justified the violence the empire inflicted upon the world, claiming it was necessary in order to accomplish the most noble of ends. An ancient writer who heaped praise on Caesar Augustus declared him to be a product of divine action, "as a benefaction to all humanity" and announced him to be "a savior who put an end to war and brought order to all things."[4] But this peace came at the edge of a bloody sword that was turned toward every people who stood in the way of the interests of Rome. Writing somewhat later, as Rome was subduing portions of Britain toward the end of the first century, Tacitus speaks of a local chieftain who described the Romans as "robbers of the world" who "make a desolation and they call it peace."[5] It is unlikely the Romans would have been capable of seeing themselves in such terms.

It is the nature of every incarnation of Babylon—including America—to see itself as a gift to the world rather than to recognize that it is frequently a threat to the world. And it is beyond question that the actions of every Babylon, every great world power, have been beneficial to some. The Revelation of John presents the business leaders as avid devotees to Babylon/Rome because they had been substantial beneficiaries (Rev 12:1–2, 4,

3. Howard-Brook and Gwyther, *Unveiling Empire*, 170.
4. Kraybill, *Apocalypse and Allegiance*, 57.
5. Tacitus, *Agricola*, 81.

11–13). The violence of the "Great Whore" furthered their interests even as they in turn promoted her glory. Imperial power insured the world would be safe for those who sought to roam far and wide to reap great profits.

Describing an event that occurred around 14 AD at Puteoli, a Roman port, the ancient writer Suetonius penned these words: "As [Caesar Augustus] sailed by the gulf of Puteoli, it happened that from an Alexandrian ship which had just arrived there, the passengers and crew, clad in white, robed with garlands, and burning incense, lavished upon him good wishes and the highest praise, saying that it was through him they sailed the seas, and through him they enjoyed their liberty and their fortunes."[6] Elements of worship found in this incident—the white robes, crown, and incense—can be seen in the worship described in the book of Revelation.

However, the praise bestowed on Caesar as the representative of the power of Babylon/Rome was misdirected adoration and, therefore, idolatrous. In striking contrast to this praise stands the worship offered to the Lamb of God,

> You are worthy . . .
> For you were slaughtered and by
> Your blood you ransomed for God
> Saints from every tribe and language
> And people and nation;
> You have made them to be a
> Kingdom and priests serving our God
> And they will reign on earth (Rev 6:9–10).

The power of Babylon/Rome, regardless of the good it may have accomplished along the way, created countless victims. Whatever peace it may have produced was preceded by death and destruction. The benefits won were not for everyone but for those who had pledged their loyalty to the empire above all. On the other hand, the Lamb who is worthy to be praised became a victim of Babylon/Rome for the sake of those "from every tribe and language and people and nation." Yet despite his victimization, he conquered without causing destruction and "made peace by the blood of the cross" (Eph 2:13–18).

And as the earlier versions of Babylon were sustained by idolatry, I find it hard to deny that the power and privileged place of America/Babylon is validated by expressions of idolatry as well.

---

6. Suetonius, *Augustus*, 98, cited in Kraybill, *Apocalypse and Allegiance*, 144f.

POLITICAL IDOLATRY AND THE PEOPLE OF GOD

Idolatry is often not easy to identify because it is not presented for what it is. It is no surprise if my suggestion that devotion to America can become a *religious* devotion of a sort that is actually an alternative to single-hearted dedication to the God revealed in Christ is quickly greeted with vigorous denials by those most affected by it. This is an understandable, perhaps necessary, response. Even the most casual of Christians know that idolatry is regarded in Scripture as spiritually repugnant. Consequently, concealment, denial, and self-deception about the *spiritual power* over hearts and minds are essential for the devotees of American Christian nationalism.

The prophet Jeremiah said, "The heart is deceitful above all things; who can know it?" (Jer 17:9). Idolatry is not readily recognized and confessed by those immersed in it. Because few behaviors and practices are intrinsically idolatrous, idolatry is easy to deny, both to self and others. Donald Evans observed that "the more powerful the idolatry the less likely it is that the idolater will recognize it in himself."[7] We humans are masters of self-denial.

Every once in a while a public figure will unintentionally bring into the light of day the idolatrous conviction that usually remains just below the surface of nationalism. For instance, New York City Mayor Rudy Giuliani—who was very prominent on the national stage after the 9/11 terrorist attacks—declared in his last mayoral speech that was given in St. Paul's Chapel, "All that matters is that you embrace America and understand its ideals and what it's about . . . . Because we're like a religion really."[8] He then qualified that claim by adding, "A secular religion." But in fact the Americanism he advocated—especially when blended with Christianity—is a deeply *spiritual* religion. But this is the spirituality of Babylon.

The First Commandment calls for exclusive devotion to the God who led the people of Israel from slavery in Egypt and insists that God's people have "no other gods before me." Gerhard Von Rad held, "The prohibition on serving any other divine power is . . . *the* commandment *par excellence* for Israel . . . there is nothing like it in the whole history of religion. It influenced to a greater or lesser degree all vital utterances on the faith of

---

7. Evans, *Struggle and Fulfilment*, 62.
8. "Text of Mayor Giuliani's Farewell Address," *The New York Times*, December 27, 2001, http://www.nytimes.com/2001/12/27/nyregion/27CND-GIUL-TEXT.html.

Yahweh."⁹ That small phrase "before me," is open to a number of possible meanings: "in front of me," "alongside me," "instead of me," "at odds with me." No one meaning need be accepted to the neglect of the others. The importance of the phrase is found in its denial of a place to any other god for those who are people of the Lord. This command doesn't just forbid exchanging the Lord for another god. It also stands against the possibility of accepting another object of adoration alongside the Lord. For those who would genuinely be faithful to God multiple claims of loyalty are to be shunned.

The Second Commandment elaborates on the First by forbidding idolatrous images. The attempt to represent God in the form of anything in all creation is forbidden because God alone decides how to manifest the divine presence and to be accessible to humankind. By prohibiting the creation of images of the divine, the identification of the king with God was undercut. No visual depiction of God was available that could be used to suggest the king's divine sanction.¹⁰ Any representation made by human hands is bound to be misleading, drawing attention away from the unseen God who alone deserves our deepest devotion. But idols are not so much statues before which to bow as they are centers of identity, unity, and security in whom to trust.

Clearly, an idol is never simply a material object nor is it lacking in power. The power of the idol is real but it is human, not divine. It neither honors God nor ennobles people. To the contrary, idolatry undermines human value: "They followed worthless idols and became worthless" (2 Kgs 17:15). An idol may undergird the interests of some but it does so at the expense of others. The problem of idolatry is fundamentally a *problem of the heart*. So Moses warned the people of Israel, "But if your heart turns away and you will not obey, but are drawn away and worship other gods and serve them, I declare to you today that you shall surely perish" (Deut 30:17–18a).

Similarly, we read that Joshua insisted, "Now therefore, put away the foreign gods which are in you midst, and incline your hearts to the LORD, the God of Israel" (Josh 24:23). Later the prophet Jeremiah spoke of Judah's idolatry as being a sin "written down with an iron stylus; with a diamond point . . . upon the table of the heart" (Jer 17:2). Many centuries later Martin Luther faithfully echoed these biblical voices by writing that "the trust and

9. Rad, *Deuteronomy*, 56.
10. Hendel, "Social Origins of the Aniconic Tradition."

faith of the heart alone make both God and idol.... That to which your heart clings and entrusts itself is, I say, your God."[11]

Surely, idolatry can be a problem in the life of an individual as he or she displaces God with some passion or loyalty that comes to dominate his or her life. Greed, the quest for sexual pleasure, even devotion to one's own family can take on idolatrous dimensions. But it is not some private passion that has crossed over an unseen threshold that receives the most sustained attention in Scripture. Rather what most preoccupied biblical writers was idolatry as a communal commitment with political consequences. Indeed, "the very notion of idolatry was originally defined in Israel's tradition as being in opposition to the God of the covenant and his public veneration."[12]

Chilean theologian Pablo Richard noted that idolatry has two different sources of meaning.[13] One is associated with the worship of false gods, gods other than Yahweh. The second pertains to Yahwehist idols. In this latter case, the idols were not the gods of other peoples that competed with the Lord, gods set over against the God of Israel. Rather those who advocated for Yahwehist idolatry did so in the name of the God of Israel. The idols were not presented as other gods but as the very God who liberated them from Egyptian bondage. Thus God was not explicitly replaced but refashioned in order to serve the interests of those in leadership and to meet the misguided desires of the people.

Repeatedly we find within Scripture the power of idolatry linked with the political power of rulers and nations. Walter Brueggemann maintained that the First Commandment—as well as the two that follow it—asserts "the oddity of God," who is not a tool for human ends and will not be enlisted and exploited for social and political projects. Rather God is to be obeyed and glorified as one who "as a critical principle deabsolutizes every other claimant to alternate power."[14] Any attempt to contain, manage, or administer God for any purpose reflects a failure to take the First Commandment seriously.

The issue of idolatry does not arise only—or even primarily—when there is a threat that God will be replaced by another. Idolatry more often shows its face when a power that offers security, identity, and meaning entices God's people and seeks a place alongside God. Multiple claims on our

11. Luther, "The Large Catechism," 365.
12. Wannenwetsch, "The Desire of Desire," 318.
13. Richard et al., "Biblical Theology in Confrontation with Idols," 5f.
14. Brueggemann, *Theology of the Old Testament*, 184.

loyalty rather than the express rejection of the one for the other is where idolatry is more likely to assert itself. It is for this reason we so often find that in Scripture idolatry is not simply a religious issue but a political concern as well. Walter Harrelson offered a contemporary re-statement of the First Commandment: "Do not have more than a single ultimate allegiance."

In keeping with this re-statement, he suggested the Second Commandment be understood in this way: "Do not give ultimate loyalty to any earthly reality."[15] Other gods that promise meaning and solicit loyalty, exert influence and compel obedience can be merged into monotheism. This happens without any explicit claim that devotion to the God revealed through Israel and in Jesus Christ is being *replaced* by another god. Idolatry can subtly subvert the fidelity and praise that God alone deserves by attaching another god to the Lord and blending the two together, as religious nationalism does.

The thirty-second chapter of Exodus deals with struggles of the newly liberated people in the midst of a transition from bondage to a fresh beginning in the promised land. In the absence of Moses, the one who had been called by God to be their leader, the people were beset with doubt and insecurity. They approached Aaron: "Come, make us gods to go ahead of us. As for this fellow Moses, who brought us up from Egypt, we do not know what has become of him" (Exod 32:1). From the gold Aaron told the people to bring to him a calf to worship was made. However, the golden calf was not presented as another god but as the God that led them to freedom.

"This is your god, O Israel, which brought you up out of Egypt," announced Aaron (Exodus 32:4). The golden calf was fashioned as a seat for and symbol of the presence of God. When the people were called together to worship, Aaron said it was to be "a festival to the LORD," not a festival to a competing god (Exod 32:5). Nevertheless, what took place was not true worship. The idolatry of the Israelites was an offense against the transcendent God who had liberated them. Their action was a rejection of their own role as a people of this God. They wanted God to be one who was readily responsive to their immediate needs and available to their manipulation.

The issue of idolatry here is not a matter of the invisibility of God versus the visibility and materiality of the idol. Visible material intermediaries were sometimes used as a means through which God self-revealed. An obvious example is the burning bush. However, in Exodus 32 it is the transcendence of God that is at the stake. The people replaced Yahweh and

---

15. Harrelson, *The Ten Commandments and Human Rights*, 192.

the divinely authorized leadership of Moses with a *version* of the God who led them from Egypt, one who would be more in harmony with their own desires. They did not straightforwardly reject the Lord for another but they reconceived God in a way that was more compatible with their own chosen ends. This version would console and comfort them and be readily available to them rather than discomfort them with the demand to trust in the face of the uncertainties of freedom. The golden calf was formed in order to lead them, not to where God would have them go, but where they wanted to go.

The problem of Yahwehist idolatry surfaces again in 1 Kings 12:26–33. Solomon's son, Rehoboam, upon his father's death took the throne of Israel and ruled oppressively. In response the tribes of the north seceded and Jeroboam became their king. Complicating this political division was a religious dilemma. Because the northern tribes had to go south to Jerusalem to worship the Lord, Jeroboam was anxious over the possibility that his people would end up recognizing Rehoboam as their king. He devised a religious solution to the problem of political power. He had two golden calves made, putting one in Bethel and the other in Dan. He then ordered that two sanctuaries be constructed as alternatives to the one in Jerusalem. Jeroboam announced to the Israelites, "It is too much trouble for you to go up to Jerusalem; here are your gods that brought you up from Egypt" (1 Kgs 12:28).

Again, we find the sin of idolatry is against the transcendence of God. Yahweh who led the people from bondage is reconceived and manipulated in order to resolve a political problem. Yahweh is not directly denied or replaced in any straightforward manner but is refashioned and used by the king in order to insure the loyalty of his subjects. Rather than confronting and opposing the tyranny of Rehoboam, the people allowed their worship to be reshaped in a manner that served Jeroboam's ends. Yahweh, therefore, is represented as a politically accommodating deity. Monotheism is not outright rejected but Yahweh is revisioned so as to be more politically useful. The divine revelation is distorted to serve interests that are not those of God. This Yahwehist idolatry is more subtle but no less significant than turning to "other gods."

And so, idolatry can take place without there being a straightforward rejection of the God revealed through the history of Israel and in Jesus Christ. Other commitments and deeply felt attachments are linked with and made a supplement to faith in God. Multiple claims of devotion undermine unqualified allegiance to the one creator and redeemer.

Every secondary claim on us must be judged by the God who alone deserves our ultimate loyalty and our whole-hearted obedience. "The First Commandment is a tacit acknowledgment that there are always claims of an ultimate sort confronting us, 'other gods,'" writes Hebrew Bible scholar Patrick Miller.[16] The issue of idolatry does not arise only when the possibility of replacing God with another is presented. Idolatry more often shows its face when a power that offers security, identity, and meaning entices us and seeks a place alongside God.

All this sheds light on the dynamic at play when Jesus was tempted in the wilderness and he was offered by Satan the power of the kingdoms. As the intellectual mystic Simone Weil insightfully claimed, "The real sin of idolatry is always committed on behalf of something similar to the State. It was this sin that the devil wanted Christ to commit when he offered him the kingdoms of this world. Christ refused."[17] But many who claim to be his followers have not refused. Neither have they acknowledged that it is idolatry in which they are engaged. While saying with Jesus, "It is written, 'You shall worship the LORD your God, and him only shall you serve,'" in practice it seems that many in America serve a god who is on exceptionally good terms with the United States.

French sociologist and theologian Jacques Ellul suggested some practical questions that can help unveil idols in our time. Among these are, "In whom, or in what, do we place our trust/our faith?" "Where do we look for security and happiness?" "Whom do we expect to guarantee our future?" "What do we think can guard our liberty?" and "Whom do we believe on the subject of truth?"[18] For many people in the United States, both inside the church and outside of it, each of these questions can be answered by saying, "America." It is this particular "work of human hands" (Ps 115:4–8) that captures the hearts and inspires sacrificial offerings of many.

Sociologists Carolyn Marvin and David W. Ingle pointed out that the highest object of loyalty among Americans—and any other people—is revealed by that for which they are willing to make the greatest sacrifices. By that measure it is difficult to argue that God attracts greater loyalty than the nation. No religious group is allowed to compel sacrifice as the nation does.

16. Miller, *The Ten Commandments*, 27.
17. Weil, *The Simone Weil Reader*, 199.
18. Ellul, "Modern Idolatry," 242.

As they observed, "Questions about sacrifice and death are profoundly religious. It is their presence that makes nationalism the most powerful religion in American culture."[19] The right to demand life-or-death sacrifice, to kill and be killed, is at the heart of nationalism. To invest in the nation the exclusive right to extract such sacrifice is indicative of the religious supremacy of the nation. "The first principle of every religious system is that only the deity may kill. . . . By this standard, nationalism is unquestionably the most powerful religion in the United States."[20] The nation motivates and calls for a degree of sacrifice that churches in America cannot hope to expect and very well may envy. But any possible envy is mitigated when nationalism is incorporated into the faith and worship of the church.

ADORATION ANY AMERICAN CAN OFFER

Worship is identifiably Christian precisely because it is shaped by the sacred story of the God of Israel as revealed to us in Jesus Christ. In sermons, hymns, prayers, confessions, offerings, and communion this God is named, praised, and appealed to as worship re-presents the story that defines what it means to be Christian. Faith in this God is essential in order for Christian worship to be engaged in with integrity. A person without faith may be present as an observer while worship occurs or may "go through the motions" without having any particular conviction or may have a degree of aesthetic appreciation for the liturgy. But to genuinely participate in Christian worship, faith in the God found in the peculiar story to which Scripture bears witness is essential.

There are countless activities we can engage in alongside those who don't share our faith and do so with wholehearted participation. I can go fishing with my friend who is an atheist and we can equally delight in catching a six-pound bass. I can sit with my Jewish friends and share a pizza as we talk about the latest exploits of our respective children. I can run in a 5K race with an assortment of "spiritual-but-not-religious" folks, fully sharing the experience with them. No specific faith commitment is required for any of these activities. Clearly none of these activities have any role in corporate worship.

We might ask, are there any behaviors that rightly belong in worship that can be done with equal sincerity and integrity by people who have no

19. Marvin and Ingle, *Blood Sacrifice and the Nation*, 9–10.
20. Ibid, 10.

faith at all in the God revealed in Christ? If the answer is yes, then we need to ask upon what basis particular actions are included in worship. If the answer is no, then we need to ask ourselves what we are doing when we include such things in worship. I am convinced that the answer is a decisive no. Songs and gestures that can be done in a conscientious way by people without faith have no legitimate place in Christian worship. They do not proclaim the truth of God in Christ. They do not engender the affections or foster spiritual formation of the sort that deepens attachment to Jesus as Lord. Their presence inevitably undercuts the character of worship. Such behaviors draw our attention to and reinforce our affection for something other than the God revealed in Christ.

No doubt there are things that take place when the church is gathered for worship that are not in themselves worship. Often at some point in a service announcements of various sorts are made. Occasionally, people involved in some aspect of the church's local ministry will be recognized and given public appreciation. Some churches designate certain worship services to specially recognize those in the local community who do or have done special tasks, such as teachers, police officers, fire fighters, or veterans. Usually such services are attempts—theologically very dubious, in my view—to use worship as a means of evangelism to draw in people who otherwise would not attend a service of worship. Yet in most instances such activities are more or less distinct from worship proper. They are appended to worship and serve a purpose distinct from offering reverent praise.

Nationalistic expressions in worship do in fact offer reverent praise. But these are manifestations of praise that can be conscientiously offered without regard to faith in the God revealed in Christ. Reciting the Pledge of Allegiance or singing "My Country, 'Tis of Thee" can be done sincerely without a hint of Christian faith. Any American can participate. Yet at the same time nationalistic expressions in worship exclude the vast majority of Christians since most are not Americans. Such worship displays adoration that any American can sincerely engage in but that all Christians cannot do with equal sincerity. This is not because they lack a relationship with God in Christ but because they lack an adoring relationship with America.

Certainly theological differences about the meaning of aspects of their faith sometimes hinder Christians being fully united in worship. But nationalistic worship separates Christians from one another by including elements utterly extraneous to Christianity itself, elements that express and strengthen a love and loyalty that is not essential to a relationship with God.

Rather than faith in the God revealed in Jesus Christ, faith in America is what is essential to the performance of these actions.

The problematic nature of this is seen more clearly by those who are not American. They are the ones quicker to recognize—as many Christians in the US do not—that the deliberate presence of expressions of national identity and pride in the corporate life of the church turns Christians who are not American into outsiders, visitors with second-class status. Non-American Christians are quick to see that patriotic worship depicts the God of all the universe as a tribal deity who bestows special attention on the nation that flies the stars and stripes. Without a devotion to America, wholehearted participation in worship is not possible in many churches in the US.

A young couple began worshiping with the congregation I serve who previously had been attending the wife's home congregation, a conservative Presbyterian megachurch. The minister of that congregation—now deceased—had a national reputation for his persistent and forceful advocacy of "Christian America." The young woman was deeply dedicated and served for a period as a missionary for her church. While involved in an Eastern European mission, she met and married an equally dedicated man, a Baptist minister from Bulgaria. Upon returning home with her new husband, they began to worship in the congregation where she had been raised. He was shocked at what he found. As his shock registered with her, she saw what was taking place in the worship life of that church through new eyes, those of her non-American Christian husband.

She was forced to acknowledge something she was not previously been able to perceive. In her words: "Some worship services of that church are more patriotic rallies than real worship to God." When worship is infiltrated by patriotism or nationalism, the door of the church ends up being opened wider to those who share in the love of country. But the door is unintentionally closed to those who do not share that particular love, regardless of their depth of Christian faith. Someone—like a Bulgarian minister for instance—is likely to feel shut out and unable to recognize the God who is worshiped in such a service as the God who "so loved the world that he sent his only begotten Son" (John 3:16).

The peculiar story presented in Christian worship becomes considerably less peculiar when it is linked to the American story. It is not quite so challenging and humbling. Humility is not easy to come by while singing, "I'm proud to be an American!" Perhaps gratitude will be inspired in a patriotism-infused worship service, but there is a danger that it will be the sort of gratitude Jesus spoke disapprovingly of when he told of two men going to the temple to pray and one uttered "God, I thank you that I am not like other people . . ." (Luke 18:11). In genuine Christian worship we acknowledge that we *are* like other people. Not great. Not good. Instead we confess we are broken, needy, undeserving, and utterly dependent on one who can do for us what we can never do for ourselves. We acknowledge that the God who loves us is certainly not concerned for us alone.

Those who want the church to pledge allegiance to the flag and to sing about or celebrate America co-opt Christian worship and turn it into something it should not be. Nationalistic worship tells a story. But it is not the same story that runs through the Bible. It is not the story of what God sacrificially did to liberate the weak, to forgive the unworthy, to reach out to despised outsiders of all sorts, reshaping them into a new community, breaking down barriers in order to create "one new humanity" (Eph 2:15). Rather it is a story of the sacrifices, the triumphs, the ideals, and the greatness of the American people who are "blessed" by God. It's a story of human worthiness, national worthiness. "America is great because America is good," said a president of the United States, paraphrasing Tocqueville. This is *not* the Christian story. Instead it is a tale that evokes idolatrous adoration befitting Babylon.

Even when national sins are publicly acknowledged in nationalistically infused worship, these tend to be sins that have nothing to do with the "heart" of what "America is really about." Rather they are presented as aberrations on the periphery that do not fundamentally detract from the greatness of the nation. We are assured that dark flaws—greed, racism, institutionalized violence, etc.—are not woven into the very fabric of what makes America *America*. This perspective permeates the worship services of thousands of churches on the weekends of Memorial Day, Independence Day, Thanksgiving Day, and other such occasions. This conviction runs counter to the story that rightfully shapes Christian worship. When it is incorporated into worship it changes the focus and the concerns rightly expressed as people of faith gather to offer thanks and praise to God.

WEAK JUSTIFICATIONS

While it is easy enough to find supporters for importing celebratory expressions of American identity and pride into the life and worship of the church, finding a coherent and well-reasoned justification of the practice is another matter entirely. Little serious theological reflection seems to have gone into it. When pressed, supporters point to several passages of Scripture that in fact offer little warrant for their practice. Chief among these are Jesus' words, "Render unto Caesar the things which are Caesar's and unto God the things that are God's" (Mark 12:17, Luke 20:25, Matt 22:15-22 KJV). These words are construed to suggest that Jesus supported giving the nation—"Caesar" being its representative—recognition alongside God. But Jesus was not speaking about a division of powers, or two kingdoms, or dual loyalties. Other than the coin bearing the image of the emperor and minted by his authority, Jesus did not grant one thing to Caesar.

There is no seed in Jesus' words from which to grow a doctrine of church and state relations, much less to justify nationalism in worship. Jesus frustrated the attempt of his opponents to entrap him with their question about whether taxes to Rome should be paid. He did not answer them on their own terms. Jesus told the people to give to Caesar only what Caesar himself created for his own purpose, currency with his face on it. In no way did the Lord suggest Caesar—or the government he represented—had a right to all he claimed. The "Caesars" through the ages have had a hunger for power, for honor, and for allegiance that has proven to be insatiable. Jesus in no way suggested that his followers should allow Caesar to determine what rightfully counts as "things that are Caesar's." Our Lord's emphasis was unmistakable in the words, "Give . . . to God the things that are God's" (vs. 21). But many Christian leaders readily offer up to "Caesar" what is God's alone and do so even in the church's worship.

Those eager to biblically justify nationalism in worship occasionally appeal to three other texts that likewise have no relevance to Christian worship.

> "Let every person be subject to the governing authorities; for there is no authority except from God, and those authorities that exist have been instituted by God. . . . Pay to all what is due them—taxes to whom taxes are due, revenue to whom revenue is due, respect to whom respect is due, honor to whom honor is due" (Rom 13:1, 7).

> "First of all, then, I urge that supplications, prayers, intercessions, and thanksgivings be made for everyone, for kings and all who are in high positions, so that we may lead a quiet and peaceable life in all godliness and dignity" (1 Tim 2:1-2).

"Honor everyone. Love the family of believers. Fear God. Honor the emperor" (1 Pet 2:17).

These passages call for submission to governing authorities, appropriate honor to leaders, and the need to pray for those in authority. They don't, however, lend support to the practice of celebrating in worship one nation, people, or government to the exclusion of others. Rather prayers and thanksgivings are to be offered for "everyone" and honor is likewise to be bestowed upon "everyone." The purpose of the prayers and honor specifically on behalf of those in positions of authority is not to celebrate a nation or to reinforce identification with it or allegiance to it. Rather these actions are done for a decidedly un-nationalistic purpose: "so that we may lead a quiet and peaceable life in all godliness and dignity."

Ministers and church leaders who speak up in support of the practice of incorporating patriotic or nationalistic elements in worship appear to be driven more by misshapen affection coupled with misguided notions of "pastoral care" than anything that might resemble genuine biblical or theological rationale. The advocates of the practice of nationalistic Christianity for the most part seem to be theologically tongue-tied.

Dr. Kenneth Hart, director of the sacred music program at Southern Methodist University, offered an explanation for the inclusion in worship of sounds and symbols of the nation. "Many churches allowed the patriotic worship as an act of pastoral care." He held, "It's a ministry. It's an emotional response to what people need and feel . . . . The church needs to respond in as many different ways as it is able."[21] But is questionable whether it is a true calling of the church to sooth troubled emotions and meet self-defined needs "in as many different ways as it is able."

Doesn't the Bible in fact teach in a host of ways that people don't even know what they truly need, much less how to genuinely satisfy those needs? Didn't Eve see that the fruit of the forbidden tree was beautiful and good for food? Didn't she *need* the fruit? Didn't the Israelites at the foot of Mount Sinai *need* a source of security that could come from a god that was more visible, tangible, and malleable, perhaps something like a golden calf? Many so called "needs" arise from failure to faithfully rely upon the true God. Many needs should not be met but challenged and redirected.

Needs should, indeed, be addressed, but this is appropriately done by drawing from resources of faith, not nationalistic forms of comfort and

---

21. Susan Hogan, "Churches Replace Cross with Flag," *The Dallas Morning News*, November 1, 2001, http://amarillo.com/stories/110101/bel_crosswith.shtml.

reassurance. It is not any part of the church's purpose to fortify various forms of tribalistic affections, pride, or security. When the church uncritically allows its ministry and worship to be determined largely by how people understand its own needs, the church is bound to go wrong. Instead of serving people as an extension of serving God, the church will simply serve the people on their own terms and God will be left behind, or worse, be remade in our image.

The church does not come to understand what people need merely by being told by them. Needs must be discerned in light of the revelation of God in Christ. The church has a distinctive ministry and that ministry is not simply to do what others can do apart from Christ. The church has an abundance of resources it can employ to meet the most varied and profound needs people experience. However, there is a no hint in the message of Christ and the apostles that lends support to the idea that the stimulation of patriotic feelings, or the reinforcement of nationalistic identity or loyalty, should be any part of the church's calling. Only by resisting the push to respond to what people "need and feel" can real needs be met in ways that reflect theological integrity. For many people it may be emotionally satisfying to hold devotion to America and worship of God in close proximity. But this is a "need" worth not meeting.

Acting in the name of "pastoral care" and "meeting needs" is not sufficient reasons to include songs, symbols, or rituals that have nothing to do with the acts and character of God or who we are as a people of faith. Christian worship is not based on what people—formed by the values and idolatrous influences of Babylon—think they need but on what God in Christ has revealed. Faithful worship re-presents the story of the God who calls a people to be in the world but not of the world, a people guided by God, not in step with the nation within which it lives. In faithful worship we come together as a people celebrating a divine love that recognizes no borders or boundaries and who "understand that God shows no partiality, but in every nation anyone who fears him and does what is right is acceptable to him" (Acts 10:34–35).

Chapter 2

Who God Is, Who We Are

"Know thyself!" is a maxim that extends back at least to the time of Plato.

How successful are we at accomplishing that task? If you were asked to say who you are in one word, what would you say? That question was put to a number of people in a national survey some years ago. A wide range of answers were given. There was no single dominant answer. That should be no surprise given the virtually endless number of possibilities. Only a handful of words garnered even one percent of the respondents. Nevertheless, the single word of self-description that was offered far more often than any other was the word "American."

Given that over 80 percent of the US population claims to be Christian, I was surprised that a much larger percent of the respondents didn't identify themselves with the word "Christian" or some other label that reflected something about their faith identity. But it was a word designating national identity that rose to the top among those who took the survey. No doubt there are a host of reasons that could be given to account for the prominence of the word *American* among the respondents. At the very least this suggests the power of nationality to define us.

Not only is this the case for individual self-understanding, it is equally true for the corporate self-understanding of the church. Does the church in the United States know itself? Is it the church in America or the church *of* America, the church *of* Babylon? A central question throughout this book is, "Who are we at worship?" As I have already noted, Christians in America often fail to see how disturbing some aspects of US church practices look to Christians who have not been shaped by American nationalism.

We cannot in any simple way separate who we are from how we worship. What is presented in worship is what our hearts are taught to adore. This adoration forms our perceptions and dispositions and forges our loyalties. It gives us a pre-reflective means of making judgments. It inclines us to cherish some things and be wary of others even before our capacity to reason enters the picture. Who we are in our deepest being and how we worship are fundamentally connected. As Kendra G. Holtz and Matthew T. Mathews have observed, "We want to know to whom or what we belong, because knowing that tells us who and what we are. The question is never whether we will offer our ultimate loyalty to some powerful ultimate in worship, but rather to what or whom we will offer such loyalty and worship."[1]

CONFUSING OUR IDENTITY

"'American' is a new kind of human being," writes theologian Peter J. Leithart.[2] Most people born and raised in the United States embrace this claim with pride. It grows out of a belief in American exceptionalism. Optimistic, inventive, determined, independent, acquisitive, confident in the rightness of every national cause, trustful of violent solutions to difficult conflicts, and certain that all right-thinking people throughout the rest of the world want to be like Americans. Christians in America also generally embody this "new kind of human being." Consequently, many have a difficult time distinguishing faith in God from faith in America.

Swiss theologian Lukas Vischer walked into a Roman Catholic church in New York City several years ago and found a large poster on the wall that he considered somewhat troubling. Many Christians from the United States could have walked in beside him and looked upon the same poster and find nothing that they did not already assume as true and good. The poster read:

Pray For Our Military — A Prayer For America

---

1. Hotz and Mathews, *Shaping the Christian Life*, 7.
2. Leithart, *Between Babel and Beast*, 57.

> We are America,
> the heart of a world seeking
> freedom and peace. We are
> the East and the West, the North and the South—
> one people embracing many. We are a legacy
> of courage with a destiny of greatness.
> We are history and prophecy, liberty and home,
> refuge and vision.
> So we lift up our light as a beacon of hope
> with this prayer to our God and Creator:
> Make us a people who care and comfort.
> Let us reach out a welcoming hand
> to the homeless, the helpless, the hungry.
> Let us fulfill God's great plan
> for our land. Let our gift to the nations be love.[3]

At first glance this text may appear benign, even commendable. No doubt there are some positive qualities and noble aspirations affirmed to the statement. Yet there are also unsettling aspects, especially considering that the poster was found in a church. The problem starts with the first line: "We are America . . . ." There would be no issue if these words were posted in a court house, post office, or public school. But the statement was put on display in a church. We who are church are *not* America. Certainly, some of us are Americans. But this identity is neither essential nor universal as we live and worship as church. When we gather as church who we are is determined by faith alone.

For the gathered community of faith being American does not truthfully define us or distinguish us from others. It does not determine our mission or shape our purpose. It does not establish our boundaries or delineate our destiny. To post a statement in a church that begins by saying, "We are America . . ." is misleading at best and expression of heresy at worst. It says to every non-native worshiper, "You are not one of us." The opening assertion on the large poster superimposes the identity of America on the church so that the one cannot be clearly distinguished from the other.

Furthermore, the statement on the poster makes bloated, self-aggrandizing claims for America. It is "the heart of a world seeking freedom and peace." There are many beyond the borders of the nation—and some within them—who would take serious exception at such an assertion. Instead of humbly presenting America as one part of a greater whole, the statement

---

3. Cited in Muller-Fahrenholz, *America's Battle for God*, 20–21.

makes it sound very much like America virtually is the world, or at least the part that makes life worth living. The rest of the world is benighted and hopeless, "so we lift up our light as a beacon of hope." America is the Messiah.

The words on the poster form a nationalist litany of audacious self-importance and pride; "We are history and prophecy, liberty and home, refuge and vision." Absent is any modesty or self-judgment. Implicit in the statement is a revelation that is not part of the legitimate legacy of the church: "Let us fulfill God's great plan for our land." What is this plan and how do we know it is of God? Certainly not by anything revealed to the church in Christ. The statement repeatedly refers to "we" and "us," inviting those in the church to collapse their Christian identity into American identity. The fact is that this invitation has been offered and accepted so many times in so very many ways, extending even into the worship practices of countless churches.

The values and convictions about who "we" are proclaimed on that poster find their way into the worship of churches throughout the United States.

Not long ago a friend went to a Sunday morning worship service that had been well advertised in the newspaper. It was billed as a "patriotic celebration." Indeed, it was one. Not only were "Stars and Stripes Forever," "Battle Hymn of the Republic," and "The Star Spangled Banner" sung, but as representatives of various branches of the armed forces were presented, one by one, the theme song for each branch was played and an announcer offered a few words of praise for the service done by that particular branch. At the conclusion of this ceremony several soldiers impressively rappelled from the ceiling of this very large church building. At a climactic point in the service an enormous American flag, which reached from one side of the chancel to the other, was majestically raised. There were even fireworks. Yes, Scripture was referenced, prayers were offered, and a sermon was delivered. The title of the sermon was, "Who Stole Our Nation?" As my friend told me about the service I could not help but to imagine that Jesus was left asking: "Who stole my church?"

Though most congregations might not be inclined to have a service of worship that equals the flamboyance of the service I just described, a large percentage of churches in the United States incorporate elements into worship, particularly during key national holidays and sometimes on other occasions, that elevate the United States above other nations, celebrate American identity, and foster national pride. In many churches the American flag is a permanent fixture that associates what takes place in worship with the nation. While this practice is widespread, its legitimacy is far from obvious. What we do in worship speaks of who God is and who we are as we live before God and others.

Faithful Christian worship forms us to be the sort of people who are capable of following no other god but the God of Israel who was disclosed most fully in Jesus Christ. When acts celebrating America are treated as aspects of worshiping and serving God, Christian identity, the nature of the church, and the character of God are misrepresented. All this negatively impacts discipleship and undermines Christian unity in a divided world, thereby hindering the church in its ministry of reconciliation.

IDENTITY IN COMMUNITY

Who we are is not individually determined. That is not to say that each of us does not have distinctive characteristics or a unique configuration of traits. However, first of all our identity is nurtured and developed in relationships of various sorts. Who I am is not separable from the relationships that make me a son, a brother, a father, a friend, a neighbor, a minister, a citizen, and more. In community we become who we are and not in self-determining isolation from others. The shaping power of communities is unavoidable. We participate in a variety of communities that impact us and our sense of self. Not only nationalism but consumerism and the ethos of entertainment are community-sustained forces that shape—and misshape—us.

The church stands as a community at odds with the communities that foster attachments and loves that undercut the love we were created to have for God and all others whom God has created. The practices of the church, and in particular the patterned behavior we participate in as we worship, produce a distinctive sort of identity in worshipers. Worship forms character by establishing certain affections in the lives of us who are worshipers. These affections are not mere emotions, though they start with emotions. Rather they are enduring features of who we are and how we see the world. Kendra Hotz and Matthew Matthews helpfully suggest twelve affections that form in us a temperament that is peculiarly Christian when they come together in us in a well-ordered way.[4]

4. Hotz and Matthews, *Shaping the Christian Life*, 8–12.

These affections include awe, humility, gratitude, a sense of mutuality and interdependence, a sense of rightness (that on whole the world is good), a sense of well-being (that there is a place for us to flourish), delight, a sense of obligation, self-sacrificial love, contrition, hope, and a sense of direction (our life has a meaningful end). These religious affections are not separable aspects of our identity but overlapping and interrelated. In worship these are affirmed and deepened, leading us, not only individually but corporately as church, to be who call in Christ calls us to be.

TRUE GREATNESS

When the psalmist rhetorically asks of God, "What are human beings that you are mindful of them?" (Ps 8:4) too often we misunderstand the intention behind the question. The query is not meant to be an occasion for us to meditate on human greatness. The Psalmist is not calling for a recitation of the best traits and greatest strengths of humankind. He did not intend to suggest that we need to identify and name the admirably distinctive qualities found in humans that have attracted the attention of God.

To the contrary, the Psalmist assumes that nothing about us humans is so great that it calls for divine attention. We are but creatures made of dust. Our existence is frail and fleeting. As Scripture elsewhere says, we are like the grass of the field that withers and like its flower that fades, present but for a short time (Isa 40:8, 1 Pet 1:24). "What are human beings that you are mindful of them?" The answer is: not much. Nothing in us warrants the attention of God. The Psalmist's very question directs us away from ourselves to the awesome God of immeasurable grace who cannot be impressed by us but who condescends, self-reveals, and loves us without regard to our worthiness. God loves in perfect freedom. Nothing about us compels divine regard.

The great temptation for us worshipers is to adore ourselves in the name of God. The celebration of God that is supposed to be directed outward turns in and becomes self-referential. This happens in a variety of ways, some of them tangentially grounded in Scripture itself. The biblical claim that we are created "in the image of God" (Gen 1:27) sometimes becomes a basis for promoting a bloated sense of self-importance. The command to "love your neighbor as yourself" (Matt 22:39) becomes an occasion to emphasize the supposed need to love ourselves first. Belief in divine providence becomes a means of selectively interpreting events to show how God has a preferential love for us over against those who are not us. Through these and other means, the greatness of God and our own supposed greatness are brought by us into the closest possible proximity. The glorification of God and self-promotion become a bit difficult to distinguish.

In sharp contrast and with frequency, worshipful words of Scripture praise God and undermine human self-importance with the same breath. I believe these words have relevance for worship tainted with nationalism:

> Have you not known? Have you not heard?
> Has it not been told you from the beginning?
> Have you not understood from the foundation of the earth?
> It is he who sits above the circle of the earth,
> And its inhabitants are like grasshoppers;
> Who stretches out the heavens like a curtain,
> And spreads them like a tent to live in;
> Who brings princes to naught,
> and makes the rulers of the earth as nothing (Isa 40:21–25).

> LORD, let me know my end,
> And what is the measure of my days;
> Let me know how fleeting my life is.
> You have made my days a few handbreaths,
> And my lifetime is as nothing in your sight.
> Surely everyone stands as a mere breath.
> Surely everyone goes about like a shadow.
> Surely for nothing they are in turmoil;
> They leap up, and do not know who will gather.
> And now, O LORD, what do I wait for?
> My hope is in you (Ps 39:4–7).

> LORD, you have been our dwelling place in all generations.
> Before the mountains were brought forth,
> Or even you formed the earth and the world
> From everlasting to everlasting, you are God.
> You turn us back to dust,
> and say, "Turn back, you mortals."
> For a thousand years in your sight
> Are like yesterday when it is past,
> Or like a watch in the night (Ps 90:1–4).

True worship puts everything in perspective. As we look to God in faith we learn to look at all things with new eyes. When we see with Isaiah "the LORD sitting on a throne, high and lofty" and we hear with open hearts,

"Holy, Holy, Holy, is the LORD of hosts, the whole earth is full of his glory," our rightful response is to confess with the prophet Isaiah, "Woe is me! I am lost, for I am a man of unclean eyes, and I live among a people of unclean eyes; yet my eyes have seen the King, the LORD of hosts!" (Isa 6:1–6). The glory of the Lord disallows any glorifying of the self or magnifying of anything that is an extension of the self.

Before the wondrous and holy God who alone deserves our worship, not only is our personal righteousness like "filthy rags" (Isa 64:6) but the righteousness of our race, class, or nation are equally unclean. The glorification of God sheds a bright light under which nothing else looks so worthy of our honor and loyalty as we had been lead to believe. The radiance of God reveals to us the irreducible difference between Creator and creature.

> You are worthy, Our lord and God,
> To receive glory and honor and power,
> For you created all things,
> And by your will they existed and were created (Rev 4:11).

There is a vast qualitative distinction between Creator and creature which we humans have attempted to minimize ever since we first heard the words, "You will be like God" (Gen 3:5). We have convinced ourselves that when certain deeds are done or conditions are met or achievements are accomplished, our godlike greatness will be established. Then our possibilities will be limitless and the acclaim we deserve will come our way.

Though it can truthfully be said that we are "fearfully and wonderfully made," the honor for this is not rightly directed to us who are "made" but to the Maker. Though we can say, "Wonderful are your works; that I know very well," these "works" are not so wonderful in themselves but are so only because of the wonder of the one who did the making. "For it was you [God] who formed my inward parts . . . . Your eyes beheld my unformed substance . . . . How weighty to me are your thoughts, O God! How vast is the sum of them!" (Ps 139: 14, 13, 16, 17). Worship has gone wrong every time people have "exchanged the truth about God for a lie and worshiped and served the creature rather than the Creator, who is blessed forever" (Rom 1:25).

This shift of focus from Creator to creature is often subtle and frequently denied by worshipers even as they are doing it. But the result is that worship no longer redefines reality. Rather it reconfirms the reality that the dominant powers of the world define: that God is with the mighty; that the prosperous are the most blessed by God; that people like us are the most virtuous; that our nation is righteous and only gets into conflicts for good and just causes; that the other people in the world ought to be grateful to us for the good we do for them. Such worship is ultimately worship of the self, worship that has "exchanged the truth about God for a lie." It is an exercise in self-adoration. This is precisely what happens as Christian worship is infused with elements of American nationalism.

CREDIBLE CHRISTIAN WORSHIP

God is not us. Yes, God is in us. Yes, God sustains us. Yes, God works through us. But God is other than us. God is wonderfully other. Acknowledging this truth is where worship begins if it is not to become a version of self-worship. And confessing Jesus as Lord and Savior is where worship that is distinctively Christian begins. In Jesus Christ the God who is other than us became one of us, revealing the truth of God to us that we otherwise could not know. This shapes the way we worship God.

Whenever worship is not at the heart of the church, the church ceases to be itself. Its purpose and identity goes astray. The church dissolves into a mere service organization or a social club. Worship is what keeps the character of the church intact and insures that the central focus of the church remains where it should be—on God. Worship does the same for the character and focus of each individual worshiper. It grounds the life and identity of the believer in God. Worship draws attention away from personal preoccupations, directing it to the one who is worthy of all praise and loyalty.

In worship we honor and praise God for who God is and what God has done. Through words, songs, and rituals, acts of worship point to the acts of God, reenacting them in the form of praise. Worship moves us toward the heart of God. This is not because we enjoy the music or find the words of the sermon amusing, or the ritual mysterious or aesthetically pleasing, but because worship moves us beyond ourselves. Worship reminds us there is a purpose greater than our purposes, a power greater than our powers, a love greater than our restricted, self-interested loves.

In celebrating who God is and what God has done we are challenged to see everything in a new way. What we do as the gathered church does not stay at church, not if we worship with an attentive faith. It provides us with a lens through which we see ourselves and the world around us and shapes our predispositions so we will live faithfully. The presence and character of

God honored in worship touches everything. Likewise, any notion of how we are to live in the world that makes sense apart from worship should leave people of faith ill at ease.

It is risky to attempt to describe Christian worship in any definitive way given the tremendous diversity of practice throughout the world. Any statement that includes certain elements as essential while forbidding others is bound to be greeted with protests from a variety of quarters. Nevertheless, to speak of worship as "Christian" suggests that there is something identifiable that warrants that label. Simply to speak, sing, pray, or employ symbols in ways we designate as being in some fashion "meaningful" is not enough to justify calling what we do "Christian worship." Worship is our response to what the God of Israel has done for us in Jesus Christ. As such what we justifiably do in worship must be grounded in the saving actions of God. Our worship answers back to the God who has called to us through the faithful life, teaching, wondrous works, death, and resurrection of Jesus Christ.

The purpose of worship is to be in the presence of God with adoring faith. There is no more central reason for Christian worship. It does not rightly serve some utilitarian function nor does it contain elements that people without faith in Jesus Christ can do equally well. If a service of worship does so that very fact is a strong indication that what is taking place is not genuine Christian worship. We do not worship in order to accomplish something that can be measured. But this does not mean worship has no effects. We become like what we adore. Worship is for God and we worship because of our love for God.

In worship we love back the God who first loved us. Our praise-giving response reflects the love given to us as we declare the worthiness of God. In premarital counseling sometimes the prospective bride and groom are asked to say *why* each loves the other. What is it about the beloved—qualities, characteristics, traits, behaviors—that evokes love? What makes this person special above all others, worthy of a lifetime of devotion? Similarly, in worship we answer such questions and do so with thankful praise. Christian worship is an occasion to re-present the God who has acted on our behalf, as Scripture bears testimony. In worship we point to the worthiness of God. Stories of the in-breaking of God to liberate, sustain, guide, and form a people are repeated. The God who is revealed through these stories is celebrated. The promises of God are reclaimed with hope and faith.

Anticipation of the culmination of God's work for the healing of all creation is reawakened as God is glorified as the source and destiny of all things.

God is worshiped as the one who is beyond human comprehension but not devoid of all definition. What can be truthfully said of God in worship can be said only because God disclosed God's self through divine interaction with Israel and ultimately in Jesus Christ. What can be known of God is what God has revealed. It is this revelation that gives Christian worship its substance as worship "in Spirit and in truth" (John 4:24). This is not to say God has never acted elsewhere, an incredible claim. Rather it is to say that the heart of Christian worship is given to us in actions that reflect God's character and intention. They are not simply invented by us for our purposes, no matter how noble we imagine them to be.

When worship serves our purposes, when our foremost concern is that our worship is "meaningful for us," God is inevitably refashioned into our image and the truth of God is turned into a lie. In such worship the Lord is not glorified. Instead we bow before another god, even though the name of Jesus may be frequently repeated. The true God is consigned to a secondary place, a supporting role to bolster whatever it is that we wish to honor. When worship serves another purpose that the singular praise of God or when an ulterior motive has intruded, this unfailingly leads to the celebration of self and our creations.

Only as we attentively and adoringly see who God is do we learn to see the world as it truly is. Instead of seeing the world as our own, our property, our putty to be molded according to our desires, we learn to see the world as God's creation. We find that "the earth is the LORD's and everything that is in it" (Ps 24:1). It is neither to be honored as divine nor exploited and abused for our greed-driven ends but treated with respect and care. Further, we learn that the world and the people that inhabit it are "fallen" and as such fail to embody God's good intention for all God has made. Pride has led humankind to turn from a gracious God to live according to a self-centered and misguided independence. Flourishing before God has been replaced by self-destruction as the strong take advantage of the weak, and the poor are used for the further enrichment of the wealthy, and the pursuit of pleasure overwhelms the impulses of compassion.

Through the stories repeated in worship that contain names like Noah, Abraham, Sarah, Joseph, Moses, Deborah, David, Elijah, Isaiah, Mary, and finally Jesus, we learn of God's persistence in love, even when there has been human rebellion and divine judgment. We learn of repentance, confession, lamentation, forgiveness, joy, and hope. We learn of God as one who draws people together, makes covenants, and creates purpose-filled community.

As the great Jewish scholar Abraham Joshua Heschel wrote, "Worship is a way of seeing the world in light of God."[5] We cannot come into the presence of God in worship, without that experience leading us to see ourselves as we had not previously been able to do. Like the prophet Isaiah before us, we perceive ourselves with a new clarity as we come before God in adoration (Isa 6: 1–8). We see ourselves as creatures, sinners, called, forgiven, incorporated into a new people, the church, the body of Christ. We learn in worship that we are not only—or primarily—individuals who have been "saved." Rather we are members of a community that has been created by Christ who demolished the barriers between peoples in order to create "one new humanity" (Eph 2: 14–18), who no longer see the world "from a human point of view" but see all things in light of "a new creation" (2 Cor 5: 16–17).

Above all, Christian worship is shaped around the story of Jesus. This story is repeated, reenacted, and celebrated. This narrative is definitive for what we mean in saying the word *God*. As the Gospels are read our eyes turn to Jesus. We pray in the name of Jesus. We are baptized in his name, dramatizing his death and resurrection as we die and rise with him to "walk in the newness of life" (Rom 6:3–4). We gather to celebrate the Eucharist, the Lord's Supper, eating and drinking, remembering what he has done for our salvation and communing around the Table with one another—and with other saints throughout the ages and throughout the world—in his presence.

In worship we learn to see that the future of the world does not reside in the hands of humans, regardless of their intentions. Rather, the fulfillment of all things is in the hands of God, the very God who calls us to live as a people faithfully subject to the rule of God. We rehearse living as people of God under the reign of the Lord, anticipating the kingdom of God while living as citizens of that realm in the present time.

Worship is both expressive and transformative. Through it we express a thankful, praise-giving faith to a God who has acted in particular ways to reveal a particular divine character. At the same time as we participate in worship—hearing, singing, giving, eating the bread and drinking from the cup of communion—transformation takes place. In worship we are faced

---

5. Heschel, *I Asked for Wonder*, 20.

again and again with who we are, to whom we belong, and to what end our lives should be directed. We enjoy a new identity that takes precedence over every identity bestowed upon us by any power or people in the world. The Scriptures speak of this as a "new nature which is being renewed in knowledge after the image of the creator" (Col 3: 10). Because of this new nature and identity, "there cannot be Greek or Jew, circumcised and uncircumcised, barbarian, Scythian, slave, free but Christ is all and in all" (Col 3:11). This nature and identity that we have in Christ means we are members of his body, the church. Thus we are united with other members of the body of Christ, not just locally but internationally.

Methodist liturgical theologian Don Saliers has suggested that the "liturgy well-celebrated should permit us, over time, to refer all things to God, and to learn how to intend our lives and the world to God."[6] When our lives have been penetrated by the practice of worship, our posture toward all things is shaped. Our affections are formed. Our devotion to and love for God will order and arrange every other love, attachment, and loyalty, confirming some, perhaps de-legitimizing others. The confession, "Jesus is Lord" proclaimed in worship becomes the practical measure to which every other claim on our hearts and lives must be subjected. This confession leads us both to serve and to faithfully resist the world that does not acknowledge the Lord. We cannot do otherwise because in worship God has shown us a different vision of the world from that in which the majority of people live. We are called to live toward that world in anticipation and hope.

Worship honors who God is and what God has done. In so doing it presents us with a wealth of possibility that contradicts every suggestion that the unjust and violent world around us is inevitable and unalterable. True worship slaps down the claim that longings for the end of gross inequality, oppression, and war are foolishly utopian by reminding us of what God has done and by calling us to live in light of a future promised by God. Worship shapes us, not to be well-adjusted residents who live complacently in the world as it is. Rather, it calls us to live as faith-filled malcontents who, like Mary, look forward to a world in which the mighty are thrown down from their thrones, the hungry are filled with good things and the rich sent away empty (Luke 1:52–53). As Walter Brueggemann has noted, "The world-making of the liturgy is also world-breaking and world-nullifying . . . . A world of justice, mercy, peace, and compassion is created in the

---

6. Saliers, *Worship as Theology*, 37.

imaginary act of liturgy. This is the real world . . . ."[7] The love of God and love for God that worship expresses and deepens prepares us to be the sort of people capable of living by faith in this world.

LITURGY OF NATIONALISM

While Christian worship offers a vision of "the real world," this remains contested territory. There is no greater contestant for the territory than the nation. The nation, too, has a liturgy of sorts through which the world is seen. There are rituals that shape the aspirations, dispositions, and actions of people. They evoke affection, and turn hearts toward some values and against others. This is not done primarily through explicit instruction. Rather gestures, images, stories, symbols, and often repeated slogans create attachments and form identity that are "caught rather than thought." Liturgical theologian James K. A. Smith has spoken of these as "pedagogies of desire."[8] These cultural practices or liturgies awaken our affections and instill love. Most of the effects take place on a precognitive level. The way we feel races ahead of the way we think. Not all of these cultural practices are directly associated with the nation as such. But none are as influential as those related to the nation.

Through cultural institutions and daily interactions what philosopher Charles Taylor calls "social imaginaries" are conveyed.[9] A "social imaginary" is an intuitive perspective, which touches the emotion and evokes devotion. It contains assumptions about how things are, how things should be, who we are, and what we should do. These are instilled and reinforced by repeated contact with others who share the same visions and through exposure to the practices that define the community. None of us become who we are on our own. The communal rituals, the expressions of admiration and praise we hear from childhood on, the often repeated stories, the obvious adoration of certain symbols are what create identity and engender love. This is not done primarily by lessons learned in a classroom.

Daily small children who have no understanding of the words they are told to speak stand with hand over heart, and with the encouragement and approval of adults in authority, they recite, "I pledge allegiance to the flag of the United States of America . . . ." Long before they can grasp the meaning

---

7. Brueggemann, *Israel's Praise*, 52, 53.
8. Smith, *Desiring the Kingdom*, 49.
9. Taylor, *Modern Social Imaginaries*.

of the often repeated phrases, they hear people they admire speaking movingly by using words like "our brave soldiers," "greatest nation on earth," "freedom isn't free." Through the years they will go to sports games or community events where they will remain on their feet as the National Anthem is sung. Annually many attend Fourth of July parades that celebrate the birth of the nation and its enduring ideals. The entertainment industry undergirds these formative liturgies with powerful movies of military bravery, sacrifice, and devotion to the nation. And in many churches in America all of this is powerfully reinforced by the association with God who apparently sanctions the message and values that have been conveyed about the nation by so many other sources. The cumulative impact is tremendous, penetrating hearts. All this conveys to us a particular vision of the good and worthwhile life and imprints a sense of what is worth living for, dying for—and killing for.

Our world is filled with institutions that would like to gain our affection and attachment. These, too, use images, music, and slogans in order to impact us. These range from the universities, to the movie theaters, to restaurants, to Federal Express and Delta Airlines. These variously provide us with services, entertainment, education, and more. From us they expect remuneration, payment for whatever it is they have provided to us. These institutions attempt to win our customer loyalty. But the word *loyalty* here is narrowly defined. At best it involves only a small sliver of our lives. Customer loyalty to one institution does not exclude customer loyalty to another institution providing a different service or experience. Nor do any of the institutions of the sort I named aim to gain preeminence in our lives so that they can prioritize the other loyalties in our lives or overthrow them altogether.

The nation-state is different. It is an institution that calls for comprehensive allegiance of a sort that supersedes every other loyalty. The nation-state is, to use the words of the first of the Ten Commandments, a "jealous God" who has little patience for competitors. This institution demands body and soul. Loyalty to it is a matter of life and death. In other words, it is *religious* devotion that is expected of citizens. The rituals and practices of the nation-state aim to form, define, and deepen our loyalty and in so doing shape our identity so that who we are above all—at least for those in the United States—is American. Of course Christianity is welcome, even applauded in most quarters. However, being Christian is assumed to be a subcategory of being American so that those in the church in the United States are *American* Christians, not merely Christians in America.

Historically, if there has been little serious conflict in the United States between Christian devotion and American allegiance it is not due to the Christian nature of America that some people imagine exists. Instead this is an indication of the extent that the church has been conformed to American ideals, interests, and identity. No clear distinction between being American and being Christian is even a possibility because the two have become one in the hearts of many. The God they worship is the American God and the nation they love is in some fashion God's nation. Consequently, many Christians find it incomprehensible that incorporating the rituals of America into the worship of the church could be anything other than a positive, edifying practice.

Nationalism generally provides answers to at least two important questions. First, is there some kind of group smaller than all of humankind that is of central importance or is there not? For the nationalist the answer is that there is such a group and that group is the nation. Second, is it voluntary or involuntary belonging that is the basis of obligation one has to his or her community or communities? The nationalist says that involuntary belonging is most important. The nation is the community to which one belongs from birth—at least that is the case for the vast majority of people—and to which one is most obligated.[10] Christians generally agree with nationalists that there is some group smaller than the entire humankind that is of central importance. But in contrast to nationalists we must insist that membership in the group and the basis of obligation to others in this particular community is voluntary. For Christians that group or community is the church.

However, for the nationalist it is not enough to view the attachment and obligation to the national community as merely important to who we are and what we do. Loyalty to the nation cannot be secondary to loyalty given to the church. National loyalty must be *most important*. Because the population is divided in many ways, political leaders are intent on uniting people by appealing to a shared identity that will supersede all other understanding of the self and "take precedence over a host of other poles of identity, such as family, class, gender, even (*perhaps especially*) religion."[11]

---

10. Miscevre, "Introduction: The (Im-)Morality of Nationalism," 5–6.
11. Taylor, "Nationalism and Modernity," 40.

The best way for nationalism to take precedence over religion is for it to wear the mantle of religion, even if unofficially. This can be done best not by an assault on religion, but by the subversion of it. Nationalistic ministers, even more often than politicians, are the most frequent agents of this subversion. On the one hand, this takes place as religious leaders make much of the ceremonial use of "God" in the national motto, the Pledge of Allegiance, in political speeches, and by treating the myths of national origin as somehow revelatory. On the other hand, the subversion is furthered by incorporating elements of nationalistic liturgy into the life and worship of the church. The result is that churches become "auxiliaries to nationalist fervor and nationalist endeavor."[12]

By prominently displaying the American flag in church, by singing the National Anthem or other songs that glorify America and foster pride in the nation, by offering special honor to the US military, and perhaps even pledging allegiance to the flag, the nation is invited to take a seat on the throne of God in such tight proximity to the Lord that distinguishing the two becomes virtually impossible. As a result, worshipers are too often formed into people who are *American* Christians rather than Christians who are united first of all, not with those with the same nationality, but with those who share their faith in the God revealed in Christ no matter their nationality.

---

12. Hayes, *Essays on Nationalism*, 119.

CHAPTER 3

Where Are We Worshiping?

As worshipers it is crucial that we ask ourselves, "Where are we?" as well as "Who are we?" That first question can be answered in a variety of ways, all of which are truthful. We are on the planet we call Earth. Many of us can say we are in the western hemisphere. Many, but fewer of us, can say we are in North America. Still fewer of us can say we are in the United States of America. Fewer still can say we are in the state of Florida. Many fewer can say we are in Coral Springs. Only one of us can say at the time I am writing these words, "I am in a Panera Bread seated at the table in the southwest corner of the building."

Hemisphere, continent, state, or city is not given regular, ceremonial attention in worship services. We might ask why the place inside national borders warrants explicit recognition in a way that apparently is unwarranted by continent or state or city. *Spiritually*, where are we in America as we live as church? How that question is answered makes a tremendous amount of difference in how we worship and in how we live. This question asks for something deeper than geographical location. It is about spiritual location. To quote the words of one liturgical theologian, "[T]he liturgy itself is a country we must learn to dwell in."[1] But how well can we learn this if nationalism infiltrates worship?

---

1. Saliers, *Worship as Theology*, 139.

Bowing Toward Babylon

AMERICAN ISRAEL

For many Christians and churches America is not Babylon but the New Israel. America is a type of the promised land, the destination of those who left the "land of bondage" where forebears experienced religious repression and persecution. Facing uncertainty and hardship, the early white European settlers made an "exodus" from the countries where they had lived. They went in search of a place where they could worship and practice their faith in freedom. Like the ancient Israelites, they arrived in a land that had some other inhabitants that they believed they must conquer and displace that God's will might be done by them, the new chosen people.

From the time Europeans put their feet onto the soil of the New World, claims of chosenness were in the air. The earliest writings from the colonists testify of their sense of identity as a special people of God serving a divine purpose. Puritan leader William Bradford wrote of the quest for a place where he and the other pilgrims who eventually formed the Plymouth colony could practice their faith without scorn and molestation. Theirs was a quest for the freedom to practice their religion. They had no interest in freedom of religion as an abstract principle to be extended to others. They sought an opportunity to forge a nation in their own godly image. With this intention, they looked to the far-flung land of America. After their challenging journey, according to Bradford, "[T]hey fell upon their knees and blessed the God of Heaven who had brought them over the vast and furious ocean and delivered them from all the perils and miseries thereof again to set their feet on the firm and stable earth, their proper element."[2]

Bradford and his fellow pilgrims, even before reaching shore in 1620, penned a brief statement that expressed their intention. They declared that their venture had been

> undertaken for the glory of God and the advancement of the Christian faith, and honor of our king and country, a voyage to plant the first colony in the northern parts of Virginia do by these presents solemnly and mutually in the presence of God and one of another covenant and combine ourselves together into a civil body politic for our better ordering and preservation and furtherance of the ends aforesaid and by virtue hereof to inact, constitute, and frame such just and equal laws ordinances acts constitutions and offices from time to time as shall be thought most mete and

---

2. Cited in Hudson, *Nationalism and Religion in America*, 11.

Where Are We Worshiping?

convenient for the general good of the colony unto which we promise all due submission and obedience."[3]

A decade later John Winthrop, while still aboard the ship Arbella, wrote in even more explicit terms of the covenant relationship with God that he believed was had by the colonists in the New World. He spoke of "the more near bond of marriage between Him [God] and us in which he hath taken us to be His after a most strict and peculiar manner."[4] Winthrop likened this relationship to that enjoyed by the people of Israel. Like Israel, this people who had embarked to America had a divinely granted special commission, a covenant with God for this work. Winthrop made it very clear that this covenant did not guarantee them unconditional privileges and blessings. It entailed great responsibility and required rigorous faithfulness so that they might be an example to others. "For we must consider that we shall be as a city upon a hill. The eyes of all peoples are upon us."[5]

As the first leader of the Massachusetts Bay colony, Winthrop sought to make clear the meaning of their enterprise and the weighty responsibility that rested upon the pilgrims. He looked upon Israel as an archetype of the people he led, and he cherished the hope that they would live in the new promised land as worthy heirs of Israel's chosen place before God. Long before his time the church had maintained that it had superseded the place of Israel as the chosen people. Winthrop, however, was the leader of a total society in which church and state, though different, were closely connected and in which Christianity informed the political as well as the religious structure.[6] Not just the church but the faith-infused commonwealth was viewed as being a foreshadowing of the kingdom of God. The line between church and state for Winthrop was not a bold one. Still the church maintained preeminence.

Though the Puritans put in place structures of government and political organization, they "became a commonwealth only in order that they might maintain themselves as a church."[7] For them, church had priority over every other structure and community. It was not for the sake of the state that the church existed. If anything, the opposite was the case. John Cotton would write, "It is better that the commonwealth be fashioned to

3. Ibid., 12
4. Ibid., 22
5. Ibid., 23
6. Bellah, *Broken Covenant*, 17.
7. Niebuhr, *The Kingdom of God in America*, 68.

the setting forth of God's house which is His church, than to accommodate the church to the civil state."[8] The maintenance of a pure and faithful church superseded every other concern. But this did not allow the Puritans—or Quakers and Separatists for that matter—to walk away from the endeavors of government. In various ways—beyond the focus of this book—they sought to both be a distinctive people of God and to order society. But in time, what started as a church against the world became a church for the world and eventually the church in America became the Americanized church.

In the years leading up to the birth of the United States it was not only biblical imagery that shaped American self-understanding. The English political tradition was profoundly influential in the legal codes and institutions that came into existence in the colonies. Imagery, terminology, and symbols were also frequently drawn from the Roman republic. The imprint of Roman classicism was obvious in the new republic. This is evidenced in the architecture of the early republican period. Of special interest was republican virtue, frugal independence, and the willingness to serve for the public good.[9]

But ultimately influences deriving from the Bible had more lasting and sweeping impact than those coming from the Roman Republic. It is striking that when Jefferson, Franklin, and Adams were commissioned by Congress to design a seal for the new nation, Franklin proposed one that would display Moses with hands lifted, the Red Sea divided, and the army of Pharaoh being deluged. The accompanying motto was "Rebellion to Tyrants is Obedience to God." Even the classicist Jefferson looked to Israel instead of Rome for his suggested design, which would display Moses leading the Israelites in the wilderness led by a cloud and pillar of fire.[10]

Associating America with biblical Israel was common fare in pulpits after the revolution. The name "American Israel" was frequently heard in churches. In a sermon from 1796, John Cushing declared that the Fourth of July should be celebrated with the self-conscious seriousness of the Jews as they observe the Passover.[11] "God led a devout people from bondage to liberty so that they might worship according to the dictates of their conscience. Though trials had to be faced and sacrifices made, in the end

---

8. Ibid., 68.
9. Bellah, *Broken Covenant*, 23.
10. Hughes, *Myths Americans Live By*, 34.
11. Cushing, "A Discourse Delivered at Ashburnham, July 4, 1796," 17.

God has exalted us and given us a rank amongst the nations."[12] Clearly the "rank" of which he spoke was an exceptional one not had by other nations.

Ezra Stiles, preacher and the president of Yale University, a few years after the Revolutionary War spoke of "God's American Israel." Drawing from the words of Deuteronomy 26:19, he anticipated that God would place the new Israel "high above all nations which he hath made." As many have, both before and after him, Stiles rehearsed the history of Europeans coming to America as an exodus and an entry into the promised land. He asserted that divine providence orchestrated every crucial event. George Washington was Joseph/Moses/Joshua. Every battle won, crucial alliance established, or key decision made was presented by Stiles as a result of the intervention of the Lord. "[W]ho does not see the indubitable interposition and energetick influence of Divine Providence in these grand and illustrious events?"[13]

Later in the nineteenth century and early twentieth century, even among the advocates of the social gospel, calls to "Christianize" America contained a tendency, not just to over-identify the church with the nation, but to elevate the nation over the church as God's instrument. After claiming that signs of the kingdom of God are the "clearest and the most convincing" in America, Washington Gladden went so far as to assert "all these glowing promises made by the old prophets of the triumphs yet to be won for the kingdom of God in the world are made to the nation and not to the church."[14]

American expansionism was viewed as the extension of "Christian civilization." It is not surprising then that denominational missionary societies supported and benefited from American imperialistic ventures.[15] Some ministers unhesitatingly suggested that soldiers sent abroad should be regarded as missionaries who go in to foreign fields. The idea held by the earliest Puritans, that they as a community of the converted were a chosen people pursuing a special task in this New World, transmuted into the idea that the United States is a chosen, specifically favored nation "destined to bring light to the gentiles by a means of lamps manufactured in America," to cite H. R. Niebuhr's often quoted words.[16] Given this history evangelism

---

12. Ibid., 18
13. Stiles, "The United States Elevated to Glory and Honor," 86.
14. Gladden, "The Nation and the Kingdom," 259.
15. Ibid.
16. Niebuhr, *The Kingdom of God in America*, 179.

and imperialism, Christianity and nationalism become hard to distinguish for many people sitting in churches in the United States.

America as a chosen nation, a new Israel, was not simply the recipient of the lion's share of God's blessings and privileges. America was understood as the special instrument of God by which all the nations of the world would benefit. Hence, the military ventures of the US were interpreted, not as being a quest for selfish acquisition, or economic advantage, or political dominance, but as efforts to spread universal ideas and values. For the most part, Americans have tended to be uncritically convinced of the nation's benevolence. This has been reflected as much—or more—in the pulpits of churches, as in the speeches of the politicians. While the destiny of the supposedly benevolent nation was sometimes manifested in the spread of its borders, even more so it was displayed in the spread of its ideals, which were understood as being reflective of the truest and deepest values of all humankind.

These convictions were proclaimed in a sermon, "The Moral Meanings of the World War," published on the cusp of the Armistice: "God is on the side, not of America against Germany, but on the side of humanity against inhumanity, on the side of justice against injustice. We shall win, not because by our selfish prayers or servile worship we shall be able to bribe God to favor our cause, but because we have allied ourselves with the cause of humanity, which is God's own cause."[17] The cause of humanity and the cause of God just happened to perfectly overlap the cause of America. Consequently, the cause of America and the cause of the church have been very difficult to distinguish for American Christians. Perhaps this is the reason why there was no widespread outcry among the churches in the United States when President George W. Bush, going beyond what previous presidents had done in using Scripture for political ends, employed words from Scripture and hymns, replacing references to Jesus Christ with those honoring America.

Particularly among leaders of the Religious Right, it is not uncommon to find them speaking of "America's covenant with God." We might ask, precisely when did God establish a covenant with America? Such a covenant cannot be established apart from divine initiative. A people cannot legitimately just claim to have a covenant with God and that claim make it so. No accumulation of quotes from early Puritan preachers, or founding fathers, or Supreme Court decisions can make an "unchosen" nation into

---

17. Hutchison and Lehmann, *Many Are Chosen*, 161.

a "chosen" one or establish a covenant not put in place by a revelation of God. While Scripture speaks of ancient Israel as "a light to the nations, to open the eyes that are blind, to bring out the prisoners from the dungeon, from the prison who sit in darkness" (Isa 42:6–7), no similar claim is made for any other nation. Still, preachers and politicians haven't hesitated to claim that America is the source of the light that shines into the darkness. In Christian Scripture when "chosenness" is mentioned, it pertains to the church, that spiritual nation that is without geopolitical borders and is international in scope (Col 3:12; 1 Thess 1:4–5; 1 Pet 1:1–2, 2:9–10).

For those who see the United States as a new Israel—or to use the more often employed phrase, a "Christian nation"—the inclusion of songs and symbols of the nation in worship is natural, not at all exercises in bowing toward Babylon. Honoring America is seen as little more than an aspect of glorifying the God who chose America, as God had chosen Israel, to be a "light to the nations." Thus, any questioning of the incorporation of nationalism in worship is not just viewed as odd by many American church members but as quite offensive.

CHOSEN NATIONS

The blending of nationalism with Christian faith is certainly not something that originated in the United States. The origins of this practice are found long before the existence of the modern nation-state. When the Roman Empire politically legitimated the church, the church was quick to return the favor. The empire went from being Babylon and beast of Revelation 13, to being friend to the faithful, to being an indispensable expression of the very reign of Christ. With the "conversion" of Constantine a new theopolitical unity began to be formed. "One God, one Logos, one emperor," was the cry. *Imperium christianum* was invested with messianic purpose previously seen as exclusively the calling of the church. The line between church and state began to be more and more permeable. As the Empire embraced the faith of the church, the church embraced the power of the Empire. What began with Constantine reached its completion with Justinian. State and church blended into a millenarian unity, a perfect duet singing in harmony to the glory of God, the ecclesiastical and the imperial, one *corpus Christianum*. The church's mission to evangelize the world and the Holy Empire's quest to subjugate the world became difficult to distinguish.

As church and Empire came to be coterminous the church allowed itself to be an instrument in the service of imperial interest. Since the Empire was Christian the church no longer needed to see itself as over against or other than the state. The church was no longer *ecclesia*, the called out. Baptism no longer functioned as an initiation into a community distinguished from the surrounding society. Worship was no longer seen as re-presenting a story distinctive from and at odds with the narrative of the Empire. In the words of Jurgen Moltmann, "In the Byzantine empire, Christianity surrendered the congregational form of living and interpreted its celebration of the divine liturgy as the true, public worship of God in empire and region . . . ."[18] What was claimed—illegitimately—by both church and state was a reality that could only come with eschatological fulfillment. "Only in the kingdom of Christ does the Christian spirit abandon its special form of life in the church, and acquire its universal political form of living. Only in the messianic kingdom will the body politic become the body of Christ."[19]

It was believed by many that the Holy Empire would last as long as human history. The idea of *translatio imperii* as used by Jerome and others held that the Holy Empire will be transferred from one empire or nation to the next in order to fight evil and keep chaos at bay. When evil can no longer be suppressed then the end is at hand. With the power of the sword and the evangelizing Word, Empire, and Church, "a religiously and politically unified *orbis christianus*, . . . would bring salvation to the nations."[20]

With the demise of the Holy Roman Empire the mantle was grasped by other so-called Christian nations, each imagining themselves to be "chosen" and central to the destiny of the world, a universal nation of sorts. In each of these nations the people saw the future of civilization and the very destiny of humankind contingent upon the fortunes of their own nation. Russia, Germany, France, and England, among others, laid claim to having been chosen by God for a high and holy purpose. Indeed, historian William Hutchison asserted that "not just 'many' Western societies, but perhaps

---

18. Moltmann, *The Coming of God*, 166.
19. Ibid.
20. Ibid, 168.

most of them, have found divine appointment a natural component of nationalist enthusiasms."[21]

Prior to the Bolshevik Revolution it was a widespread conviction among the Russian Christians that their nation was the rightful heir to the holy Christian empire.[22] The Russian people were not simply one nation among many, but a representative people who contained the essence of humanity and through whom all humanity would benefit. Dostoyevsky could write that Russians are "the only God-bearing people on earth, destined to regenerate and save the world."[23]

In Germany prior to the end of World War II the evangelical wing of the Protestant church was the strongest advocate of religious nationalism. Drawing on Old Testament themes of covenant, church leaders celebrated the German people as the chosen of God. As the home of the Protestant Reformation, Germany was the most Christian of nations. There was a widespread belief that God had intervened at crucial junctures in German history to insure the preservation and prominence of the nation. Just prior to World War I references to "God our old ally" could be uttered with deep confidence, a conviction carried on the belt buckles of German soldiers: "Gott mit uns"—"God with us."[24] Preachers did not hesitate to speak of Germany as "the Israel of the New Covenant."[25] After the nation was defeated in World War I, even as church leaders called for national repentance, many German Protestants began to envision and ready themselves for revenge.[26] They did not waver from the belief they were God's chosen people until it was put to rest when German church leaders signed the "Stuttgart Confession of Guilt" late in 1945.

Belief in France's chosenness reaches back to the thirteenth century, at least to the reign of Philip the Fair. The early formulation of the sense of being chosen by God moved France to "derive its worth from its faith and its fidelity to God's divine will . . . . Little by little the ['most Christian'] developed into a reason for their calming certainty that France would always play an important role in God's plan for the order of the world."[27] Joan of

21. Hutchison and Lehmann, *Many are Chosen*, 15.
22. Kalb, *Russia's Rome*, see introduction.
23. Cited in Lieven, *America Right or Wrong*, 34.
24. Lehmann, "God Our Old Ally," 87, 91.
25. Hoover, *God, Germany and Britain in the Great War*, 93.
26. Lehmann, "'God Our Old Ally,'" 106.
27. Beaune, *The Birth of an Ideology*, 192–193.

Arc was frequently pointed to as evidence of God's miraculous intervention to save France as God had saved Israel. Later, though the Republican vision of France clashed with that of the Catholic vision, that did not stop people like prominent nineteenth-century historian Jules Michelet from speaking of the mission and identity of France in religious terms: "No doubt every great nation represents an idea important to the human race. But great God! how much more true is this of France! Suppose for a moment that she were eclipsed or perished; the sympathetic bond of the world would be loosened, broken and probably destroyed."[28]

England's claim to be the peculiar chosen people of God originated in its resistance to the Roman Catholic Church. When King Henry VIII repudiated the authority of the Pope and stepped in as the supreme ruler of the church in England the foundation for the claim of chosenness was laid. With the head of the church and the head of the state now being one and the same person, the traditional claims of the church as being the people of God were more easily applied to the nation.

Henry VIII had no real interest in reforming the church. Others, however, did. Impetus for reformation was provided by William Tyndale, who went to Germany, studied with Martin Luther in Wittenberg, and worked on an English translation of the New Testament that first appeared in print in 1526. Several years later he completed a translation of the Pentateuch, first published in 1530. With each edition of his translation he provided prefaces and prologues in which he made suggestions about how to best interpret Scripture. In them he promoted Luther's teaching of justification by grace through faith alone. But he was also taken with the theme of covenant and the idea of the chosen people.

The prologues and prefaces of his 1534 edition argued that the central theme of Scripture is the covenant God makes with his people. Tyndale did not see this as something restricted to the people of ancient Israel but held that God could extend this covenant to others such as England if they would repent and reform. While Tyndale never expressly argued that England was God's chosen people, by the time Henry VIII died and Edward VI took the throne—at only nine years of age—the idea that England was chosen by God was widespread.

A number of the advisors to the young king were sympathetic to the Reformation cause. Edward sent Archbishop of Canterbury Thomas Crammer to seek advice from Reformed leaders in Zurich, Switzerland.

---

28. Cited in Kselman, "Religion and French Identity," 70.

He was urged to purge the church of non-biblical tradition and restore the ancient faith. If such actions were implemented, England would show itself to be chosen by God. When Edward died and Queen Mary harshly resisted reforms and persecuted reformers, many fled to Protestant cities on the continent.

When Mary died they returned, determined to radically reform the Church of England. These earliest Puritans managed to institute some reforms, though their efforts largely failed. By the end of the sixteenth century some of these Puritans concluded that they must separate from the Church of England in order to establish a true and faithful church. Other Puritans remained within the national church and continued working for reform. Whether they worked within or outside of the Church of England, their aim was to lead the people to embrace faithful practices as a covenant people and so reap the benefits of being the chosen of God.

Under King James I the Puritans were harassed in various ways, but when his son Charles I took the throne, opposition to the Puritans intensified. All this led a group of Puritans to leave England. But many remained and with them the idea of England as a chosen nation continued to make an impact. This idea even influenced the minds of those who were not themselves Puritans. Elizabethan Bishop John Aylmer would go so far as to claim, "God is English."[29] While the Puritans did not attain their ends, nevertheless anti-Catholic forces kept the Church of England from the hands of Rome. And these continued to preserve the belief in "England's unique status as the successor Chosen People of God to the Old Testament's Chosen People."[30]

Long after the days of the Puritans, the claim of English chosenness remained well and alive. The expansion of the British Empire and Christian foreign missions were deeply entwined in the minds of many Christian leaders. The imperialistic spread of "civilization" and the propagation of Christianity tended to be viewed as mutually supportive ventures. At a Missionary Society gathering in 1897 Wesleyan minister W. L. Watkinson, speaking in reference to Isaiah 19:23–25, declared, "England stands much in the same position that Israel did. It is the spiritual centre of the world . . . . God in His government has also given to us special powers for the diffusion of the Gospel."[31] Twenty years later J. Paterson-Smyth wrote, "In

---

29. Longley, *Chosen People*, 126.
30. Ibid, 38.
31. Cited in Walls, "Carrying the White Man's Burden," 41.

the mysterious calling and election of God, Britain is the elect nation of the world today. We say it in all wonder and humility. For it is not we, but God who has done it."[32]

AMERICA AS BABYLON

In contrast to those who consider America to be a New Israel, I am contending it can more appropriately be seen as the new Babylon. Clearly this is not a national self-understanding fostered by a host of early American preachers, to say nothing of presidents, politicians, or Supreme Court justices. But Babylon as a metaphor for a superpower empire in which the people of God reside as aliens is, as I have already argued, firmly rooted in Scripture and an apt label for America.

Babylon is not so much a specific place as it is a spirit. As a spirit, Babylon was found in Persia, Greece, Rome, and in every arrogant empire, including the United States, though many—especially those who most benefit from the empire—are blind to the truth. As Daniel Berrigan wrote, "Those who dwell in Babylon do not know they are there."[33] The ease with which many churches blend sounds, symbols, and gesture that pay tribute to America into worship provide evidence that there is no shortage of Christians who don't know where they are. There are good and lovely things in Babylon. Knowledge, creativity, and culture exist in abundance. There is religion in Babylon but it is a religion that sanctifies and undergirds the values of the empire while disguising the truth that God's ends are not being honored by the structures that are in place.

Babylon has great power, far beyond that of her neighbors who she is able to dominate (Rev 17:2, 18). This dominance takes place both by means of seduction—in the book of Revelation Babylon is presented as the great whore—and by means of violence. Due to the benefits of cooperation and loyalty, Babylon allures many people and ensnares their hearts. Like ancient Tyre, where "merchants were princes" (Isa 23:8), so in Babylon "the merchants of the earth have grown rich from the power of her luxury" (Rev 18:3b). They both feed the wealth of Babylon and are fed by it; their fortunes and fate are inexorably tied to the empire (Rev 17:4; 18:11–17). When her power and prominence falters under the judgment of God, the first to mourn are those who "grew rich by her wealth" (Rev 18:19). I cannot

---

32. Paterson-Smyth, *God and the War*, 12.
33. Berrigan, *The Nightmare of God*, 107.

believe it will be otherwise in America where business interests drive public policy to such a degree that the needs of ordinary citizens and residents are often marginalized, if not altogether ignored.

In a very Babylonian fashion the military budget of the United States dwarfs that of every other nation in the world. In fact it rivals the defense budgets of all other nations of the world combined. Human services are deprived of much-needed funds in order to keep the vast flow of money directed toward military bases, weapons, and personnel. Yet most Americans have great pride in the nation's powerful armed forces. According to polls, Americans place more trust in the military than they do in any other institution in society. Church and organized religion fall far behind.[34]

In fact the fawningly idolatrous adoration many Americans have toward the military is seem in a meme that has often been posted on social media sites: "Only two defining forces have ever offered to die for you: Jesus Christ and the American Soldier: one died for your soul, the other died for your freedom." Whether the wars fought by the United States have been "for your freedom" is highly questionable. Regardless, comparing the deaths of soldiers who died while trying to kill other people to the death of Jesus Christ who practiced nonviolent love and died at the hands of a violent state is blasphemous. But that fact is lost on Christians who have absorbed nationalism into their faith. Stanley Hauerwas insightfully stated that war is "America's central liturgical act necessary to renew our sense that we are a nation unlike other nations."[35] And the bloodshed in this "liturgical act" is not primarily that of the American solders but that of those on the receiving end of American deadly force. As with every earlier Babylon, America is sustained by blood.

It needs to be said that every Babylon has redeeming features. None entirely lack traits deserving of praise. There is certainly much that is good and commendable about America. Nevertheless, there is much about America that warrants the label "Babylon." All great powers have characteristics of Babylon to one degree or another. Not all of them are equal in corruption, the abuse of strength and arrogance. But as evangelical leader Tony Campolo once remarked, "Even a very good Babylon is still Babylon."

As faithful worshipers we neither allow ourselves to be shaped into ordinary residents and citizens who beam with pride in our nationality and

---

34. "Confidence in Institutions," Gallup, June 2015, http://www.gallup.com/poll/1597/confidence-institutions.aspx.

35. Hauerwas, *War and the American Difference*, 4.

compliantly support every venture of the nation nor do we utterly reject America. We live in tension, between yes and no, between full assimilation and total withdrawal.

Knowing that we are not in some kind of New Israel, we acknowledge that where we live is less like home than it is like a place of captivity. This being the case, we are careful not to become too much at ease. Rather it is crucial that we remain wary of those aspects of the culture that can—and often do—subvert our faith. We live in the awareness that we must at crucial points resist rather than support dominant values and prevailing visions of national interests. We reject programs and policies that lead to the flourishing of some at the expense of others. Rather than proudly celebrating America, we need to endure the suspicion, criticism, and disdain that frequently befall those who boldly refuse to extol America as "the rightfully preeminent place in the planet" the home of the "chosen people" who "bear the ark of the Liberties of the world."[36]

By repeatedly reenacting the Christian story, worship shapes us to be a people capable of resisting the seductive lure of America rather than to be deeply assimilated into a Babylon masquerading as a New Israel. In worship, through song, prayer, Word, and Eucharist, we encounter Jesus and are drawn to follow in his way. We learn to be more like Jesus and less like the "heroes" who kill other children of God for the sake of national interests. Worship turns our hearts from the sort of pride that is grounded in a place so we can say with Scripture, "Let the one who boasts, boast in the LORD" (1 Cor 1:31).

Again I must emphasize that as we live and worship in American Babylon, we don't simply reject in an unqualified way the culture and values we find all around us. Neither do we retreat into Christian ghettoes of "purity." In a world that God created and called "good," there is no place so marred by sin that there is not room for affirmation and support. We do not take a posture that is only "for" or only "against." Whether we are critical, constructive, accepting, or resistant in any given instance depends upon the character of the aspect of the culture we face and the situation at hand. Faithful discernment is required.

Our aim is not to destroy but to build up. But we do this as a people who are called to recognize we are "citizens . . . of the household of God" (Eph 2:19), people whom God has "transferred . . . into the kingdom of his beloved Son" (Col 1:14). Yet for now we continue to dwell in this world. As

---

36. Melville, *White Jacket; or, The World in a Man-of-War*, 144.

we do so, the previously mentioned guidance of God through the prophet Jeremiah to the captive people of Israel, can provide wisdom to us: "But seek the welfare of the city where I have sent you into exile, and pray to the LORD on its behalf, for in its welfare you will find your welfare" (Jer 29:4–5, 7).

We do not rightly seek "the welfare of the city"—in our case, American Babylon—by being just another part of the nationalistic pep squad. Rather the church must assert its distinctiveness from American identity and interests. As Miroslav Volf has observed, "Literally, everything depends on difference.... The gospel is always also about difference; after all, it means the good news—something good, something new, and therefore something different!"[37] It is not by being like other Americans in most significant ways that we are constructively, transformatively, and affirmatively present. Our distinctiveness grows out of our loyalty to Jesus Christ who was sent as the love and truth of God incarnate for the entire world and not just for the Babylons of the planet. This distinctiveness is expressed and reinforced as we gather to worship the God who loves the world and gives American Babylon no special regard.

Too often the wisdom of ancient Christians has eluded us. They understood that no land in which they lived deserved to be celebrated—especially in worship!—in a way that other lands were not. Describing the posture of Christians, an ancient document said of them, "They reside in their own countries, but only as alien citizens, and they endure everything as foreigners. Every foreign country is their homeland, and every homeland a foreign country."[38]

LOCAL WORSHIP

The church universal is always manifested in particular communities of faith. Each of these communities have characteristics derived from the location and culture in which they are found. Social structure, patterns of interaction, language, artistic expression, and more impact the local church. It is impossible and undesirable for a local church to rid itself of all the distinctive characteristics of the culture in which it is embedded. The church universal does not exist apart from particular communities of faith. Each community is a microcosm of the whole. The fullness of Christ is

---

37. Volf, *A Public Faith*, 95
38. Richardson, ed., "Letter to Diognetus," 227.

present where ever faithful people gather in his name to worship. The worship is expressed in forms that have the peculiarities of a place. Yet what is expressed in worship points to the faith of the church universal. Appropriate attachment to the local and incidental characteristics of a congregation does not undermine, but reinforces unity with the universal.

There are no timeless, placeless expressions of worship. Protest against nationalistic, America-centric worship must not be mistaken for a denial that worship is local. Unavoidably, the praise of God is given form in language, gestures, and music that developed in a real time and place that differs from other times and places. Though these diverse and distinctive expressions adoration to God is offered. Liturgy always uses the resources of the particular culture in which the worship takes place.

Naturally around the world there are variations in worship that result from factors other than strictly theological differences. Christian worship has been and must be accommodated to the peculiar times, cultures, and languages in which it is practiced. Its capacity to express and transform is lost apart from such accommodation. Worship would be incapable of communication if it were not shaped in some fashion by its context, adopting speech, music, symbols, and forms. But all accommodation is not equally legitimate. Worship that undergirds local loyalties, reinforces division or enmities, sanctions the dominance of some parties over others or otherwise authorizes the suppression of those who are weak, is a misguided worship that subverts the truth of the gospel.

Any worship that claims to be Christian but does not celebrate God as the one who sent Jesus to demonstrate indiscriminate love for the world and does not lead us to love neighbor—near and far—should be held suspect. Any worship that loosens the unity we have with others in Christ while at the same time affirming and strengthening the tie with another people and/or power different from Christ and his body is worship not worthy to be called Christian. The truth of God is always greater than the local modes of communication can convey. None of them is uniquely suitable for worship. All of them contain potential hazards and deficiencies. So while it is important to recognize that worship is local, the peculiarities of the local culture must function as servant, not master. Otherwise, that which passes as the praise of God will become the captive of the spirit of the age and place where it occurs.

Worship inevitably involves our creativity and artistic efforts. But the end to which our efforts are exerted must be found in the revelation of God. Other values and aims are distractions from or distortions of our rightful focus: what we see of God through God's interaction with Israel and embodiment in Jesus Christ. Our creative freedom in worship is not boundless but conditioned by the one truly worthy of our adoration. In worship we acknowledge divine mystery rather than create it. We joyfully respond to God rather than create an experience of joy.

Worship is directed toward what is given, what is divinely disclosed. Our response is inspired and shaped by one who is not us. Yet our creative expressions of praise grow out of the culture in which we are found. The artistic resources of that culture are employed with all the freedom that faith affords to glorify God. The musical expression, language, and forms will differ from place to place. Nevertheless, "All our imagination and energy are concentrated on the One who stands in our midst and bids us to respond."[39] In worship we find ourselves invited and being prepared to participate with God in ways of self-giving love, mercy, and compassionate service.

Through hymns and songs, Scripture reading, and sermons, offerings given and communion received, we learn to see and to be in the world before God. But a failure to be vigilant about the words and forms used in the assembly of the church can subvert the transformative effects of worship. Instead a narrower vision and a smaller god will produce deformative effects. Rather than God being glorified, projects and interests that contribute to human self-aggrandizement will be furthered and excessive local loyalties and counterfeit consolation offered.

I knew a minister in a university town in Oklahoma who was a big football fan. Each Sunday morning after the home team won a game, he would stand in front of the congregation and make a great show of putting on a stole in the school colors. Inevitably the people would laugh and applaud. The gesture was all in harmless fun. The intramural sports rivalry that the minister exploited was surely not a denial that Jesus is Lord.

At the same time, can it honestly be denied that values were being celebrated and attachments reinforced that have absolutely nothing to do with the legitimate reasons for worship? Were not the emotions that related to team loyalty stroked and reinforced? Was this gesture not something that marginalized those who didn't share the team loyalty being ritualized by

---

39. Saliers, *Worship as Theology*, 198.

the minister? Even though this action was done in a spirit of playfulness—and I believe playfulness can have a rightful role in worship—his actions shifted attention away from the one who is the proper object of praise and from the true identity of the worshipers. His actions also cracked open the door for other less benign intrusions.

Faithful worship is entered into through "embodied cultural forms that open up levels of reality they do not 'contain' in themselves."[40] Because God is the rightful object of worship, every expression of worship falls short of being adequate. The music, symbols, and gestures are strained and stretched by the awareness of the grandeur of God. The cultural forms used in worship, though located in the customs of identifiable times and places, point beyond to one who shatters all limits. When worship not only uses the forms of a particular culture, but employs them in a way that expressly celebrates a culture and place above others then worship fails to honor the truth of the gospel.

Faithful worship breaks open the cultural forms that express praise and discloses a new world under the reign of God. No human community or culture is fully in harmony with God. All of them remain unworthy of being elevated in worship. "If liturgy is to be divine/human interaction, the modes of appropriating and sharing the mystery in and through language, symbol, and song must be the people's. . . . At the same time, the symbolic action of liturgy points to realities in tension with all inherited cultural assumptions and patterns of perceptions," remarked Don Saliers.[41] Bringing elements of nationalism into worship not only incorporates local forms but reinforces assumptions and patterns of perception. In so doing, a new world is not disclosed but the old world is falsely sanctified.

When the local church goes beyond expressing by means of inherited cultural forms the faith it shares with the universal church and instead celebrates the peculiarities of the local, Christian unity is hindered and glory to the God of all is undercut. No longer is the local church a microcosm of the whole. Instead it honors part at the expense of the whole. There is a vast difference between a faith community employing the language, musical instruments, and styles or gestures that are rooted in the indigenous culture, on the one hand, and, on the other, celebrating and honoring in worship one race, ethnic group, or nation over others. As Gordon Lathrop observed,

---

40. Ibid., 209.
41. Ibid., 214f.

"The Christian meeting place is centered, yet it points away from here."[42] When elements of nationalism intrude into the church, the church meets and ends up pointing in the wrong direction. The following several chapters will examine particular expressions of nationalism to show how they undercut the faithful praise that should be happening in Christian worship.

---

42. Lathrop, *Holy Things*, 210.

Chapter 4

What Time Is It? Holidays or Holy Days?

Each year my mother bought a new calendar to be prominently displayed in her kitchen. She would page through it and mark days that were of particular importance for our family. My birthday, as well as those of my sisters, was noted. The birthdays of my grandparents, aunts and uncles, and at least some of the cousins, also were marked on the appropriate place. Anniversaries of marriages, deaths, and family tragedies were marked. When the special dates neared, my mother would send cards, make a cake, buy gifts, or make phone calls to recognize the occasion. Of course some of the days required more time and attention for their proper observation than others. My mother believed that acknowledging these special days strengthened the family and in some fashion lifted up people and events that make us as a family *us*.

WE ARE WHAT WE CELEBRATE

Calendars are agenda laden. They offer a perspective on what is important. This is the case whether the calendar is like my mother's family calendar, work calendars, school calendars, national calendars, or the calendar of the church year. Calendars shape how the past is remembered, how current

What Time Is It? Holidays or Holy Days?

priorities are determined, and how we see our place in the world. They codify which events are to be considered most seminal, which people are most worthy of admiration, which values should be shared. All this is reinforced by rituals and practices related to the holidays, such as speeches and the act of decorating graves on Memorial Day or watching fireworks displays on Independence Day. Calendars help deepen affections and shape character, molding those who observe them into a certain kind of people.

"Shared rituals, symbols and collective memories form a key part of the formation of a nation's sense of self. They are chosen as a reminder of unity, ideology, and heritage. As regular and recurring dates, National Days give the nation a heartbeat—a calendric rhythm of self—awareness and pride," notes Alex Salmond.[1] The disjointed busyness that dominates the lives of many of us can undercut a sense of shared purpose and self-understanding. Special days on the national calendar can serve to reorient and remind people of some important things they have in common.

National days, or what I call nationalistic holidays, remind people they are part of a much larger community that significantly defines who they are in the world. "They are also a way of communicating to the wider world the nation's values, attitudes and strengths. In this sense they also become a channel for aspirations, an opportunity for transformation and a way of positioning a country on the global stage," notes Salmond.[2] In other words, nationalistic holidays serve not only to express and reinforce the unity and identity of a people, they also function to let others know who "we" are in contrast to "them." They function to draw attention to what makes "us" special.

Nationalistic holidays tighten communal bonds, and, like religious services, they "reinforce the commitments that have been diluted" at other times, and they offer a window into "the beliefs and other attributes of a given society."[3] Holidays invite participants to share the values and history that are being promoted through the observations. While some holidays don't reinforce commitments—such as Mardi Gras or Halloween—nationalistic holidays most certainly do. Notable among these are Independence Day, George Washington's birthday, Memorial Day, Flag Day, Veterans Day, and Thanksgiving Day.

---

1. Salmond, "Preface," xiii.
2. Ibid.
3. Etzioni, "Holidays and Rituals," 9–10.

Bowing Toward Babylon

Whether sacred or secular, no two holidays serve the exact same role. Just as Easter and Christmas serve different purposes, so, too, do Veterans Day and Thanksgiving Day. Each one lifts up a specific value or corporate memory at a different time of year. Yet the different holidays are mutually reinforcing. Each of them contributes to a narrative that conveys a vision of the world and a version of what matters and what should have a place in our hearts. Together the holidays help deepen attachments while—potentially at least—loosening other attachments. And that is the problem insofar as the worshiping church is concerned.

The effectiveness of national holidays to reinforce values and shape identity may have been lessened in recent decades because public observances are not so widely attended as they were in the past. Holidays are more often celebrated in families and small groups in backyard barbecues or picnics in parks. These gatherings generally have little focus on commitment to national community. Nevertheless, privatized holidays are not entirely ineffectual so long as more broadly shared commitments are acknowledged in some fashion, according to sociologists like Talcott Parsons.[4]

By far the best attended public celebrations of nationalistic holidays take place in churches. The number of people who show up for community-sponsored parades and ceremonies for nationalistic holidays is inconsequential in comparison to the crowds that gather for religious services each week. Though the stated purpose for church services is the worship of God, on the Sunday closest to Independence Day, Memorial Day, Thanksgiving Day, and perhaps other national holidays, the theme often is less determined by explicit Christian teachings or Scripture than by the national values and visions conveyed by the particular holiday. What is said of God is colored by what is affirmed and celebrated in America-centric worship. On nationalistic holidays, it is apparent that the liturgical colors are red, white, and blue.

The church calendar and the national calendar have very different ends. When nationalistic holidays are celebrated in worship, attachment to America, other Americans, and things American compromises and conditions the rightful work of worship. Instead of allowing the calendar to be used to convey the Christian story and foster attachments and affections suitable for people loyal to Jesus Christ, another story—the American story—gets interwoven into Christian time-telling. The result is *not* the cultivation of wholehearted dedication to Jesus Christ and his worldwide

---

4. Parsons, *Structure of Social Action*, Vol. 1, 438–41.

What Time Is It? Holidays or Holy Days?

church but the fostering of a narrower, nationalistically shaped devotion. How we see God and how we see ourselves is impacted by the special days we observe in worship.

TELLING TIME IN CHURCH

One Sunday morning while I was on vacation years ago my family took the opportunity to go to a church we had never attended. There was a megachurch in the area I'd heard much about, and my wife and I decided to visit there for worship. I'm married to a wonderful, intelligent, strong, and lovely woman who is constitutionally incapable of being on time. So we were running late. When we arrived we found a parking lot the size of one at the average shopping mall. We hustled across it toward the church building with our children in tow. Finally, we walked through the doors.

There in the narthex—well, they didn't call it a narthex, but the lobby—I stopped in my tracks. A collection of men were decked out in military uniforms. The one in the lead was holding a large American flag. They were about to process into the sanctuary as patriotic music was pulsing from within. I had forgotten it was the Fourth of July weekend. My family showed up at the church on what we thought was the Lord's Day. We *didn't* follow the color guard into the sanctuary.

The way the calendar is celebrated can either foster or enfeeble faithfulness. People of faith recognized this truth long before there were Christians who gathered to worship. It is notable that in the midst of the dramatic narrative of God's liberation of the people of Israel from slavery as found in the book of Exodus, liturgical instructions are given regarding how to celebrate this act of God. The description of the climatic tenth plague is interrupted with a command establishing a new calendar and detailing how Passover should be observed (12:14–20). Then, after continuing the story up through the drowning of the Egyptian army, the narrative ends as liturgical instructions are again provided regarding the celebration of Passover (12:43–49). Scott Bader-Saye notes, "Time itself has been transformed by this event. Through the practice of Passover, Jews from antiquity to the present participate in a ritualized simultaneity that cannot simply be circumscribed by nation."[5]

From this kind of time-telling heritage of faith arose the development of the church year. To cite Bader-Saye again, "The church's conception of

5. Bader-Saye, "Figuring Time: Providence and Politics," 97.

time must show itself able to produce communities that bear witness to a redemptive politics, a way of being in the world that trusts the future precisely because of the ways it narrates the past."[6] From denomination to denomination and congregation to congregation there are differences as to how—or which days of—the various celebrations during church year are observed. Still the vast majority of churches observe periods of time during which a special focus is placed on aspects of the Christian story and conviction in order to strengthen faith, form affections, shape character, and promote the unity of the church.

Designating Sunday as the Lord's Day is an ancient Christian practice. Very early in the life of the church this day was embraced as the day especially appropriate for Christian worship. It was, after all, on the first day of the week that Jesus was raised from the dead. Early Christians remembered that it was also on the first day of the week, seven days after the resurrection, that Jesus appeared to the disciples, breathed on them and said, "Receive the Holy Spirit" (John 20:22). Ignatius wrote in the early second century of the Lord's Day as the time on which "also our life arose through him and his death."[7]

Occasionally the Christian day of worship was referred to as the Eighth Day of the week. It was seen not as a "Christian Sabbath," but as a day beyond the Sabbath rest when a new creation begins. The early Christian writing that is known as the Epistle of Barnabas declared that "we observe the eighth day as a time of rejoicing, for on it Jesus both arose from the dead and, when he had appeared, ascended into the heavens."[8] The new age began when God liberated Jesus from the grave, initiating the renewal of creation which will culminate in a new heaven and a new earth.

Sunday worship foreshadows and anticipates the future God has promised. As Marianne Micks has written, "The day is seen as essentially a repeated entry into tension—an eschatological tension between the already and the not-yet. It is a day on which Christians rejoice and give thanks for the resurrection of Jesus Christ, for God's new creation, but also a day on which they acknowledge the urgency and responsibility which the End imposes."[9] Celebrated as the day of resurrection Sunday becomes a time that provides a glimpse of glory which makes us realize more clearly that

---

6. Ibid., 98.
7. Cited in Micks, *The Future Present*, 38.
8. Ibid.
9. Ibid, 40.

it is not yet fully present. Understood as the Lord's Day and the Eighth Day, Sundays are transformed from ordinary days to become a means of communicating the Christian story, conveying a Christ-centered vision of reality, and galvanizing the community of faith.

Easter has been celebrated since the second century. It was not, as some have claimed, derived basically from a pagan rite of springtime. Rather, from the beginning it was closely connected with the Jewish feast of Passover, initially celebrated on the same day as the Jewish feast. All the Gospels report that the crucifixion and resurrection of Jesus took place during the week of Passover. Later the Apostle Paul wrote, "Christ, our Passover lamb, has been sacrificed. Therefore let us keep the Festival" (1 Cor 5:7–8). Not the rejuvenation of nature but the Jewish memorial feast celebrating the liberation from Egyptian bondage was the immediate backdrop for the Easter celebration of the liberation of Jesus from the tomb. The resurrection of Jesus from the dead is at the very heart of Christian conviction and so it is no surprise that Easter as a special time of observance was the earliest and remains the most important day on the Christian calendar.

In the fourth century the church at large began to observe a festival to celebrate the incarnation of the Lord, not only the birth of Jesus. However, early Christian writers did propose different dates for the birth of Jesus. Many scholars believe the church in Rome settled on December 25 to commemorate his birth to undercut the influence of the Roman festival of *Dies Natalis Solis Invicti* (Birthday of the Unconquered Sun). This date for Christmas was gradually accepted throughout the church in the West. In the East the church remained less concerned about which day Mary gave birth and instead celebrated Epiphany on January 6 as an occasion set apart to draw worshipful attention to the mystery of the incarnation.

Pentecost, as a time to celebrate the outpouring of the Holy Spirit and the birth of the church, began to be observed at least from the time of Tertullian in the third century. This day was originally the Jewish Feast of Weeks (Shavuot), falling on the fiftieth day of Passover. It was during the Feast of Weeks that the first fruits of the grain harvest were dedicated (Deut 16:9). This was also a time for celebrating the giving of the Law. The second chapter of the book of Acts reports that the disciples of Jesus were gathered in an upper room in Jerusalem when they began to hear what sounded like a very strong wind. Then, appearing like flames of fire, the Holy Spirit descended upon each of them. This experience inspired the disciples to praise God and preach in tongues—languages—that could be understood in the dialects of all the people who had come to worship in Jerusalem from other places in the Roman Empire.

These celebrations developed over time and were used to more comprehensively instruct, inspire, renew, and deepen faith. Currently, for many church traditions in the West the Revised Common Lectionary is employed to help Christians learn to tell time in a distinctively faith-filled way, aiding spiritual formation.

The church year can be divided into three main periods. The first is the incarnational cycle from the four weeks of Advent through Christmas to Epiphany, which focuses on the incarnation and the birth of Jesus but also looks to his coming in the future. This cycle concludes with Transfiguration Sunday. The second, the paschal cycle, starts with Ash Wednesday, which begins the forty day Lenten season. The last week of Lent is Holy Week and includes Palm/Passion Sunday, Maunday Thursday, and Good Friday. The paschal cycle reaches its high point with Easter and continues through Pentecost. The third cycle, Ordinary Time, occurs during two periods, from Trinity Sunday to Christ the King Sunday, the week before Advent begins, and includes some Sundays after January 6 in some traditions.[10] This period is not "ordinary" in the sense of being plain, humdrum, or dull. Rather, the name comes from the fact that the Sundays of this period are designated by ordinal numbers (first, second, third, etc.). There are differences between the Roman Catholic, Orthodox, and Protestant liturgical calendars and some variations among Protestant churches. However, they all have in common the intention of celebrating the story of Jesus and fostering affection for and attachment to Christian convictions.

Interspersed throughout the church year is what has been called the Sanctoral Cycle during which the lives of the saints are celebrated. Protestants have traditionally objected to designating a spiritually superior class of people as "saints" over against ordinary Christians, contending that all baptized believers are saints. In free churches such as my own tradition, Dr. Martin Luther King Jr. Day is likely the only day to be observed on our essentially nonexistent Sanctoral calendar. All Saints' Day was established due to the fact that in the early church there quickly became more martyrs than individual days on which to honor each of them. Hence, a time was designated to recognize them all as a group. In the Roman Catholic Church All Saints' Day is followed by All Souls' Day when all deceased Christians are remembered. Protestants are more likely to collapse the two occasions

---

10. Duck, *Worship for the Whole People of God*, 130ff.

into one, commemorating all the departed faithful on All Saints' Day, remembering that we live and worship before a "great cloud of witnesses" (Heb 12:1).

The liturgical calendar—despite its denominational variations—provides the gathered church with opportunities to journey with Jesus into a variety of situations as a community of faith united in adoration and affection. The special days and seasons helps us to tell time, not in a way that leads us to celebrate distinctive American values and visions, but in a manner that re-presents the sacred narrative and convictions that make us who we are as a people of faith and that unites us with others who confess Jesus as Lord where ever they dwell.

WRONG CALENDAR, WRONG STORY

When nationalistic holidays are celebrated in worship the Christian story is altered by the inclusion of another story, the adoration of the church becomes divided. Who we are as church becomes obscured when a calendar is observed in church that honors persons, events, and values that have little or nothing to do with the sacred narrative and the loyalties that bind us together with others who follow Jesus where ever and whoever they are. Affections not suitable for the whole people of God are fostered in services of worship that are shaped by nationalistic holidays.

This is not to say that no mention in church should be made of nationalistic holidays or that these occasions cannot in any way be used as teaching opportunities. Preaching on the importance of memory on Memorial Day, freedom on Independence Day, or on gratitude on Thanksgiving Day need not be shunned if the messages are faithfully derived from Scripture and not merely an affirmation of the national ethos. Rather I am claiming that these holidays should not be occasions to celebrate national identity or for bestowing honor on the ventures, values, and heritage peculiar to America. Such aims have no place among those who come together as the body of Christ. When Christians in America gather in worship what makes them special is not something that a nationalistic holiday highlights but solely what is given in Christ and shared by all who are in Christ throughout the world.

The convictions that unite Christians regardless of nationality, race, or class rightly determine the content of every service of worship. In contrast, among the purposes of nationalistic holidays is to integrate diverse people by having them join together in celebrating a common loyalty that does not eliminate but supersedes other attachments and identities citizens may hold. As sociologist W. Lloyd Warner put it, "The ceremonial calendar of American society . . . *more sacred than secular*, is a symbol system used by all Americans . . . . [T]his calendar functions to draw all [American] people together to emphasize their similarities and common heritage; to minimize their differences; and to contribute to their thinking, feeling and acting alike."[11] Not only is the national calendar more sacred than secular, it can end up being more sacred than other sacred calendars, subverting them for nationalistic ends.

What sociologist Amitai Etzioni says of ethnic and racial celebrations has relevance to the Christian community: "Holidays can serve to modify the relationships between societal part and the whole." Often "conscious and systematic efforts are made" to insure that particular group celebrations do not "undermine commitment to the whole." He mentions the importance of symbolic expressions of the nation being present, specifically mentioning the display of the American flag during ceremonies and prayer. He points out the usefulness of displaying the symbols of the group alongside the flag as well as some statement like "God bless America" to indicate the group's "loyalty to the whole, stressing that their group upholds dual loyalties, and hence, its particularistic commitments do not conflict with its commitment to the larger national society."[12] However, in Christian worship the "commitment to the whole" is not the whole nation but the global church that the particularistic loyalty to America—or any other nation—threatens to undermine.

The spirituality expressed in nationalistic holidays is a competing, not complementary, spirituality to that rightly practiced in the life of the church. The unity that is affirmed and reinforced through nationalistic holidays is not an aspect of, but is potentially at odds with, "the unity of the Spirit through the bond of peace" (Eph 4:3) of which Scripture speaks. For Christians unity with those who share their faith rightly transcends the various identities and commitments found among them. A shared attachment to a nation is *not* the blest "tie that binds our hearts in Christian love" in "the fellowship of kindred minds . . . like to that above," as the hymn puts it.

11. Warner, *American Life*, 7.
12. Etzioni, "Holidays and Rituals," 17.

What Time Is It? Holidays or Holy Days?

The nationalistic holidays most frequently celebrated in churches in the United States are Independence Day, Memorial Day, and Thanksgiving Day. Each of these days plays a distinctive purpose in the life of the nation. In the following we will briefly examine the origin and function of each of these holidays and speak to the reasons their observance in Christian worship is problematic.

INDEPENDENCE DAY: THE MYTH OF "OUR" ORIGIN

For Americans the very words "Fourth of July" always mean much more than the fourth day of a midsummer month. The words are synonymous with Independence Day, the birthday of the United States. While it was on July 2, 1776, that the Second Continental Congress voted to approve a resolution of independence and not until nearly a month later before all the signatories had placed their names on the document, nevertheless the date shown on the Declaration of Independence is the day when the wording of the document was approved. In the early years of the nation the most important patriotic holiday was not Independence Day but the birthday of George Washington. In fact Independence Day didn't become an official national holiday until 1870, though it had been celebrated since 1777 in some places.

Still, it was a notable day in the life of the nation and through the years its importance increased as the day became more broadly celebrated. Not long after the Revolutionary War some religious leaders offered spiritual interpretations of Independence Day. In a message delivered on July 4 in 1796 Congregationalist preacher John Cushing celebrated the nation's birth as an American Passover. He said, "It is a day to be remembered throughout all generations." Cushing insisted, "God dealt with no people as with Israel. But in the history of the United States, particularly New England, there is as great similarity perhaps in the conduct of Providence to that of the Israelites as is to be found in the history of any people. Truly, God has done wonderful things."[13]

Among the activities normally found in Independence Day observances in earlier times were prayers, the reading of the Declaration of Independence, orations—sometimes with considerable depth and sophistication—on America origins, heroes, and accomplishments, a militia

---

13. Cushing, "A Discourse Delivered at Ashburnham, July 4, 1796," 17, 18.

shooting exhibition, or military parade. Pictures of George Washington were often displayed, as was the American flag. The flag was rarely seen by most people at other times of year prior to the Civil War. Patriotic music was often played and sung. Occasionally, there would be a community picnic.

In more recent decades family picnics and attendance at a community fireworks displays are largely all that most Americans do to celebrate Independence Day. However, that is not the case for many who attend worship. In church services on the Sunday nearest to the Fourth of July in many—if not most—American churches Independence Day is celebrated in worship. People who never sing elsewhere will sing patriotic music in church. Special attention is given to the American flag. Furthermore, while most people have never heard an Independence Day oration by a politician at a civic gathering will hear one in church in the form of a sermon.

Examples of the sorts of messages that come from the pulpits across the country are not difficult to find. Internet websites such as sermoncentral.com, preaching.com, sermonsearch.com, and many others contain messages for Independence Day. Generally the sermons of more recent decades lack the substantial insight and broad historical perspective of many of the available examples of earlier orations. Nevertheless, they serve the same basic purposes: to celebrate the birth of the nation and extol American exceptionalism in order to inspire national pride, deepen affection and loyalty, and solidify unity.

While there is considerable diversity among Independence Day sermons, frequently claims are made by preachers that America was founded as a Christian nation on biblical principles, a dubious assertion at best. Preachers will often proclaim, "America was protected and directed by God from the beginning," and that America was settled by people seeking religious freedom in contrast to the "other nations that came into existence by conquest for selfish and ambitious motives."[14] In truth there were as many or more early settlers who came to America "for selfish and ambitious motives" as there were those who came "seeking religious freedom."

Further, the religious freedom sought by the Puritans was freedom for their own practices, not for the religious practices of others, a fact neglected by ministers who seek to keep the myth of America's beginnings

---

14. "Blessed is the Nation," Sermon Central, July 2009, http://www.sermoncentral.com/sermons/blessed-is-the-nation-part-1-melvin-newland-sermon-on-independence-day-59326.asp?Page=2.

untarnished. Assertions that hold that America is the most welcoming and generous of all nations abound in these sermons, though this claim was far more true of the nation in the past than in the present. Founding fathers, presidents, and other luminaries are copiously quoted—and sometimes fabricated quotes are used—to show the godly nature of America, if not in practice at least in intention.

In many pulpits on the Sunday nearest to the Fourth of July the importance of America is elevated and claims about God's special providential work in, for, and through America are common features in the messages preached. Assurance that God has a special covenant with America is routinely offered from pulpits on Independence Day. As Adrian Rogers, preacher and three-term president of the Southern Baptist Convention claimed, "May I tell you again, without stutter, stammer or equivocation, that no nation in the history of the world ever had such a Christian beginning as our God-blessed America. The American dream was placed in the bosom of our founding fathers by the Almighty Himself."[15] In a variety of ways pride in American identity is fostered through the Independence Day sermons. In sermons preachers often make it clear that America is exceptional and has been given a special place in God's providential work to spread freedom throughout the world, peaceably if possible, by force of arms if necessary.

Not surprisingly, it is common for ministers to remind their listeners that while they should love and be loyal to America, they should always be even more faithful to God. However, very rarely is there a suggestion that Christians will ever have to make a choice between the two. Rather, there is a prevailing assumption that the will of God and the interests of America are altogether compatible. Furthermore, what is virtually never heard in an Independence Day sermon is any admonition calling American Christians to be more loyal to the church than to America or to remember that our spiritual attachment to followers of Jesus throughout the world is more precious than a shared identity as Americans.

Independence Day celebrations in worship are occasions to distort Christianity by exalting the nation over the church as an instrument of God for the healing and hope of the world. All too often the sermons for the day present a nationalistic false gospel. Branden P. Anderson is correct in saying "this nationalist discourse, which emanates from within the

---

15. Adrian Rogers, "Blessings for America," Sermonsearch, http://www.sermonsearch.com/sermon-outlines/14949/blessings-for-america/.

church itself, constitutes a syncretistic salvation narrative, distorted from the Christian faith, entailing a theopolitic that supplants the church with the American nation as the extension of a misappropriated biblical Israel."[16]

MEMORIAL DAY: RIGHTFUL REMEMBERING?

Memorial Day is a specially designated occasion for honoring the people who died in combat while serving in the military. It originated in the aftermath of the Civil War, first in the South and shortly thereafter in the North. Several cities lay claim to being the founding place of Memorial Day, including Charleston, South Carolina; Boalsburg, Pennsylvania; Columbus, Georgia; Carbondale, Illinois; and Columbus, Mississippi. On May 26, 1966, President Johnson signed a presidential proclamation designating Waterloo, New York, as the birthplace of Memorial Day. Prior to this action, the 89th Congress had adopted House Concurrent Resolution 587 which officially recognized a 100-year tradition of Memorial Day observances in Waterloo.

A study based on careful research has called into question origination claims and concludes that nearly all of them are based more on legend than history.[17] Originally called Decoration Day, particularly in the North, this was an occasion for recognizing the Civil War dead and for placing flowers on their graves. In the North the observances were sponsored by the Women's Relief Corps, the women's auxiliary of the Grand Army of the Republic. In the South the Ladies Memorial Association held an important role in the development of Memorial Day celebrations. In the first years after the Civil War Memorial Day speeches became an occasion for veterans, politicians, and ministers in the North, on the one hand, and in the South, on the other, to remember those who died on battlefields and recall the "atrocities" of the enemy.

In the twentieth century the focus of Memorial Day broadened to honor all Americans who died while in the military service. Sociologist W. Lloyd Warner observed, "Memorial Day is a cult of the dead which organizes and integrates the various faiths and national and class groups into a sacred unity."[18] The primary theme of the holiday is the freely given

---

16. Anderson, *Chosen Nation*, 150.
17. Bellware and Gardiner, *The Genesis of the Memorial Day Holiday in America*.
18. Warner, *American Life*, 8.

sacrifices of the soldiers for the good of the nation. These sacrifices are held up to be honored and, when necessary, emulated by those who are still living.

From the beginning Memorial Day was more of an expressly spiritual affair than Independence Day. The somber parades have generally had religious overtones and speeches given at community gatherings frequently have had references to Scripture. This nationalistic spirituality is heightened in tone and content when Memorial Day celebrations are brought into worship. As with Independence Day, the many churches that observe Memorial Day display the American flag, sometimes having the congregation stand to recite the Pledge of Allegiance. Patriotic music is included in the service as the voices of the worshipers are joined in singing lyrics that extol America and ally God with the nation.

The number of people attending Memorial Day ceremonies has diminished in recent decades. While there are towns and cities that still hold Memorial Day parades, in other places parades have been discontinued due to lack of participation. The majority of people exposed to Memorial Day observances encounter them in worship. Sermons for the day are characteristically filled with expressions of thanks for the soldiers who died in war and declarations about their heroism. Messages commonly honor the sacrifices of the fallen by linking battlefield deaths with the self-denial Jesus called his disciples to practice. The sacrifices of soldiers engaged in warfare are often compared favorably to the sacrifice of Jesus Christ.

A cursory review of the sermon websites I mentioned above will reveal the great extent nationalistic commitments merge with claims of Christian faith claims in Memorial Day sermons. Preacher David Whitten compared death of soldiers to the incomparable sacrifice of Jesus: "Thank God for those who died to make us free . . . . Similarly the price Jesus paid afforded our salvation."[19] *Similiarly?* Such a comparison diminishes the astonishing nonviolent, self-giving act of God in Christ in order to bestow exaggerated honor on those who died in bloody conflict. But such comparisons are a regular feature in Memorial Day messages that issue from pulpits.

Despite the fact that freedom of religion was not at stake in a single American war, Whitten declared, "Because men died for this country we

---

19. David Whitten, "Every Sunday is a Memorial Day," Sermon Central, May 2002, http://www.sermoncentral.com/sermons/every-sunday-is-a-memorial-day-david-whitten-sermon-on-holidays-civic-47023.asp.

have a right to preach God's word freely."[20] Misleading assertions of this sort are not uncommon in Memorial Day sermons. After making some blatantly slanderous claims about the aims and intentions of antiwar activists, in a sermon titled "So Much to Remember," preacher Jerry Shirley insisted, "We should make much of our war heroes before our children . . . . We are proud of our heritage and those who have so honorably defended our freedoms."[21] Instead of fostering affections for peacemakers who deplore war, the preacher urges Christians to instill in the hearts of the young national pride and foster a disposition to support those willing to make war.

Not just appropriate honor but excessive glorification of soldiers who died in battle abounds in many sermons for this holiday. Exploits of soldiers who caused considerable death and damage to the enemy before succumbing to mortal wounds themselves are sometimes described to those gathered for worship. Dramatic, savior-like accomplishments are ascribed to soldiers. In a sermon called "A Memorial Day Challenge" preacher Marvin Patterson cites a litany he attributes to an unnamed Marine.

> It's the soldier, not the reporter who has given us
> Freedom of the Press.
> It's the soldier, not the poet, who has given us
> Freedom of Speech.
> It's the soldier, not the campus organizer, who has given us the
> Freedom to Demonstrate.
> It's the soldier, not the lawyer, who has given us the
> Right to a Fair Trial.
> It's the soldier who salutes the flag,
> Who serves beneath the flag,
> And whose coffin is draped by the flag,
> Who allows the protester to burn the flag.[22]

In keeping with broader recent American trends, Memorial Day activities in churches often honor not only soldiers who died in war, but all soldiers. With more truth than is offered in many Memorial Day sermons, cultural critic David Masciotra observed that the armed conflicts involving American soldiers since World War II "had nothing to do with the safety or

---

20. Ibid.

21. Jerry Shirley, "So Much to Remember," Sermon Central, May 2006, http://www.sermoncentral.com/sermons/so-much-to-remember—memorial-day-jerry-shirley-sermon-on-holidays-civic-91583.asp.

22. Marvin Patterson, "A Memorial Day Challenge," Sermonsearch, http://www.sermonsearch.com/sermon-outlines/76814/a-memorial-day-challenge/.

freedom of the American people.... If a soldier deserves gratitude, so does the litigator who argued key First Amendment cases in court, the legislators who voted for the protection of free speech, and thousands of external agitators who rallied for more speech rights, less censorship and broader access to media.... [I]nsisting all members of the military are heroes too often reinforces the American values of militarism and exceptionalism." And these are not the rightful values of the church nor an appropriate focus for liturgical remembrance.[23]

The church has a particular responsibility to remember truthfully, not in a way that fosters either national pride or the demonizing of others. As we gather for worship the memories we lift up are those that call us to be attentive to the working of God, lead us to seek the comfort of God, and move us to be more faithful to God, not to any other power. Michael L. Budde observes that "the control of death's presentation and meaning remains central to reinforcing the claims of modern citizenship above all other allegiances and identities."[24] For the church in worship it is the Christian story, not the American story, that sets the context of our presentation of death and its meaning.

Memorial Day exercises in worship, like those in non-church settings, are all too often exercises in false memory. While lost loved ones are rightly grieved and courageous and sacrificial actions are justly admired, it is definitely not true that all American wars have been for just causes or fought in a just manner. All who have served in the armed forces are not heroes by any reasonable definition of the word. To "remember" in a way that suggests otherwise, as many sermons have done, is deceptive and destructive, bestowing honor where honor is not due and illegitimately glorifying not only warriors but American wars. Theologian Miroslav Volf has insightfully written, "To remember something incorrectly is, in an important sense, not to remember at all—[W]e do not remember to the precise extent that what we remember is incorrect... so that we unwittingly pass fictions for truths."[25]

The church has set aside a time for remembering the dead. That time is All Saints' Day. This celebration of remembrance is not for those who

---

23. David Masciotra, "You Don't Protect My Freedom," Salon, November 9, 2014, http://www.salon.com/2014/11/09/you_dont_protect_my_freedom_our_childish_insistence_on_calling_soldiers_heroes_deadens_real_democracy/.

24. Budde, *The Borders of Baptism*, 184.

25. Volf, *The End of Memory*, 47.

died for the nation in wars, but for those who died in Christ. On this day we honor those who went before us on the journey of faith and who are examples for us as we endeavor to walk in the way of the Prince of Peace.

THANKSGIVING DAY: BEING GRATEFUL FOR US

The theme of gratitude and the practice of giving thanks to God for the abundance of God's gifts to us are deeply biblical. "O give thanks to the LORD, call on his name, make known his deeds among the peoples . . . . O give thanks to the LORD, for he is good; for his steadfast love endures forever" (1 Chr 16:8, 34). "I will praise the name of God with a song; I will magnify him with thanksgiving" (Ps 69:30). "Let us come into his presence with thanksgiving; let us make a joyful noise to him with songs of praise!" (Ps 95:2). "Everything created by God is good, and nothing is to be rejected, provided it is received with thanksgiving" (1 Tim 4:4). I find myself compelled to agree with Richard L. Eslinger: "The church's appropriation of Thanksgiving is certainly the least problematic of any attempts to 'Christianize' distinctly civil religious holidays."[26]

However, to say that celebrating Thanksgiving Day in worship is "the least problematic" does not mean it is *unproblematic*. Speaking of Thanksgiving Day, a generally liberal Roman Catholic priest wrote, "The national feast is so basically religious, so fundamentally American, and so agreeably Catholic that it should rank as one of the significant feasts of the liturgy."[27] But the fact is that just to the extent that Thanksgiving Day is "fundamentally American" it is incapable of being genuinely Catholic or catholic. Gratitude is catholic and ecumenical; the American holiday of Thanksgiving Day is not.

For the church to celebrate this occasion as an American holiday leads to the diminishing of distinctively Christian motifs. It is notable that most frequently used hymns for Thanksgiving—"We Gather Together" and "Come, Ye Thankful People, Come"—lack specifically Christian themes. Further, the narrative from which Thanksgiving Day arises is peculiarly American and as such importing it into worship helps facilitate and foster a unity, identity, and affections not inherent to the faith and life of church. The story of the so-called "First Thanksgiving" is part of the American

---

26. Eslinger, "Civil Religion and the Year of Grace," 378.
27. Bordelon, "Thanksgiving Day," 655.

origin myth and often is presented as a piece of a salvation story with similarities to the narratives of the people of Israel in the wilderness.

After their first harvest in 1621, the Pilgrims celebrated with a feast that lasted three days. William Bradford wrote a matter-of-fact account of the events. "He intended not to establish an institution, but only to note the passing of yet another providential moment among many," observed historian Anne Blue Wills.[28] Yet the story of the Pilgrims and American Indians feasting together and thanking God for the plenty after that first harvest is recounted as though this event was the beginning of an annual celebration. In fact the Pilgrims sporadically celebrated "thanksgivings" for a variety of reasons. They also declared days for prayer and fasting.

It is, indeed, true that Massasoit the Wampanoag leader had provided food to the colonists during the first winter when supplies brought from England proved to be inadequate. Likewise, it is true that the Pilgrims were taught how to catch eel and grow corn by Squanto of the Patuxet tribe who lived among the Wampanoag and served as an interpreter for the Pilgrims. He had learned English while enslaved in England. But the idyllic harmony portrayed in the often repeated telling of the "First Thanksgiving" serves a nationalistic origin myth of a golden age rather than a fuller truth.

In response to this mythic version of the First Thanksgiving Native Americans, James Lee West offered a version of events that does not serve nationalistic ends:

> My people have grown weary of hearing the songs of Thanksgiving. My people have grown weary of looking back at the first winter when the white man came singing songs of praise to a white man's God who had blessed the new experiment in the "bleak wilderness" where no man had set foot. My people have grown weary of a celebration that can speak over and over again of a great tradition and a great nation "born under God" for the good of all mankind and that can turn men's hearts and minds to years of building a great American dream without turning their hearts and minds to the blood and death upon which that dream is built.
>
> We remember very well that Massasoit helped to save those first white men by teaching them to survive in the wilderness they feared so much. But we also remember that he could not teach them that their "red brothers" were more than animals. We remember that two generations later in King Philip's War Massasoit's

---

28. Wills, "Pilgrims and Progress," 140.

own people fought back at these white men who had no regard for our humanity or civilization.[29]

Rather than being a celebration that developed directly from the experience of the early Pilgrims, Thanksgiving Day was a nineteenth-century invention. In the minds of the Pilgrims to establish an annual day of Thanksgiving would be to take God's providential mercy for granted. "It would tend to make people overconfident of God's blessings and insufficiently conscious of their constant dependence upon his mercy," wrote Diana Muir.[30] It is noteworthy that when President George Washington issued his Thanksgiving Proclamation in 1789, as well as the earlier Thanksgiving Proclamations of the Continental Congress, no mention is made of the so-called "First Thanksgiving" as a historical precedent. Even in the Thanksgiving Proclamation issued by Abraham Lincoln in 1863 there was no reference to the Pilgrims' harvest feast.

For the most part Thanksgiving celebrations were proclaimed by governors of states rather than by presidents. They were not always annual events and the date of observance differed from state to state. It was only in 1863 that Thanksgiving Day became an annual holiday, established by President Lincoln. To a great extent this was due to the lobbying efforts of Sarah Josepha Hale, editor of the most widely read periodical in the country at the time *Godey's Lady's Book and Magazine*, later called the *Ladies Home Journal and Practical Housekeeper*. "Thanksgiving for Hale signified one's active participation in the fulfillment of America's destiny as the greatest of all nations."[31]

The annual celebration of Thanksgiving Day was never simply an occasion to express gratitude to God. Nationalistic aims shaped the holiday. Schools used Thanksgiving as pedagogical tool to instruct and socialize immigrant children, southerners, Catholics, and others on the margins, imparting feelings of national unity and loyalty.[32] The advocates for an annual Thanksgiving Day believed that the US had been chosen by God and used the holiday to instill that belief in those who newly arrived in the country. However, as historian Anne Blue Wills observes, "Where the Pilgrim soul sought God, the nineteenth-century Pilgrim heirs sought a certain kind of Americanness.... As this festival united U.S. citizens, set them apart from

---

29. West, "A Native American's Reflection on Thanksgiving," 12.
30. Muir, "Proclaiming Thanksgiving Throughout the Land," 195.
31. Wills, "Pilgrims and Progress," 147.
32. Pleck, "Who Are We and Where Do We Come From?" 46.

the rest of the world and fit them for a certain way of life, it also knit itself into their memories and tempered their behavior. Thanksgiving encouraged submission, not to a sovereign providence, but to the project of the nation."[33]

While fostering and expressing gratitude to God in worship for the saving deeds and ongoing blessings of the one revealed in Christ is of central importance, inspiring people to be thankful as Americans for things related to America is *not*. We thank God for who God is and for what God has done. Generating thanks based on national myths that hide more truth than they display has no role in the worship life of Christian churches. Rather, as we gather as a people of faith in thankful praise, we do so in unity with others throughout the ages and throughout the world who follow Jesus.

It is as we worship God, remaining attentive to the Christian story and conscious of our fellowship with brothers and sisters of every race, class, and nation, that we who seek to follow Jesus Christ are reminded of who we are and how to live. Celebrating the calendar of Babylon by observing American nationalistic holidays in worship will not help us develop the affections, sense of self, or sort of unity suitable for a people pursuing a Christ-centered faith. Those ends of faith are far better served by telling time in worship according to the calendar of the church without observing the nationalistic holidays that serve ends foreign to Christian faith.

---

33. Wills, "Pilgrims and Progress," 142, 154.

CHAPTER 5

Displaying the Banner of Babylon

Several years ago the organizers of the National Day of Prayer were selling on their website a framed picture entitled, "True Prayer." It was a photograph of a darling, very young girl with eyes closed, caressing an American flag on her cheek. How is this an image of "true prayer"? What kind of prayer can this be? To whom is prayer being offered? Only in the view of those whose faith has been significantly misshapen by nationalistic devotion to Babylon could prayer be identified in any way with cuddling the national flag. Yet many churches have in a fashion cuddled the flag by displaying it before the congregation gathered for prayer and worship.

Ministers who believe the flag has no place before the church at worship and have acted to remove it have often paid a heavy price at the hands of those who are determined to have the congregation continue the cuddling. As one commentator on the American religious scene said, "In the culture where I live, a pastor of a typical church who removed the flag would be fired. A pastor who started a process aimed at removing the flag would be starting a process to find another job. Removing the flag would be seen as something like a declaration of atheism or endorsing Al-Qaeda. Or both. Multiplied. By ten."[1]

---

1. Michael Spencer, "What About the Flag in the Sanctuary?" Ministry Matters, July 1, 2011, http://www.ministrymatters.com/all/article/entry/1407/what-about-the-flag-in-the-sanctuary-or-how-to-get-fired-really-fast.

Displaying the Banner of Babylon

A few years ago a minister in Florida removed the American flag from the sanctuary of the church he served, and the negative response was so intense that it led to a police investigation.² Many congregants were angry. The minister received several harassing notes. One of them threatened, "Resign this Sunday or else." Though this minister attempted in sermons and discussions to offer theological reasons for his actions, the opposition continued unabated. Finally, he took a leave of absence and eventually resigned. One person who posted a response to the newspaper online report of this conflict, wrote, " . . . so why are people taking flags down??? Get a grip America as the time has come to remember our basics of our foundation."

What is it about the flag that has anything to do with the "basics of our foundation" as a people called together in Christian worship? The insistence that the flag be displayed in church reflects a widespread willingness to honor a national symbol as sacred in a setting where nothing should be considered sacred but God alone. But when American Christian nationalism is incorporated into faith, misplaced adoration is inevitable. Again it must be said, this is the essence of idolatry. Sociologist Wilbur Zelinsky observed that "as *the* organizing symbol of our nation-state and of the Americanism that is its civil religion, the flag has preempted the place, visually and otherwise, of the crucifix in older Christian lands."³

The national flag, the banner of Babylon, has become an essential symbol of many congregations at worship. When that which is holy to the nation becomes holy in the worship of the church confusion about who God is and who the people are as they gather in worship will surely be the result. The America flag in worship is the most evident ongoing manifestation of the church's willingness to bow toward Babylon.

HOW THE AMERICAN FLAG GOT INTO THE CHURCH

The first European settlers in America not only held no flag as sacred but intentionally acted to insure that flags would not draw undue honor. Puritan leaders altered colonial flags to remove any religious symbolism. John Winthrop's successor as chief magistrate of the Massachusetts Bay Colony

---

2. "Resign This Sunday or Else," WTSP Tampa Bay, May 14, 2008, http://www.topix.com/forum/city/deland-fl/T9OT1MOT54FP54A8C.

3. Zelinsky, *Nation Into State*, 196.

ordered the cross to be removed from a flag in Salem in 1634.[4] His aim, and that of other like-minded leaders, was to insure that flags were purely functional and did not evoke anything akin to religious devotion. For well over 200 years from the time when Puritan leaders acted to desacralize flags, no flags were found in churches.

Not only was the flag not brought onto church property or welcomed in worship spaces, the national flag did not always enjoy the place it now holds both in the American landscape and in the hearts of Americans. As historian Cecilia Elizabeth O'Leary noted, "Rallying around the flag, the ritualistic core of the modern patriotic movement, was slow to develop."[5] In fact for the eighty-five years or more after the Revolutionary War, many Americans may have lived their entire lives without ever seeing an actual national flag. On patriotic occasions like Independence Day, speeches, poetry, and early America patriotic art would be present but the flag was often absent. The most important patriotic symbols in the early decades after independence were images of George Washington, personifications of liberty, and the bald eagle, not the flag.

Francis Scott Key's words in "Star Spangled Banner" helped bring the flag into greater prominence. For decades the flag had a purely utilitarian purpose, mostly used for identification purposes on commercial ships and the navy. The use of the flag slowly grew throughout the first half of the 19th century. The army did not use the American flag until 1834, preferring regimental banners. In the 1840s the flag began to be more evident during election seasons. The flag was first used on a battlefield during the Mexican-American War (1846–1848). As conflict grew between the North and the South prior to the Civil War, so, too, did an emphasis on the flag increase among Unionists. However, it was the attack on Fort Sumter on April 12, 1861 that led to the dramatic emphasis on and use of the American flag. For those in the North, the conflict was a "War against the Flag."[6]

Attributing religious meaning to the America flag began shortly after the start of the Civil War. In *Harper's* magazine, July 1861 in an article entitled "Our Flag and What it Symbolized" the editor ventured well beyond the factual observation that thirteen stripes symbolize the original thirteen colonies and the number of stars represent the current number of states in the union. He wrote, "God has given us our guiding light and our moving

---

4. Guenter, *The American Flag, 1777–1924*, 26.
5. O'Leary, *To Die For*, 20.
6. Guenter, *The American Flag, 1777–1924*, 65.

mind and will continue and renew them still. More deeply perhaps than we are conscious, we feel this two-fold gift when we look at the flag of our Union .... Those stars speak to us of laws of equity as fixed as the eternal heavens, and those stripes as they wave in the breeze, tell us of that mysterious breath which move through men and nations that may be born, not of flesh, but of God."[7]

With the onset of the Civil War the meaning of the American flag began to swiftly evolve from being a functional emblem of the nation into a symbol of religious significance. In no small part, this occurred because "in the churches, where voices joined in prayer and supplication for victory, the American flag quietly appeared, not just as a secular symbol, but an affirmation of a belief in God's ordained plan for the future reconciliation and growth of the Union."[8]

No longer was the flag just a national banner displayed on ships, forts, and sometimes on federal government buildings. It began to appear on college flagstaffs, over hotels, in front of banks, in school rooms, on private homes, and along streets. It was with this outburst of enthusiasm for the flag that it was introduced into churches. The stars and stripes was brought into sanctuaries and placed upon chancels. It was flown from steeples. The religious passion for the flag increase as the passion for war rose.

Northern seminaries also began to fly the American flag. Harriet Beecher Stowe, author of *Uncle Tom's Cabin*, wrote a hymn sung to the music of "America" that was used during the raising of the flag at Andover Seminary. The lyrics explicitly linked the flag to the providential working of God.

> God bless our star-gemmed banner,
> shake its folds out to the breeze,
> From church, from fort, from house-top
> O'er the city on the seas;
> The die is cast, the storm at last
> Has broken in its might;
> Unfurl the starry banner,
> And may God defend the right.
>
> Then bless our banner, God of hosts!
> Watch o'er each starry fold,
> 'Tis Freedom's standard, tried and proved

---

7. Cited in ibid, 83.
8. Ibid, 66.

On many a field of old;
And thou, who long hast blest us,
Now bless us yet again,
And drown our cause with victory,
And keep our flag from stain.[9]

Baptist, Episcopal, Dutch Reformed, Roman Catholic, and other churches began to display the America flag in or around the church. Though this had previously not been a practice, political—and, more specifically, wartime—passions ran ahead of theological clear thinking. Almost entirely absent were voiced concerns about the integrity of worship. Support for the Union was given priority. So with little critical reflection churches embraced the flag. A rare expression of objection to the eager adoption of the flag by churches came from the New York *Commercial Advertizer*. The editor was not a supporter of the Union cause.

He was particularly provoked when the Grace Episcopal Church in Manhattan voted to fly the flag from the top of the church spire. With some difficulty two painters attached the flag atop the cross, to the cheers of a crowd gathered below. In response, the paper declared, "The historian of the day will not fail to mention, for the edification of men of future ages, the fact that the flag, which was once the flag of our Union, floats boldly above the cross of Christ on Grace Church steeple."[10]

While there was no broad and conspicuous outcry of opposition to the introduction of the American flag into churches, still some churches did not adopt the practice. Nationalists saw this omission as a problem. In the decades following the Civil War, patriotic societies began an aggressive campaign to elevate the honor bestowed on the flag and proliferate its display. With militant determination patriotic societies—the Grand Army of the Republic (GAR) and the Daughters of the American Revolution (DAR) in particular—promoted the introduction of the flag in every possible public space.

Placing American flags in churches was particularly important for those intent upon elevating reverence for the Stars and Stripes. Ministers were often eager accomplices in these efforts to turn the flag into a holy symbol. In a flag ceremony at the City College of New York on June 8, 1888, the Rev. Dr. John R. Paxton urged, "Now let us come and gather under its

---

9. Collins, *Threads of History*, 88.
10. Cited in Guenter, *The American Flag, 1777–1924*, 85.

blessed folds. Let us be tangled in the stars and covered with its stripes."[11] George Gue, pastor of Rock Island, Illinois persuaded the Central Illinois Conference of the Methodist Episcopal Church on September 30, 1889 to endorse the following resolution: "Resolved, that we, as a conference, do recommend that the American flag be placed in our churches and Sunday Schools as an emblem of our Christian civilization."[12]

The following year, he published *Our Country's Flag*, a large book that contained, among many other patriotic items, an illustration of an American flag flying from the spire of a Gothic church. Also included in the book was a poem, "Our Country's Flag on God's Sacred Altars," by J. W. Temple, which encouraged the merging of Christianity and patriotism by displaying the flag in churches. The flag evangelists knew attempts to foster the glorification of the flag would be most successful if it was brought into the presence of people at worship.

Near this same time, a tireless promoter of patriotism, New York City auditor of the board of education George T. Balch, concerned about "human scum, cast on our shores by the tidal wave of a vast immigration," was busily at work. He wrote *Methods for Teaching Patriotism in Public Schools*, a manual endorsed by the GAR and used widely. Not only did it suggest ways of honoring the American flag in public school, recommendations for home, and church were included as well.

The aim to sacralize the flag by associating it as closely as possible with God is clear on many pages of the primer: "The first lesson of patriotism should be taught at the mother's knee when innocent lips are taught to lisp 'Our Father, who art in Heaven.' Teach them to love the word 'country' . . . . Let the America flag be constantly in sight—in the home, in the street, in the school house, in the church. Let our love for God be mingled with our love of country. Let the flag be placed with the Holy Bible, one the emblem of loyalty and that freedom which God intended for his creatures, the other the teachings of humanity and God's divine love for his children." He insisted, "Let the cross, precious emblem of our savior's suffering, be entwined with the starry fields of the American flag, which represents the blood bought liberties we enjoy." Also found on these pages is the insistence that "our country's flag must find a place in your ranks, side by side with your grand standard of the blessed Emmanuel, the Prince of Peace."[13]

11. Ibid, 105.
12. Ibid, 106.
13. Ibid, 119.

During the 1880s pictures of the American flag began to appear much more frequently in books and popular journals, particularly for those published for children. Stories that were written to foster patriotism increasingly gave the flag a more central role. Devotion to flag and devotion to country were characteristically equated. Sometimes the flag was attributed with almost mystical power. In the 1890s the status of the flag continued to grow to such an extent that in some patriotic stories, "the American flag becomes a central prop, often granted a 'persona' more God-like than human."[14]

The nationalism inspired by the Spanish-American War led to the further proliferation of the flag and provided a compelling occasion for the continuing introduction of the American flags into churches. War was—and continues to be—an important driving force in the propagation of flag displays in churches and elsewhere. In the years during World War I the campaign to place the flag in every possible public arena continued even more aggressively. So many flags were needed during the war that the price for flags more than doubled.[15]

At this time period a number of ritualistic programs glorifying the American flag were written for and performed in churches and other large groups. In 1917 *Building of the Flag, or Liberty Triumphant* was produced by Homer A. Rodeheaver as a "patriotic exercise for juniors."[16] The production thoroughly blended Christian's language and symbols with songs and rituals of flag adoration. A "Christian flag" was suspended above the stage. As the ceremony proceeded, children brought paper strips and pasteboard stars and gradually built a large American flag. The Pledge of Allegiance was recited. A banner with a selection of Scripture led a procession, Bible passages were read, and patriotic songs were sung, including the "Flag Drill Song," which offered praise for both the American flag and the "Christian flag." The final verse completely merges Christianity and American nationalism: "Lift them higher, Christian flags so true, Red, white and blue, Both dear to you! Liberty to all mankind proclaim Thro' the dear Redeemer's name."

The following year, H. Augustine Smith, a Boston University professor, wrote *A Pageant of the Stars and Strips*.[17] It was billed as "A patriotic

---

14. Ibid, 111.
15. Ibid, 163.
16. Rodeheaver, *A Patriotic Exercise for Juniors*.
17. Smith, *A Pageant of the Stars and Stripes*.

service for Churches, Church Schools, Public Schools, Boy and Girl Scouts, Civic Celebrations." In the first portion of the presentation a summary of the development of the American flag was reviewed through staged scenes and songs. Children in scout uniforms, men in military khakis, and finally representatives of church dressed in vestments entered and all stood in front of GAR veterans to sing "Onward Christian Soldiers."

The second portion of the presentation involved children building an American flag, much as was done in Rodeheaver's production. As school girls came in, two at a time, to construct the flag, portions of Secretary of State Lane's Flag Day address were read. The ceremony concluded with all who were present reciting the Pledge of Allegiance, followed by everyone singing "The Star Spangled Banner."

The high point—or low point?—in flag worship was given form in William Norman Guthrie's 1918 *The Religion of Old Glory*.[18] The performance of this ritual was authorized by the bishop of New York of the Protestant Episcopal Church. This presentation drew together readings from the Old Testament, rituals from secret societies such as the Masons, and expressions of polytheism. Guthrie unambiguously identifies the American flag as the flag of God and equates glory given to the flag as glory bestowed on God: "Live for it, die for it! . . . That Old Glory float and live in the very wind of God's breath/As the symbol of the 'faith to which we are born,'/ And all mankind, thank God, along with us!"

The Chief Officiant welcomed all present "to express in word and action the religious meaning of our national emblem, Old Glory." Among the elements in this service were a Ritual Father and Ritual Mother, representing Adam and Eve, who helped place thirteen pillars around a flagpole. The American flag was displayed at the altar. "Behold with reverence and grateful pride the emblem of this Elect Nation," uttered the chief officiant. "The nation chosen by God for a mighty purpose."

The ceremony included genuflections before the flag and prayers *to* the flag. Red, white, and blue flowers were place on the altar. The chief officiant kindled a fire on the altar and burned incense, directing the smoke toward the flag. The Star Spangled Banner was sung as the Father and Mother offered ritual gestures in the direction of the flag and the chief officiant "throws a devout and passionate kiss to the flag." After "The Battle Hymn of the Republic" was sung, the service concluded with the singing of a poem

---

18. Guthrie, *The Religion of Old Glory*.

composed by Guthrie which several times repeats the words, "We worship thee flying from flagstaff, mast and steeple." The chorus declared,

> Hail, great in song and story,
> Dear flag of brave and free—
> O Stars and Stripes, Old Glory,
> We offer our all to thee.

While Guthrie's ritual received no broad embrace, voices expressing concern about hyper-Americanism and excessive honor being bestowed on the flag were mute among the religious mainstream. The most blatantly idolatrous manifestations of adoration of the flag were greeted with either open arms or silent consent. The campaign during the first decades of the twentieth century to elevate the status of the American flag through flag codes, rituals, and desecration laws received widespread support from churches at virtually every turn. With every spike in patriotism—usually during a time of war—more previously flagless churches open the doors to welcome the red, white, and blue "holy" banner.

ENFORCING FLAG HONOR

As the America flag became increasingly sacred, so too did concern about protecting the flag from desecration grow in intensity. A national flag with the simple utilitarian purpose of being an emblem of a country has no need for desecration laws. But as the American flag came to be more closely associated with God and divine purposes, concern that the flag be properly adored and that any evidence of disrespect be penalized moved more to the forefront in the work of patriotic and veterans organizations. Disrespect for the flag was not regarded as just boorish but seen as blasphemous.

Initially these groups urged voluntary respect for the flag but eventually discontent heightened considerably about how some people treated the flag. In particular using the flag to advertise products from cod liver oil to whisky seemed to treat the flag with casualness not appropriate for a symbol that had been elevated to holy status. Further, in the eyes of its most ardent devotees, the flag seemed to be insufficiently honored in political campaigns. Sometimes the names of candidates were printed across American flags. Perhaps this benefitted the candidate by associating his name with the stars and stripes, but in the view of those intent on making the flag holy, using the flag for blatantly partisan ends seemed to diminish the sacredness of the flag. No concern, however, was expressed over associating the flag with God, thereby increasing its aurora of holiness for the flag while diminishing the holiness of God by reducing God to a tribal deity.

At the end of the nineteenth century veterans, hereditary, and other patriotic organizations began to lobby for laws to stop the uses of the flag they considered to be desecration. The first anti-desecration legislation was presented in the House of Representatives in 1878 by Representative Samuel Sullivan Cox of Ohio. It died in committee. A similar bill was introduced two years later by Hiram Barber Jr., a congressman from Illinois. It, too, failed to become law. During the next decade anti-desecration legislation began to be given better reception. However, the success was on the state rather than national level.

At the forefront of the flag protection movement was wealthy retired newspaper advertising executive Charles Kingsbury Miller. Using explicitly religious references in an 1898 address, he maintained, "Those three sacred jewels, the Bible, the Cross, and the Flag, command our national reverence." He went on to say of the flag "that the emblem of our republic should be kept as inviolate as was the Holy of Holies in King Solomon's temple."[19] It was not uncommon among the advocates of flag protection laws to compare the adoration due to the flag like that given to the cross.

By Flag Day 1905, thirty-two states had flag protection laws. That same year Congress codified into law a ruling by the US commissioner of patents and trademarks that his office would no longer register any trademarks on commercial products that included an image of the flag.[20] However, despite the considerable lobbying efforts, no flag protection legislation was voted into law by the US Congress until 1968.

Though many states instituted flag protection laws, state appeal courts overturned a number of convictions, emboldening both politicians and businesses who were inclined to use the flag for their own interests. However, in 1907 the US Supreme Court—in *Halter v. Nebraska*—upheld the constitutionality of flag desecration laws. The court declared that the flag must be protected like religious symbols are kept holy: "The flag is the

19. Welch, *Flag Burning*, 35.
20. Leepson, *Flag*, 156ff.

emblem of national authority. To the citizen it is an object of patriotic adoration, emblematic of all for which his country stands—her institutions, her achievements, her long roster of heroic dead, the story of her past, the promise of her future."[21]

Subsequent to that decision, a number of states put into place more strict flag protection laws. In 1918 Texas passed a "disloyalty act" that raised the penalty for flag desecration from thirty days to *twenty-five years in prison*. The law did not limit what fell under desecration to actual behaviors. It also applied to any person who used "any language," whether in private or public, that "cast contempt" on the American flag.[22]

That same year, E. V. Starr was convicted in Montana under a similar law because he refused to kiss a flag after a mob attempted to force him to do so. The reason the mob attacked him is unclear from published reports, though some researchers have speculated that it was for political motives. Regardless, he resisted, saying, "What is this thing anyway, nothing but a piece of cotton with some paint on it and some other marks on the corner there. I will not kiss that thing. It might be covered with microbes." For this he was sentenced to the state penitentiary for up to twenty years of hard labor. When his case was appealed to a Judge Bourquin, he expressed his dismay at the "horrifying" sentence and criticized the mob that attacked Starr. Nevertheless, with reluctance he decided that he could not reverse the lower court's ruling.[23]

These and similar actions found some support in the words of President Woodrow Wilson, who declared at the onset of World War I, "If there should be disloyalty, it will be dealt with a firm hand of stern repression."[24] Some people took it upon themselves to be the agents of that repression as they defended the sacredness of the American flag. The most troubling incident took place near St. Louis in April 1918 when a mob of about 300 people converged on the home of Robert Paul Prager in the town of Collinsville, Illinois. He was a thirty-one year old German-American and unemployed miner.

Prager had given a speech at a socialist meeting earlier on the evening he was attacked. Some of his remarks were taken to be proof of his disloyalty. The mob dragged him from his home and forced him to walk

---

21. Cited in O'Leary, *To Die For*, 234f.
22. Ibid, 234f.
23. Ibid., 236.
24. Cited in Leepson, *Flag*, 190.

barefoot down the city street carrying two small American flags. He was also wrapped in a large American flag and forced to kiss it as he made his way down the street. Eventually, the police appeared and took him into protective custody. However, the mob later broke into the jail, took Prager, put a rope around his neck, and hanged him from a tree. A large American flag was laid over his casket at his funeral. Eleven men were arrested by the police and charged with his murder. They were tried and found not guilty by a jury in Edwardsville, Illinois.

The campaign to give the flag ever more glory continued on through the 1920s with the American Legion—the "spiritual successor" of the GAR—at the forefront of the efforts. At its founding meeting the organization expressed its intention to work for "God and Country."[25] The Legion's national director of Americanism, World War I veteran and former Maryland state senator Gerland W. Powell, wrote a book entitled *Service for God and Country* in which he offered advice on flag etiquette. He called for a national conference to design a uniform national code of flag etiquette.

Such a conference took place on June 14, 1923 in Washington, DC. Along with the American Legion, nearly seventy other organizations took part in the meeting. The US Army and Navy sent representatives. Representatives from organizations as diverse as of the Boy Scouts of America, Parent-Teacher Associations, and the Ku Klux Klan were present as well. Alvin Owsley, American Legion national commander, issued a statement, saying the intention of the conference was to "develop a definitive code of rules so that every man, woman and child in this country may know how to honor and revere the American flag."[26]

The conferees managed to agree on a flag code regarding the ways, positions, times, and occasions to display the flag. The following year another meeting was held that included over fifty more veterans and hereditary and patriotic organizations. At that time minor revisions were made to the earlier version. It was not until 1942 that the Flag Code was signed into law by President Franklin D. Roosevelt. While there were no penalties written into the code for violations of its provisions, its very existence made official the expectation that the American flag was to be treated with honor and reverence, certainly far beyond what was expected for a flag by any other nation at that time. The United States was not only the first nation to codify flag etiquette, it was also the first to create a Pledge of Allegiance, the subject of

25. Ibid, 194.
26. Ibid, 198.

the next chapter. The vast number of other nations still have neither a code nor a pledge.

The United States was also the first to have a designated Flag Day, a holy day expressly for the stars and stripes. President Woodrow Wilson presided over the first official national Flag Day on June 14, 1916, though it was not yet a legal public holiday. Nevertheless, the special day was observed in many places throughout the United States, and it became a popular day for political speeches and patriotic ceremonies. Flag Day would not be recognized by Congress and the President until 1949.

During a Flag Day speech in San Francisco on June 14, 1948, President Harry Truman declared "that the flag has significance now, and has had always a significance that no other flag in the world ever had." He went on to say the American flag is "the most beautiful flag in the world, and a *flag that stands for everything that is sacred on this continent* and stands for everything the world should strive for as a whole."[27] Such an idolatrous remark goes virtually unnoticed in America where no amount of praise for the flag is recognized as too much.

Just as Flag Day wasn't signed into law until decades of sustained advocacy, so, to, Congress did not pass a federal flag desecration law until July 4, 1968, despite the fact that such laws were on the books in every state. The impetus for the national law was found in a series of flag burnings that had taken place since 1965, primarily to protest the war in Vietnam. The law allowed for fines up to one thousand dollars and a year in jail. The political rhetoric leading up to the vote was extreme in tone and content, reflecting the idolization of the flag prevalent in America.

Representative E. Y. Berry of South Dakota claimed that those who burned the flag were "Setting fire to the institutions, beliefs and laws of our Nation as well."[28] Tennessee Representative James Quillen asserted that "anything short of a firing squad" would be "agreeable to me" as a penalty for burning the flag.[29] Other congressmen proposed that there be almost no limits on the allowable punishment for abusing the American flag. Congressman James Haley of Florida dismissed limits altogether and proposed, "Load a boatful of them and take them 500 miles out into the ocean and

---

27. Cited in Leepson, *Flag*, 221
28. Goldstein, *Saving Old Glory*, 126.
29. Ibid, 127.

handcuff them, chain the anchor around their neck and throw them overboard and tell them to swim [to a country] whose flag they can respect."[30]

During this period state laws in Alabama, Oklahoma, Indiana, and elsewhere increased penalties from a maximum of thirty days in jail and a hundred dollar fine to a maximum of between two to five years in jail and between three thousand and five thousand dollars fines. While virtually all the state flag desecration laws forbid making marks or putting pictures on the flag, using the flag for commercial purposes, as well as burning the flag, enforcement was inconsistent and arbitrary. Nearly all the prosecutions for flag desecration were of people involved in peace demonstrations.

In a controversial five-four decision fourteen years after the end of the Vietnam War—June 21, 1989—the Supreme Court ruled in the *Texas v. Johnson* case that burning the flag in protest is a form of symbolic speech covered by the First Amendment right of free speech. In his oral argument before the court, Solicitor General Kenneth Starr insisted that support for flag protection laws in effect turns the flag into a "golden image" that requires the worship of the people but "once people are compelled to respect a political symbol, then they are no longer free and their respect for the flag is quite meaningless."[31]

Feelings among those on the Court who were in the minority were strong. In writing his dissenting opinion, Chief Justice William Rehnquist declared, "The flag is not simply another 'idea,' or 'point of view' competing for recognition in the marketplace of ideas." So repugnant did he regard flag burning that he grouped it together with murder and embezzlement. He pointed to the flag's "unique position as a symbol of our nation" and noted the "mystical reverence" with which countless Americans have viewed it.[32]

The public outcry over the Supreme Court decision was immediate, as was the response of elected officials. Robert Justin Goldstein wrote in his history of flag desecration laws, "Certainly no Supreme Court decision within recent memory was so quickly and overwhelmingly denounced by the American political establishment."[33] In response Congress passed and President George H. W. Bush signed into law the Flag Protection Act of 1989. It read, "Whoever knowingly mutilates, defaces, burns, or tramples upon the flag of the United States shall be fined under this title or impris-

30. Ibid.
31. Ibid., 218.
32. Boime, *The Unveiling of the National Icons*, 65.
33. Goldstein, *Saving Old Glory*, 205.

oned for not more than one year, or both."[34] However, the following year the Supreme Court in the *U.S. v. Eichman* decision ruled five-four that the law was unconstitutional. The day after the decision President George H. W. Bush called for a constitutional amendment to protect the flag because, he said, the flag "is too sacred to be abused."[35]

In the summer of the following year, the first proposed flag desecration constitutional amendment was introduced into the US Congress. It read that "the Congress and the states have the power to prohibit the physical desecration of the flag of the United States."[36] It received a majority votes in both houses of Congress. However, it failed to receive the necessary two-thirds vote necessary for constitutional amendments. The amendment has been repeatedly introduced in Congress, falling short of the needed votes each time.

Despite the unconstitutionality of them, flag desecration laws remained on the book in many states and they were occasionally enforced. In fact vigilante justice against flag burners was essentially encouraged by resolutions placed before the legislature in several states. A Louisiana measure lowered the normal penalty for assault from $500 to a $25 fine for those assaulting flag burners.[37] Louisiana state representative Frank Patti declared, "If I saw somebody burning the flag I would stomp the hell out of them." In states where such measures failed, some politicians publically condoned violence against those who abuse the flag. Miami Beach mayor Alex Daoud held, "People who burn the flag should be shot."[38]

The excessive concern about the "desecration" of the flag, the willingness the impose criminal penalties on those who dishonor it, and the desire to do violence to those who burn the flag in protest all reveal an extreme adoration and idolatrous veneration of the flag prevalent in America. Flag protection has often been promoted—deceptively—in the name of guarding society from moral decline. In keeping with this Senator Orrin Hatch declared, "We live in a time where standards have eroded. Civility and mutual respect—preconditions for the robust views in society—are in decline

---

34. https:www.congress.gov/bill/101st-congress/house-bill/2978.
35. Leepson, *Flag*, 237.
36. Ibid., 238.
37. Welch, *Flag Burning*, 104.
38. Ibid.

.... absolutes are ridiculed. Values are deemed relative. Nothing is sacred. There are no limits."[39]

But in fact those who have burned the American flag have *not* done so in the name of relativism or because they have no values and believe nothing is sacred. Rather they have done so because they believe actions and policies have been pursued by the US government that are offensive to the highest of values. They have burned the flag, not because they believe "nothing is sacred," but because they believe there are things more sacred than the flag, and more deserving of protection, and that these have been harmed by the nation represented by the flag.

In other words, when the American flag is burned in protest this is an expression of an alternative morality that stands firmly opposed to national interests being placed above the lives and interests of the peoples of other nations. It is not emblematic of a sweeping rejection of all things American or evidence of a general breakdown of morality. Flag burning is a symbolic gesture that is given more power precisely because the American flag has been inappropriately attributed with sacred value far beyond the utilitarian purpose of the flag. However, as a form of protest it is ineffective and counterproductive, prone to misunderstanding on the part of the general public.

Regardless of the high regard given, indeed, the holy status attributed to the American flag by much of the nation, the flag still doesn't mean the same thing to everyone, otherwise there would be no debate over infractions of flag etiquette or flag protection laws. Scott Tyler, a young artist who created an installation in 1989 titled, "What is the Proper Way to Display the U.S. Flag" and placed a flag on the floor, later burning an American flag on the steps of the US Capitol building, contrasted his view of the flag to those who saw it representing freedom, noble values, and sacrifice:

> For me, when I think about the U.S. flag, it's the flag which flew above the Supreme Court as it ruled that there were no rights a black person had which a white person was bound to respect.[40] It was the flag on the planes that dropped napalm on the Vietnamese. It was the flag that most recently presided over the genocide in Iraq.[41]

While his view of the American flag seems to me to be excessively negative and one-dimensional, the fact remains that for him and for many others,

---

39. Ibid, 150.
40. Dred Scott decision, 1857.
41. Boime, *The Unveiling of the National Icons*, 79.

the flag is an obstacle, not an aid to approaching God in corporate worship. By putting the flag in close proximity to the cross or other Christian symbols a barrier is placed before those who do not see the flag as a sign of values that are universal and worthy of loyalty but who want to approach the God of all in worship.

Even in the aftermath of the 9/11 terrorist attacks, when flags were omnipresent, Katha Pollitt, a columnist for *The Nation*, a liberal periodical, refused to display the flag. As she told her daughter who suggested flying it from their living room window, "Definitely not, I say: The flag stands for jingoism and vengeance and war. There are no symbolic representations right now for the things the world really needs—equality and justice and humanity and solidarity and intelligence."[42] For her and others who view the flag in similar ways, the flag is not an emblem of peace and justice or a sign of welcome for all.

The church should not seek to cater to the perspectives of the more extreme viewpoints in society. But neither should the church include in its life and worship symbols of the values and loyalties of the mainstream of society when those values and loyalties are not expressive of the faith of the ecumenical church. The church is to be *church*, not an auxiliary to America, actively promoting attachments and expressing adoration particular to America and not distinctive and peculiar to the church loyal to the God revealed in Christ.

FLAG IDOLATRY IN THE CHURCH TODAY

There is poem I have seen included in church newsletters and bulletins variously entitled "I Am Old Glory" or "I Am the American Flag" and attributed to Don S. Miller.[43] The piece glorifies the flag in the strongest possible terms.

> I am the flag of the United States of America
> My name is Old Glory.
> I fly atop the world's tallest buildings.
> I stand watch in America's halls of justice.
> I fly majestically over great institutes of learning.
> I stand guard with the greatest military power in the world.
> Look up! And see me!

42. Leepson, *Flag*, 260.
43. http://www.usa-patriotism.com/poems/cf/old_glory1.htm.

> I stand for peace, honor, truth, and justice.
> I stand for freedom.
> I am confident . . . I am arrogant.
> I am proud.
>
> When I am flown with my fellow banners,
> my head is a little higher,
> my colors a little truer.
>
> I bow to no one.
> I am recognized all over the world.
> I am worshipped.
> I am saluted.
> I am respected.
> I am revered. I am loved.
> And I am feared.

What does it say that a church could distribute a piece of writing such as this, a personified self-adulation of the American flag, claiming, "I bow to no one! . . . I am worshipped! . . . I am revered!"? If this is not suggestive of idolatry, what is? Yet as I have already observed, where idolatry is operative it is not likely to be acknowledged as such. In fact no matter how present and active idolatry is in church, it is essential that its existence be denied, given the strong condemnation it receives throughout Scripture.

In fact the power of idolatry is best preserved by refusing to acknowledge its presence even when it is manifestly operative. Speaking of flag-centered nationalistic religion, Carolyn Marvin and David Ingle write, "When it [i.e., idolatry] threatens to surface, it is vigorously denied. . . . Though it uses Christian vocabulary, its themes are common to many belief systems." The refusal to acknowledge idolatrous devotion for what it is "obeys the ancient command never to speak the true name of God."[44] As I noted earlier, even while prancing around the golden calf, the ancient Israelites told themselves that what they were engaging in was a "feast to the LORD" (Exod 32:5). It seems that many American churches may be continuing in that very old tradition.

Idolatry functions best when it is practiced as an aspect of devotion to the true God. Imaginative attempts to interpret the American flag as a Christian symbol continue to be offered. In a leaflet by Flip Benham of

---

44. Marvin and Ingle, *Blood Sacrifice and the Nation*, 2–3.

Operation Save America, he wrote, "Our liberty in America was bought for us, first by Christ Himself freeing us from sin, and then by the sacrifices of those who followed hard after him. Life and blood go hand in hand. The American flag epitomizes this liberty." Further, he asserted that the flag's "seven red stripes signify . . . Christ's blood." He went on to claim that when enemies of America see the American flag "they see Jesus."[45] If people look at the American flag and see Jesus, the Jesus they see will not be one that resembles the Jesus presented in the Gospels. Linking the death of the non-violent Jesus to battlefield deaths, as is often done by devotees of American Christian nationalism, deeply distorts the incomparable significance of the cross.

As a national emblem, the flag is far more associated with war than any other American symbol. The Statue of Liberty, the Liberty Bell, even the bald eagle are not associated with war and warriors nearly to the degree as the flag. No one is said to have died for the Liberty Bell but it is common to speak of soldiers who have "died for the flag." While all national symbols are problematic when brought before the Christian community in worship, even more so is the flag because of its connections with war in the minds of Americans. And when there are conversations about removing the flag from sanctuaries where it has been displayed, one of the chief objections to doing so comes from people who claim the flag should remain to "honor those who died for it."

During Flag Day ceremonies held at Fort McHenry in Baltimore on June 14, 1985, President Ronald Reagan said, "And let us never forget that in honoring our flag, we honor the American men and women who have courageously fought and died for it over the last 200 years—patriots who set an ideal above any consideration of self and who suffered for it the greatest hardships. Our flag flies today because of their sacrifice."[46] Such sentiments motivate many church members who insist that the flag remain before the congregation in worship. However, they give little thought about what the church is saying by flying a banner to honor those who "courageously fought and died" while engaged in killing others who were not American but who also "courageously fought and died," and for whom Christ died.

American practices related to the flag have been Christianized to promote the stars and stripes banner as spiritually important. Legends of uncertain origin are circulated in some Christian quarters to advance the

---

45. Bentham, "I Am Not Ashamed of the American Flag."
46. Leepson, *Flag*, 247.

dubious claim that the colors selected for the American flag have some particularly Christian meaning. Likewise, though the Federal Flag Code—first adopted by Congress in 1923—has been reinterpreted by some nationalistic Christians to impose specifically religious meanings on each fold of the flag. This interpretation has been repeated in some military funerals. For instance, one fold is said to be a symbol of our belief in eternal life. Another fold represents an emblem of eternity and glorifies God the Father, the Son, and Holy Spirit. These latter-day religious interpretations of flag etiquette serve no other purpose than to blend American nationalism with Christianity thereby providing the illusion of legitimacy for the flag as a Christian symbol suitable for the church at worship.

Defenders of the flag in worship typically make their case by confusing categories. For instance, in making a case for the American flag in church one minister passionately insisted, "The flag in a sanctuary portrays a people 'under God' embracing the deepest values of life for themselves, their nation, and people of other nations.... The flag conveys inclusiveness .... The flag conveys opportunities and freedom for all. None is excluded .... The American flag in a church reminds us of the source and the cost of our freedom."[47] Whatever truth there is to be found in his words about the flag, it is not the truth of the church.

While he claims the flag "portrays a people 'under God,'" it is not the people who confess Jesus as Lord that it portrays. It only portrays Americans, both those who have faith and those who have none. To the extent that the flag "conveys inclusiveness," it does not convey *Christian* inclusiveness which is far broader than that which is found in the United States. As an American Christian of Indian descent observed, a church displaying the flag says, "You are welcome here—provided you bow to that flag. That is invariably how non-nationals, for whom our society pointedly reserves the term 'alien,' regard the flag."[48] Finally, while the flag may well remind Americans of the political freedom that is the work of human hands, it does not represent the freedom brought to us by Jesus Christ and enjoyed by people of faith without regard to nationality. The American flag in worship distracts from the truth affirmed by the church in every nation.

Is there a "moderate" position that can be taken, one that recognizes the dangers of the idolatrous inclinations of nationalistic excess in churches while supporting the presence of the American flag in worship? Russell

47. Roland, "Yes, a Flag in the Church," 23.
48. Nandy, "A Flag in the Church," 44.

D. Moore, dean of the School of Theology at Southern Baptist Theological Seminary has attempted to present such a stance. He maintains, "The flag can prompt the church to pray for and honor [national] leaders. The flag can prompt us to remember that our national identity is important but transitory."[49] Perhaps. But are these things actually what the American flag is most likely to prompt as it stands before the people of faith gathered in worship? As Carolyn Marvin and David W. Ingle stated in their important study of the flag, "Groups within the nation"—such as churches—"seek to bend the totem to their will" but their efforts inevitably fail.[50]

The emotions, values, and inclinations that the American flag generally evokes when it is displayed in a more secular setting likely will be the same ones it will prompt in worship: national pride and an America-centric perspective on life and loyalty. What the presence of flag is less likely to evoke in a community of faith are dispositions and affections distinctive of a people committed to following Jesus. The flag is unlikely to remind us that the God we worship does not hold America in special regard but is equally the God of all nations. The flag in worship is not going to prompt us to remember that nationality is peripheral to our purpose and identity as the gathered church. It is not likely to prompt us to pray for the leaders of all nations that they work together in harmony for the good of all. It will not remind us that people of faith who live under other flags are equally our brothers and sisters. Rather the American flag will much more likely distract the congregation from these truths.

Mark Tooley, president of the Institute on Religion & Democracy, has claimed, "Churches display their own country's flag because that is where God has placed them, and that is the nation entrusted to their care. It's doubtful that 'visiting Koreans' or any nationality would object to a US flag any more than an American visiting overseas would object to seeing that nation's flag displayed."[51] He assumes that the display of national flags is somehow "normal." But in fact the display of national flags in Christian worship is *not* a practice found in most nations and many Christians from other nations have expressed discomfort and surprise when seeing the American flag in US churches. Still, even if displaying the national flag was

---

49. Moore, "Fly It Responsibly," 83.

50. Marvin and Ingle, *Blood Sacrifice and the Nation*, 7.

51. Mark Tooley, "U.S. Flags in Churches?," Juicy Ecumenism, July 4, 2013, http://juicyecumenism.com/2013/07/04/u-s-flags-in-churches/.

a common practice in the churches of other lands, it would be contrary to the nature of the church and without theological basis.

The American flag was introduced into churches without any theological justification, a manifestation of being "conformed to the world" rather than "transformed" (Rom 12:2). Ridding the churches in the United States of the national flag is a task that should be taken on by those who care about the integrity of Christian worship. Many people in churches will passionately resist and some will vilify the ministers who advocate the removal of the flag, all the while denying that idolatry is at play. I cannot help but recall the words of a chairman of the governing board of a local congregation in the midst of a discussion about the prospect of removing the American flag from the sanctuary. In an unguarded moment of patriotic fervor, he thundered: "Some things Jesus Christ himself can't make me do!" That says it all.

CHAPTER 6

Pledging to Babylon's Banner

Several years ago the congregation I was serving decided to redesign the church website. I thought it might be wise to take a look at what other churches were doing so we could appropriate—plagiarize?—some of the best ideas. Much of the content I found was pretty much what I expected: worship times, calendars of activities, descriptions of ministries, brief biographical information about the church staff, and some words about the church's vision and basic beliefs. What I didn't expect was that a significant number of the church websites also included the Pledge of Allegiance to the Flag of the United States of America.

While the Pledge wasn't listed along with the basic beliefs of these churches, clearly it was crucial to their convictions and identity. Usually on these church websites the Pledge was accompanied by a graphic of the American flag. Occasionally, a pledge to the so-called Christian flag and a pledge to the Bible were included as well. The Pledge of Allegiance didn't appear only on websites of conservative evangelical churches. Some websites of mainline Christian churches displayed the Pledge as well. No explanation for its inclusion was ever offered. Apparently, no explanation was thought to be necessary because the reason should be self-evident. Bowing toward Babylon as expressed in the Pledge of Allegiance is *in fact* a fundamental commitment of many churches.

Pledging to Babylon's Banner

While it is likely that fewer churches in the United States recite the Pledge than display the American flag, still on Sundays nearest to patriotic holidays a considerable number of congregations will stand facing the flag in a nationalistic expression of commitment. As one editor of a Christian magazine put it in his defense of saying the Pledge in church, "[W]e offer Caesar all that is his. 'I pledge allegiance to the flag of the United States of America . . .' With quickening pulses—yes, even with glistening eyes—we place our hands upon our hearts, and with millions of our fellow Americans, we repeat the soaring words."[1]

But in fact including the Pledge of Allegiance to the Flag in worship has absolutely nothing to do with "giving to Caesar what is Caesar's" (Matt 22:21) but rather the ritual grants to "Caesar" that which is due to God alone. The prayer for and submission to governing authorities urged in Scripture falls considerably short of the ritualized adoration of the American flag expressed in the Pledge. Nor is using the Pledge in worship a way in which we acknowledge that we are citizens of two worlds. If a flag was needed to serve that end, the flag of the United Nations might be a better choice than the flag of any single nation.

Rather, introducing the flag pledge into worship aids and abets the state in its perennial endeavor to secure the unqualified loyalty of its residents, triumphing over any other attachment in the hearts and minds of the people. The Pledge is a means of forming and expressing the identity of a people. The words "under God" in the Pledge in no way limits the attachment and loyalty being engendered on behalf of the nation. Rather the great adoration given to the flag in the very act of repeating the words of the Pledge helps revision who the God is whom the people have gathered to worship, misshapes the identity of worshipers, and cripples the Christian imagination. Any God who would be pleased to be worshiped along with the Pledge of Allegiance to the Flag cannot be a God who relativizes national identity or could expect obedience at odds with national interests. This beloved nationalistic ritual is another manifestation of the church in America bowing toward Babylon.

THE PLEDGE'S BACKSTORY

Most Americans would probably be surprised to learn that very few other countries have a pledge of allegiance to their flag. The United States was

---

1. Smith, "We Pledge the Flag; We Say the Creed."

the first nation to have such a ritual and not many others have chosen to follow suit. The degree of adoration given to the national flag seen in the United States is not found elsewhere. Surely, patriotism exists elsewhere but it is not focused on the national flag as it is in America. The flag in other countries serves a utilitarian purpose and does not necessarily engender the emotional attachment that would lead to the moistening of the eyes at the sound of the words, "I pledge allegiance to the flag . . . ."

As I discussed in the previous chapter, the American flag was not the most important patriotic symbol nor particularly visible in national life prior to the Civil War. It was not displayed in public schools and often it was not found on federal government buildings, much less on homes. After the war veterans organizations like the Grand Army of the Republic and patriotic societies such as the Daughters of the American Revolution led a campaign to elevate the status of the American and encourage the display of the flag in as many venues as possible. Flag codes, Flag Day, and flag desecration laws were promoted in an effort to emphasize that the flag should be recognized as a sacred emblem comparable to the most important religious symbols.

The Pledge of Allegiance to the Flag was developed as a part of this effort to foster the glorification of the national banner and thereby to instill patriotic values. In particular a concerted effort was made to inculcate children into the cult of the flag. Children's literature was an important tool in this effort. The widely circulated children's magazine *St Nicholas* began to publish an increasing number of stories that involved the American flag. Likewise, the graphics that included the flag grew in number, as did poems glorifying the flag.

Forms of honoring the flag were suggested in the pages of *St. Nicholas*, including taking off one's hat to the flag. In an article the magazine describes a military ceremony, "Swearing Allegiance to the Colors," and urges emulation in public schools, teaching students to salute the flag.[2] The enthusiasts for the flag believed that to maximize its positive impact upon the formation of the young the flag must not only be present but also be honored through some form of ritual performed by the children.

It was New York City auditor George T. Balch, a veteran and spokesman for the GAR and author of *Methods of Teaching Patriotism in the Public Schools*, who first proposed an organized flag salute for students. He did not want the practice to be enforced from top down but to be the result of

---

2. Clark, "Honors to the Flag in Camp and Armory," 760ff.

a choice of the students confirmed in a school election. In what was called "The American Patriotic Salute," students touched first their foreheads, then their hearts, reciting together "We give our Heads!—and our Hearts!—to God! And our Country!" Then with right hand extended toward the flag, somewhat elevated and palm down, the students declared, "One Country! One Language! One Flag!"[3]

In his history of the American flag, Scot Guenter noted that by calling for a pledge to God and country Balch "sought to mingle these allegiances in the early training of the young."[4] By linking God and country so explicitly and intimately in the ritual it would help form the affections and loyalties of the young in a way that piety and patriotism would be virtually indistinguishable. "For a nation that possessed supreme confidence that America was God's chosen nation, putting god first entailed a conflict of loyalties..." observed Richard Ellis, and such a conflict was supposedly impossible.[5] The flag should be honored as an emblem, not just of the United States, but one associated with God as well, according to the nationalists. Balch's efforts were "conscious and deliberate ideological engineering."[6] However, the use of his salute did not gain widespread popularity.

Prior to the Columbian Exposition in Chicago in 1892, *The Youth's Companion*, the magazine with the highest circulation in the country at that time, put tremendous energy in promoting the Columbian Public School Celebration. The magazine was a leading instrument in the schoolhouse flag movement. James Upham, the head of the magazine's advertising (premium) department, came up with the idea of linking the school house flag movement with the Columbian Exposition. The magazine advertised and sold American flags at a significantly reduced cost. In its pages students and teachers were urged to put the public schools at the center of the celebration of the four hundredth anniversary of Columbus's voyage to America by insuring that every school displayed the flag.

At the forefront of this national effort was Francis Bellamy, a Baptist minister and Christian Socialist who joined the magazine's promotion staff. In contrast to the patriotism of George Balch, which placed an emphasis on military-like discipline and individual freedom, Bellamy "envisioned a 'social citizenry,' in which every member of society would share a common set

---

3. Balch, *A Patriotic Primer for the Little Children*, 16.
4. Guenter, *The American Flag, 1777–1924*, 119.
5. Ellis, *To the Flag*, 123.
6. Hobsbawm, *Nations and Nationalism Since 1780*, 91–92.

of institutions and services that would guarantee everyone a decent standard of living."[7] He believed *The Youth's Companion* could be instrumental in fostering "civic-minded patriotism."

Bellamy worked tirelessly to promote the Columbian Public School Celebration. Not only did he reach out to students and teachers, he obtained the support of the World's Congress Auxiliary to the Columbian Exposition, the US commissioner of education, and the president of the National Education Association (NEA) and the endorsement of the NEA. Not only was the GAR endorsement sought but the organization was requested to insure that veterans would be personally present for the flag raising and ceremony. Under Bellamy's leadership, organizers reached out to ministers across the country to enlist them to urge their congregations to participate in the celebration at the public schools.

Bellamy personally met with President Benjamin Harrison to secure his endorsement, which the president gave without hesitation. Bellamy went a step further and asked the president to declare Columbus Day a national holiday. He was told by the president that such a thing was beyond his power to do. Congress would have to authorize it as a holiday. Bellamy began lobbying members of Congress to authorize the holiday as a part of their support for the Columbian Public School Celebration. He tailored his message in such a way that enabled him to gain bipartisan support. A joint resolution was passed by leaders of both houses of Congress on June 29, 1892 that authorized the president to designate Columbus Day as a national holiday.

President Harrison named October 21 as the date for the holiday, linking the celebration of the "discovery" of America with the schoolhouse flag movement. In a statement that concealed more about history than it revealed, President Harrison declared, "Columbus stood in his age as the pioneer of progress and enlightenment." He went on to say that "the system of universal education is in our age is the most prominent and salutary feature of the spirit of enlightenment.... Let the flag be flown over every schoolhouse in the country and the exercises be such as shall impress upon our youth the patriotic duties of American citizenship." President Harrison went on to explicitly enlist churches: "In the churches . . . let there be expressions of gratitude for Divine Providence for the devout faith of the

---

7. O'Leary, *To Die For*, 158.

discoverer, and the divine care and guidance which has directed our history and so abundantly blessed our people"[8]

More than half the schools in the country committed to participate in the flag raising and pledge ceremony. School bands practiced patriotic music and students memorized the words of the Pledge of Allegiance. "Whereas only four years earlier the flag had seldom been flown over schoolhouses, on Columbus Day, 1892, more than one hundred thousand schools raised the flag."[9] Bellamy wrote specific instructions for the entire ceremony. There were several speeches, patriotic songs, Scripture readings, and prayers incorporated into the service which led up to the Pledge of Allegiance and the prescribed gestures to be used at the high point of the celebration. This was then followed by the doxology. The ceremony was concluded with a benediction given by clergy.

The Pledge had actually been recited by around 35,000 students several days earlier in New York City on the first of a three day Columbus Day celebration. But the more notable event was on what was believed to be Columbus's birthday October 21 when millions of students throughout the country joined together in speaking the words of the Pledge.

James Upham had attempted to write a pledge before he gave up in frustration and passed the task on to Bellamy. They were of one mind that it should be "a vow of loyalty, or allegiance, to the flag, based on what the flag . . . stood for" and that the words should not only be an expression of loyalty but name "the reason for loyalty." The owner and publisher of *The Youth's Companion* Daniel Ford reviewed the work, approved it and put in in print for the first time in the September 8, 1892 issue.

As Bellamy originally wrote it, the Pledge had twenty-one words: 'I pledge allegiance to my Flag and the Republic for which it stands, one nation, indivisible, with liberty and justice for all." After he heard the Pledge spoken by students in Boston on October 21, he added another word: "to" just before the words "the Republic." Later, in 1923 and 1924, two other changes were made by the delegates to the National Flag Conference in Washington, DC at the urging of the American Legion and the Daughters of the American Revolution. The words "my Flag" were replaced with "to the flag of the United States," to which two further words were later added, "of America."

---

8. Brown, *The Public School Journal*, 91.
9. O'Leary, *To Die For*, 169.

The Pledge's meaning and motives are mixed. While Bellamy was a socialist and a case can be made for the view that he "intended the line 'One nation indivisible with liberty and justice for all' to express a more collective and egalitarian vision of America" that would "promote a moral vision to counter the individualism embodied in capitalism,"[10] this oversimplifies the matter. Bellamy later wrote that he originally thought about including the phrase from the French revolution, "Liberty, Equality, Fraternity" but decided "with liberty and justice for all" was a better choice because it was "applicable to either an individualistic or a socialistic state, and could not be gainsaid by any party."[11]

If Bellamy didn't seek to insert socialism into the Pledge, he certainly did intend to strike a blow against the greed and materialism that he saw taking a greater role in the life of the nation. In a speech to the National Education Association just weeks before he wrote the Pledge, Bellamy called for a civic patriotism that he contrasted to "narrow, grasping, selfish" approaches to life. "True Americanism," he declared, "is . . . opportunity for the realization of justice; opportunity for the free use of all native powers; opportunity for the rounded development of every individual . . . [and] the putting steadily the thing that is fair, the thing that is just, into legislation."[12] While the speech was not socialist, it did offer a progressive vision of America in contrast to the celebration of capitalism.

A few months later in a speech to the Women's Literary Union, Bellamy criticized the nation's adoration of "the shameless, indecent almighty dollar" and called for a "new Americanism" that didn't equate "liberty" with the pursuit of personal gain. He objected to the way some people used the word *liberty*. "It had meant liberty for great corporations to oppress the people . . . liberty for the atoms on the top of the sand heap to press down harder and harder the atoms below." Bellamy understood "liberty and justice for all" to mean "every man shall have the equal right to work and earn bread for his family; that every child shall be taken and given as good a chance as the government can afford."[13]

---

10. Dreier and Flacks, "Patriotism's Secret History," 40.

11. Ellis, *To the Flag*, 29, cited from Bellamy to Mrs. Lue Stuart Wadsworth, July 12, 1923, Bellamy Papers.

12. Francis Bellamy, "Americanism in the Public Schools," 61–63, cited in Ellis, *To the Flag*, 29.

13. Mr. Bellamy's Lecture: "The Spirit of Americanism," cited in Ellis, *To the Flag*, 31.

Whatever role Bellamy's socialism played in his writing of the Pledge was less significant than his racist and xenophobic concerns. The Pledge of Allegiance was devised as a means of combatting the perceived threat presented by immigrants who were regarded as racially or ethnically inferior. "Absent large-scale immigration, it is difficult to imagine adults bothering to write a pledge of allegiance for schoolchildren," observed Richard Ellis.[14] While Bellamy readily acknowledged that America was a land of immigrants, he noted that "there are immigrants and there are immigrants." Those who came to the shores of America in earlier decades were primarily from northern European countries, well-suited for assimilation. But he was anxious about the waves of immigrants coming from Italy, Poland, Russia, and elsewhere.

"Where all classes of society merge insensibly into one another every alien immigrant of inferior race may bring corruption to the stock," wrote Bellamy. He insisted, "The people must . . . guard, more jealously even than their liberty, the quality of their blood."[15] Fear of people coming to America with a divided loyalty served as a crucial motivation behind all patriotic education and in particular the use of the Pledge of Allegiance to the Flag. Bellamy claimed that he saw "astonishing results" among children who engaged in flag exercises in public schools. He believed their eagerness to salute the flag had "as great a potency to Americanize the alien child as it has to lead regiments to death."[16]

Bellamy was well aware of the fact that the children who repeated the words of the Pledge did not understand the meaning of the phrases they recited. Yet, he said that "the whole thing sinks in as a general impression, which by repetition becomes a memory that sticks by as they grow older . . . . It is the same way with the catechism, or the Lord's Prayer."[17] Several years later a similar observation was made by Gridley Adams, chairman of the US Flag Code Committee, who said of the Pledge that "just as in advertising 'repetition makes reputation,' so does reiteration of any creed make it become part of the subconscious."[18] The aim in having children—particularly immigrant children—focus on the American flag and offer ritual

14. Ellis, *To the Flag*, 49.
15. Editorial, *Illustrated American*, August 28, 1897, 258.
16. "The Newest Movement." Bellamy Paper. Cited in O'Leary, *To Die For*, 177.
17. Bellamy, "A New Plan for Counter-Attack on the Nation's Internal Foes," Bellamy Papers. Cited by O'Leary, *To Die For*, 178.
18. Adams, *New York Times*, September 13, 1936, IV, 9. Cited in Ellis, *To the Flag*, 80.

adoration in gestures and words was to forge a deeply engrained, emotionally attached American identity that would supersede any other identity and loyalty. This is very fitting way to honor a "jealous god" of nationalism.

PASSION FOR THE PLEDGE

Within a few decades of its introduction, the Pledge of Allegiance to the Flag became the preeminent expression of patriotism for most Americans. It has been observed, "People's attitude toward the Pledge often parallel their basic beliefs and feelings about their country."[19] But not only do the attitudes people take toward the Pledge reflect their beliefs and feeling about the country, more important for the church, people's attitude toward the Pledge reflect their views of God, idolatry, and their understanding of their identity as people of faith.

While the Pledge originated as a voluntary ritual whose use was to be encouraged, not mandated, state and local governments, as well as school boards of education began to require the Pledge in public schools. Washington and Delaware were the first states to enact laws that required students to recite the Pledge of Allegiance. By 1935 ten states and the District of Columbia mandated that the Pledge be spoken, some requiring it be done daily, others less frequently. In many other places the Pledge was mandated by local or state school boards. The Pledge was seen as, in the words of the United States Flag Association, "an antidote against bolshevism, communism, and all other 'isms' except Americanism."[20]

But not everyone could get behind the aggressive campaign to advance Americanism. While those who resisted saying the Pledge did not share the identical reason for doing so, the majority of the resistance came from deeply dedicated religious people. Not only does "civil religion in the realm of flag adoration lend itself to strict political orthodoxy," it also lends to nationalistically shaped ideas of religious orthodoxy.[21] Consequently, resistance to saying the Pledge was met with punitive intolerance from school officials and disapproval among many church members.

In 1918 a Mennonite girl in West Liberty, Ohio refused to say the Pledge. She was sent home from school. The following days she would return but she was repeatedly sent home when she refused to recite the

---

19. Jones and Meyer, *The Pledge*, 15.
20. "Pledge Flag with Curtis," *New York Times*, June 7, 1930.
21. Welch, *Flag Burning*, 43.

Pledge with her class. Eventually, her father was prosecuted and convicted for failing to keep his child in school. He appealed his conviction and twenty-five-day jail sentence, arguing that it was the school officials, not he, who hindered his daughter from attending school. His appeal was rejected by the judge who accused the father of poisoning his daughter's mind with thoughts of disloyalty.[22]

Mennonites continued to have conflicts with authorities over the Pledge during the next decades. Thirty-eight children in Greenwood, Delaware in 1928 were expelled from school. The Mennonites contended that pledging to the flag implied "a pledge to defend it against all its enemies, which would mean to resort to arms and take human life." As such, it was a violation of their convictions. The Mennonites started a private school in order to avoid arrest as they sought the reinstatement of their child in the public school. The American Civil Liberties Union offered to represent the children in a lawsuit against the school. However, the beliefs of the Mennonites forbade them from resorting to secular courts to resolve conflicts.

Other small religious bodies objected to the Pledge of Allegiance as well. In 1926 Denver, Colorado around fifty children who were members of a group called the Jehovites were expelled from school for refusing to salute the flag. The Jehovites held that the flag ritual was an expression of idolatry, a charge that their detractors claimed was "the limit of absurdity." The conflicts cooled off during the summer—and after the threat of a suit—and the children were allowed to return to their classes the following school year.[23]

Around this same time a religious group called the Elijah Voice Society argued that the Pledge fostered a nationalism that "tends toward militarism and war" and to teach "America First" was to instill "the spirit that makes world wars and other wars possible." When a nine-year-old boy, Russell Tremain, whose parents were members of the group, refused to say the Pledge, he was expelled from his school in Bellingham, Washington. His father refused to cooperate with the school and he was arrested and jailed for "contributing to the delinquency of his son." The judge gave the state permanent custody of the boy and his parents were forbidden from visiting him. The judge, W. P. Brown, ridiculed the religious convictions of the parents and insisted that refusing to salute the flag would lead to total

---

22. Ellis, *To the Flag*, 85.
23. Ibid., 86.

disregard for all law. It took over two years of legal action to get the boy returned to his parents.[24]

Other episodes of religiously based refusal to pledge to the flag in schools occurred in Oklahoma, Kansas, California, New York, and Illinois. However, the most frequent and well-known instances of resistance to the Pledge and reprisal by flag supporters involved the Jehovah's Witnesses. Their resistance did not begin until 1935 when the leader of the Witnesses, Joseph Rutherford, honored the Witnesses in Germany for refusing to give the "Heil Hitler" salute. He then pointed to the similarity to the American flag salute and declared that they were both idolatry and showed "unfaithfulness to God." Later that same year an eight-year-old student in Lynn, Massachusetts, a Jehovah's Witness named Carlton Nicholls, refused to say the Pledge because, he said, his faith taught him "he could only adore and bow down to Jehovah."[25]

Rutherford commended the boy's action and held him up as a model for other Witnesses to follow. Within months Jehovah's Witnesses were being expelled from public schools across the nation for refusing to recite the Pledge. In some instances there were violent responses toward the resisters. Some children were whipped as well as expelled from school and parents were fined. Several children in Canonsburg, Pennsylvania were taunted, threatened, and beaten by teachers and the principal of the school. The principal choked one girl for her refusal to say the Pledge. In Pittsburgh the school board started "proceedings toward having children sent to the House of Corrections."[26] Also, several teachers were fired for refusing to lead the Pledge of Allegiance.

The American Civil Liberties Union (ACLU) stepped up to represent Jehovah's Witnesses in a number of cases regarding the mandatory flag salute. Generally, their efforts faltered in court. The Nicholls case managed to reach the Massachusetts Supreme Court before it ended in defeat. Writing on behalf of the Court, the Chief Justice totally disregarded the concerns of the Witnesses, maintaining that religious freedom was not at stake in requiring the Pledge be recited. Arrogantly assuming that the Court was in a better position to deem what is religious that the practitioners of a religion, he wrote,

24. Ibid., 87f.
25. Ibid., 92.
26. Ibid., 93.

> The flag salute and pledge of allegiance here in question do not in any just sense relate to religion. They are not observances which are religious in nature. They do not concern the views of any one as to his Creator. They do not touch upon his relations with his Maker. They impose no obligation as to religious worship.... The pledge of allegiance to the flag... is an acknowledgment of sovereignty, a promise of obedience, a recognition of authority above the will of the individual, to be respected and obeyed.[27]

Given that the Pledge was introduced to the nation in a service that included prayers, Scripture readings, speeches that made reference to God, and the singing of the doxology, any claim by the court that the Pledge was not at all religious seems disingenuous. Further, to insist that the court was better equipped to determine what is or is not religiously relevant does not undercut but rather it reinforces that Witnesses' contention that the state was seeking to displace God with a false religion that regarded the authority of the state supreme. In other words, the issue was in fact a matter of idolatry.

After years of fighting on behalf of the Witnesses, a crucial case pursued by the ACLU made it to the Supreme Court—*Minersville School District v. Gobitis*—but ended in defeat when the Court issued an eight-one ruling, reversing the decision for the Witness by a lower court. Felix Frankfurter was selected to write the court's opinion. He supported requiring students to say the Pledge based on the need for national unity. He held that "national unity is the basis of national security" and held that without a "unifying sentiment... there ultimately can be no liberties, civil or religious."[28] National unity was affirmed by the Court as a value superior to religious liberty. This placed those who objected to the Pledge for reason of faith in a position where they had to choose between being faithful to what they understood God to require and complying with what the state required.

This court decision was apparently viewed by people in some quarters as permission to force Witnesses to say the Pledge and to intimidate, humiliate, and physically punish those who resisted. It was not only children who were penalized for refusing to say the Pledge in public schools. The passion for the Pledge led to numerous instances of appalling brutality being inflicted upon other Jehovah's Witnesses. Vigilante mobs, often with

---

27. Cited in Ellis, *To the Flag,* 95.
28. Ibid., 103

the support of local law enforcement, threatened and sometimes viciously abused those whose faith led them to refuse the salute the flag.

In Richmond, West Virginia, Witnesses were roped like cattle and marched to the mayor's office. There they had castor oil poured down their throats by member of the American Legion and then led in front of a crowd of people from the town who further humiliated them. In Litchfield, Illinois sixty Witnesses were attacked by a large crowd. One of the Witnesses had his head repeatedly slammed into his car hood for nearly half an hour. The crowd overturned and destroyed the cars of the Witnesses so they had to take a bus to leave town.

Aggressive supporters of the Pledge rioted against Witnesses in Kennebunk, Maine and burned down their kingdom hall. In Nebraska in 1940, a man was sadistically castrated for his refusal to pledge to the flag. Members of the American Legion were at the forefront of the persecution of the Jehovah's Witnesses. This led a US Attorney General in Texas to make a radio appeal to Legionnaires in which he told them not to "let your patriotism get the best of your judgment" and to keep their distance from Witnesses. But his words apparently had little effect. The head of the Legion's National Americanism Commission encouraged Legionnaires to "keep up the good work" of harassing Witnesses who were, according to him, "teaching disloyalty."[29]

The intimidation, harassment, and violence inflicted upon the Jehovah's Witnesses in the aftermath of the *Minersville School District v. Gobitis* case led several Supreme Court justices to have second thoughts about their decision. Several of them made public their change of mind. Consequently, when the *West Virginia v. Barnette* case was brought before the court the majority of the justices were not inclined to reaffirm their support for those who sought to enforce a mandatory flag pledge. On Flag Day, June 14, 1943, the six-three Supreme Court decision was announced. Justice Robert Jackson wrote the decision of the Court.

Jackson held that the state could not compel the Jehovah's Witnesses to salute and pledge to the flag, not only because to do so in contrary to the freedom of religion, but because to do so "invades the sphere of intellect and spirit" the First Amendment was intended to protect. He insisted that a faithful adherence to the Constitution demands the recognition "that no official, high or petty, can prescribe what shall be orthodox in politics, nationalism, religion, or other matters of opinion or force citizens to confess

---

29. Cited in ibid., 107.

by word or act their faith therein." He went on to say that the "freedom to differ is not limited to things that do not matter much. That would be a mere shadow of freedom. The test of its substance is the right to differ as the things that touch the heart of the existing order."[30]

This decision put an end to the legally enforceable mandatory flag pledge. However, the liturgical power of the Pledge and the widespread passionate devotion to it was not eliminated by making the observance officially voluntary. "In fact, the Pledge ritual is a prayer that sanctifies the flag while stigmatizing desecration as a heretical and iconoclastic act."[31] But not only is desecration stigmatized, all failure to bestow upon the flag the conventional ritualistic honor continues to be viewed with contempt by many.

The pressure to participate in nationalistic rituals is great, whether mandatory or not. This is particularly true for students. As Leonard A. Stevens noted in the epilogue of his study of the impact of the required flag pledge on the Jehovah's Witnesses, even non-compulsory flag exercises can be subtly coercive because "most young people, who naturally try to do as others do, are under a great deal of social pressure to conform to the ceremony."[32] As they engage in the liturgy of the nation, reciting words they don't understand, predispositions, attachments, and values of the young are precognitively formed.

The potential of becoming the object of disdain and the focus of threat is not lost on those who are for any reason disinclined to participate in flag ceremonies. The hostility toward noncompliance raises its head often enough to remind us we cannot assume anyone can withhold the conventional adoration to the flag, complete with ritual honor, without consequence. For instance, consider the fallout from a news story about Washington High School in Sioux Falls that misrepresented a school board decision. The reporter claimed the board decided to drop the Pledge from high school classrooms.[33] In fact the Pledge of Allegiance to the Flag had not been a required part of daily activities since the 1970s.

Board members explained that high school teachers were free to lead their classes in the Pledge, but that they didn't want to add another

---

30. Cited in Stevens, *Salute!*, 134.
31. Boime, *The Unveiling of the National Icons*, 35.
32. Stevens, *Salute!*, 139.
33. Wes Williams, "False Fox News Story About 'Banned' Pledge of Allegiance Results In Death Threats," November 22, 2013, http://www.addictinginfo.org/2013/11/22/fox-news-school-board-death-threats/.

requirement for high school classrooms. But a national TV news organization picked up a story and presented it as an example of an anti-patriotic drift in public school. The school board experienced serious backlash. School board member Kent Alberty told a news station that board members had received hate mail and death threats, largely from outside the area. Alberty revealed that one of the threats called for all of the school board members to be lined up and shot.

ADDING GOD TO THE PLEDGE

While Bellamy's pledge didn't include the word "God," this fact was not due to any desire on his part to keep religion at bay. The manner in which the Pledge was introduced to the country thoroughly blended Christianity and Americanism. In the mind of its author, the Pledge was not a ritual to be used in public schools alone. As Bellamy explained, "In its sheer ethics, the Pledge has a home in the Churches, and its doctrines should be urged by the clergy."[34]

With the addition of the ambiguous phrase "under God" in the Pledge, some American Christians assume the appropriateness of the ritual in worship is beyond dispute. But it is not clear what "one nation under God" actually means. Neither is it clear that the word "God" in the Pledge refers to the One who is the rightful focus of Christian worship. There is good reason to believe that it does not.

Many Americans are unaware of the fact that "God" was absent from the Pledge until more than sixty years after the oath was created. The phrase was added on Flag Day, June 14, 1954 when President Dwight D. Eisenhower signed a resolution from Congress pertaining to the wording of the Pledge. The action was the climax of an effort by the Knights of Columbus, the largest American Roman Catholic organization for laymen.

Several years earlier the Knights passed a resolution "urging all assembly meetings [of the Knights of Columbus] in the United States to include [under God] in their recitation of the pledge."[35] This led to an extensive lobbying effort to gain support from Congress for adding the words "under God" to the ceremony.

The Knights of Columbus were not the only ones involved in advocating for the inclusion of God in the Pledge. Others were active in the effort

---

34. Cited in Ellis, *To the Flag*, 123.
35. Cited in Jones and Meyer, *The Pledge*, 144.

as well. A notable contribution was made by the pastor of the New York Avenue Presbyterian Church in Washington, DC. On a Sunday when President Eisenhower was seated in the congregation, the Reverend George M. Docherty declared, "There is something missing in the pledge, something that is the characteristic and defining factor in the American way of life." With the absence of God, "I could hear little Muscovites repeat a similar pledge to their hammer-and-sickle flag in Moscow."[36]

The references to Moscow were lost on no one, especially the President of the United States. The Cold War was being fought on many fronts. "Godless communism" was viewed as an ominous threat that demanded that opposition be mobilized in as many ways as possible. While the military remained at the ready, the battle above all was an ideological one. And what ally was better to have in such a battle than God?

At the White House signing ceremony President Eisenhower suggested how God would be added to the arsenal of America.

> From the day forward, millions of school children will daily proclaim in every city and town, every village and rural schoolhouse, the dedication of our Nation and our people to the Almighty.... [I]n this way we are affirming the transcendence of religious faith in America's heritage and future; in this way we shall constantly strengthen those spiritual weapons which forever will be our country's most powerful resource, in peace or in war.[37]

On that very day, a new American flag given by the American Legion especially for the occasion was raised by an honor guard to fly above the dome of the Capital building. Political dignitaries watched as a military band played "Onward Christian Soldiers," after which the new version of the Pledge of Allegiance was recited, including the words "under God."[38]

The vast majority of Americans were pleased with the revision to the Pledge. A few people of faith saw problems, recognizing that adding the words "under God" did nothing to actually honor God. Instead political ends were being advanced. "God" was used to bolster Americanism over against Communism. The interests of the nation rather than the glory of God was being served. To put it in another way, the insertion of "God" in the Pledge of Allegiance uses God's name in vain, offending against the Third Commandment.

36. Burrell, *The Words We Live By*, 67.
37. US President, *Public Papers of the Presidents of the United States*, 563.
38. *New York Times*, June 15, 1954.

Bowing Toward Babylon

Writing on the addition of "under God" to the Pledge, Lee Canipe observed, "The elusive and rather vague Supreme Being of Cold War America conveniently defied definition. In the religious vernacular of the day, the only discernible thing for which America's God stood for was ... America."[39] Nevertheless, most churchgoers deeply influenced by American Christian nationalism infused the American God with Christian meaning to make it clear that the God they gather to worship on Sundays is partial toward America.

Such a "God" is in fact an idol bearing little real resemblance to the God revealed in Christ. The "God" of the Pledge offers the illusion of transcendence where there is none and instead serves the singular purpose of elevating America over against all possible contenders in the hearts of those who utter the words. When the words of this nationalistic liturgy are repeatedly uttered, affection for America is deepened and at the same time the association of the nation and God is reinforced in the perception of those who participate in the ritual.

Many religious people who fail to distinguish the God of nationalism from the God revealed in Jesus Christ are desperate to keep the word "God" present in as many governmentally sanctioned venues as possible. It is no surprise that they met with outrage the June 2002 ruling of the U.S. Ninth Circuit Court of Appeals that the inclusion of the words "under God" in the Pledge is unconstitutional. Despite the fact that during most of history of the Pledge those words were not in the Pledge, eliminating them was denounced as an offense to "our godly heritage."

James Dobson, founder and president of the conservative Christian organization Focus on the Family, declared, "This abominable ruling by an imperious court is a slap in the face to all Americans and people of faith. It's time for citizens throughout the country to condemn the increasing tendency ... to secularize and demean our deeply held values."[40]

We might ask, "Which deeply held values?" The mere use of the word "God" does not lend support to deeply held values derived from the confession of Jesus as Lord. The word lends support to the Republic symbolized by the flag of the United States of America. Rather than objecting to the removal of "under God" from the Pledge because to do so would "secularize and demean our deeply held values," Christians would do better to

---

39. Canipe, "The Pledge of Allegiance in Cold War America," 314.

40. Quoted in Kellogg, "Response Swift to Pledge Ruling," cited in Canipe, "The Pledge of Allegiance in Cold War America," 308f.

recognize that the presence of "God" in the Pledge falsely sacralizes that which is not sacred and thereby demeans the word "God." The only god who is honored by the phrase "under God" is the deified nation. As Stanley Hauerwas observed, "Americans continue to maintain a stubborn belief in a god, but the god they believe in turns out to be the American god. To know or worship that god does not require that a church exists...."[41]

"God" was not included in the Pledge to call people to worship. Instead the reason for the inclusion was because "God" was useful in an ideological conflict. Historian Derek H. Davis rightly contended, "God is not simply a resource that we can harness to serve our national interests. God always remains above culture and nation, which remain under his scrutiny and judgment. Americanism can never be synonymous with God .... 'God,' a sacred name for people of faith, becomes in the Pledge of Allegiance only a receptacle for popular patriotic fervor, bereft of any real theological meaning."[42]

When the courts have ruled in favor of the inclusion of "under God" in the Pledge, they have not done so because of the profound meaningfulness of the word "God." The opposite has been the case. "God," the courts have essentially declared, is allowable because using the word is a sentimental gesture without religious substance. "God" serves a ceremonial and patriotic purpose rather than a designation for that which is most holy and worthy of praise. The Supreme Court evoked an undefined concept of "ceremonial deism" to allow the use of the word "God" in official government related venues.[43] The court has judged that "God" is constitutionally allowable because "God" is useful to solemnize a public occasion but otherwise is devoid of substance.

CREED NOT PLEDGE

Many churches that eschew confessing the ecumenical creeds in worship—like those in my own Disciples of Christ tradition—have no problem occasionally reciting the Pledge of Allegiance to the Flag. But whatever the shortcomings that might be found in the creeds—and I'm speaking particularly of the Apostles' Creed and the Nicene Creed—pale in comparison to distortion of Christian faith represented by including a confession in

---

41. Hauerwas, *War and the American Difference*, 16.
42. Davis, "The Pledge of Allegiance and American Value," 665.
43. *Lynch v. Donnelly*, 1989.

worship that can be equally made by people with no faith in Christ whatsoever but cannot be made by people of faith from other nations. The primary reason for rejecting creeds was because they build walls of exclusion by functioning as "tests of fellowship." In fact the Pledge of Allegiance, even if it does not outright exclude, marginalizes in the worshiping body those who are not Americans.

The ecumenical creeds, on the other hand, rightly serve as identity statements, not first of all as tools of exclusion. This is not to deny that creeds have functioned to combat teachings deemed to be contrary to the accepted teaching of the church. But to a great extent in Protestant churches more recently the creeds are used more as expressions of unity than as means of division. They voice convictions that have united Christians throughout the nations and throughout the ages. The liturgical function of creeds is not to build walls but to give voice to the global, transcultural core of Christian conviction. The use of the ecumenical creeds in worship is not to express the personal faith of every individual who speaks the words—many have reservations about one article or another—but to confess the faith of the church. As Geoffrey Wainwright put it,

> The liturgical use of the traditional creeds is a sign that it is indeed the Church of Jesus Christ to which the believer belongs—a Church whose transcendence of time and death is experienced in faith's sense of the risen lord's presence and (it may be) the communion of the saints as predecessors in the way. Synchronically, the use of the common creeds is a sign of Christian identity throughout the inhabited earth. The believer is thereby enabled to find his ecumenical identity, his solidarity in the universal Church. His worship and witness become part of the world-wide liturgy and mission.[44]

Common confession of the creeds doesn't entail a common understanding of all the affirmations in the creeds. There is room for considerable diversity in thinking. Creedal unanimity and theological plurality can exist side by side as we who confess Jesus as Lord move toward ever fuller unity in faith and life. As individuals we would likely express our faith and beliefs with words and phrases that reflect our own experiences and context. "But when the church is summoned to rise and profess its common faith, it does not do so in a cacophony of simultaneous personal testimonies, but in words

---

44. Wainwright, *Doxology*, 190.

that belong to the community of saints, including both the living and the dead."[45]

The creeds as summaries of Christian faith are vital, enduring but imperfect and culturally conditioned expressions of faith. We will not all understand the creeds used in worship in the same way as all others who speak the identical words, nor are we ourselves likely to understand the claims in the creeds now as we have in the past or will in the future. Nevertheless, they foster an identity that is based on the claims at the heart of the biblical story of salvation. This is an identity that transcends and challenges identities derived from attachments that have nothing to do with faith in the God revealed in Christ.

When confessing the creeds in worship the church speaks as church celebrating the being and acts of God for our salvation. In doing so it acknowledges who we are as a people called by God in Christ. We are "the holy catholic church, the communion of saints," "one holy, catholic and apostolic Church." By giving voice to historic expressions of the faith the local church in one place is reminded that the convictions at the core of its life are shared by believers in many places and times. We are one with them.

The local church is part of a far broader body, extending through space and time, a body set apart for a God-given purpose. Confessing the creeds, Aidan Kavanagh observed, "checks any temptation the assembly may be under to withdraw into itself and to worship with self-complacency. It cautions the assembly never to forget that it is nothing less than a chosen race, a royal priesthood, a holy nation, God's own people who exist to declare the wonderful deeds of him who has called it out of darkness into his marvelous light (1 Peter 2:9)."[46]

Confessing the creeds is not first of all a cognitive exercise, as those who have intellectual reservations about their various articles often believe. On this point a discussion found in David Foster Wallace's novel *Infinite Jest* is revealing. Taking place in Ennet House, home to a variety of self-help, twelve-step programs, Geoffrey Day disdainfully reflects on his experience at the facility.

A skeptic about the rituals of Alcoholics Anonymous, with a sense of intellectual superiority he complains, "So then at forty-six years of age I came here to learn to live by clichés. To turn my will and life over to the care of clichés. Easy does it. First things first." Day prefers to keep his intellect at

---

45. Byars, "Creeds and Prayers-Ecclesiology," 89.
46. Kavanagh, *On Liturgical Theology*, 141.

the forefront. He wants to face his problem by figuring it out, comprehending the matter, and beating the addiction with knowledge, not enduring meeting after meeting. Why can't he just be provided with information "instead of the glazed recitation of exhortations to attend these vague future revelatory meetings?"[47]

Intellectually offended by the clichés of the recovery program, Day insists that he simply can't believe, even if he wants to. Don Gately, an Ennet House mentor, concedes that the AA rituals cannot be captured in conceptual ideas that can be expressed in an intellectually satisfying way. He says, "Trust me because I been there, man. You can analyze it til you're breaking tables with your forehead and find a cause to walk away, back Out There, where the Disease is. Or you can stay and hang in and do the best you can." The narrator concedes, "Simple advice like this does seem like a lot of clichés—Day's right about how it seems . . . . If Day ever gets lucky and breaks down, finally . . . . Gately'll get to tell Day the thing is that the clichés directives are a lot more deep and hard to actually *do*. To try and live by instead of just say."[48]

Confessing the creed with it phrases that perplex and evoke intellectual objection is a practice deeper than some imagine. Creating attachment and developing character-shaping affection more than the transmission of ideas are what is taking place in rituals of every sort. This is not to say intellectual content has no importance. It is, however, to say that who we are, how we see the world, and the way we are inclined to live in it are not instilled in us by concepts taught to us so much as by practices we habitually engage in with others.

I'm not suggesting that the inclusion of the ecumenical creeds in worship is essential for a church to be faithful. Though this practice can be of great help for expressing and reinforcing the identity of the church, other means of doing this are also available. The reading of Scripture and hymn-singing serve a similar purpose. And, as with the creeds, the words of hymns and Scripture are not our words as individuals but the words of the church. They call for our respect and attention even as they sometimes evoke our questions. Regardless, they remind us who we are as people of faith in the God made known in Christ. In contrast, including the Pledge of Allegiance in worship turns our attention and affections to the nation and the nationalized god as we bow toward Babylon.

47. Wallace, *Infinite Jest*, 270, 1001.
48. Ibid., 1002, 273.

Chapter 7

Singing the Songs of Babylon

There is an often told apocryphal story of the little boy in a worship service who was seated beside his father, as he frequently was at sports games. The minister called upon the congregation to stand and sing the National Anthem. With gusto the boy added his voice to the others in the congregation. As soon as the song came to an end, he loudly shouted, "Play ball!"

Those of us who have had considerable experience with children in worship won't find this story all that far-fetched. And those of us who have considerable experience worshiping in American churches won't find it at all far-fetched to hear of the National Anthem being sung during a service. But I am convinced that such an action is every bit as misguided as holding a ballgame in the sanctuary.

The concern for liturgical integrity is lost on those who think devotion to God and love of nation can be seamlessly joined. They may think the desire to keep patriotic music out of worship is either an expression of an overly scrupulous concern for liturgical correctness at best, or at worst, evidence of anti-Americanism.

It is neither. The real issue, as I have repeatedly observed, is the nature and identity of the church. What is sung in worship says something about who God is and our singing should faithfully express what—and whose— the church is and serve no other purpose. When other needs are met or other loyalties are given voice, the true reason for worship is undermined. Music is an important focus for those who seek to maintain the integrity of Christian worship over against the encroaching influence of American Christian nationalism.

Among those who seek to encourage nationalism or patriotism, the impact of music has not been overlooked. The importance of patriotic music for character formation has long been recognized by American music educators. A. E. Winship wrote at the dawn of the twentieth century, "Patriotism is devotion with a human christening. It idealizes, almost deifies, one's country. It enkindles the worshipful side of our being.... We do not sing 'America,' 'The Star-Spangled Banner,' 'Dixie,' ... as much as we ought .... 'America' in the school makes my anti-American sentiment impossible. No teaching of history will do for patriotic sentiment what a daily school song can do."[1]

Regardless of the place patriotic music has in public school, music in Christian worship has a very different purpose. The power of patriotic songs to deepen nationalistic devotion and to undercut the possibility of other values and loyalties raising up as challengers, works in church as well as in school. But in a community of faith that proclaims, "Jesus is Lord!" we should ask why such a thing would be allowed. Nothing should be permitted in worship that fosters a disposition to honor or support anything that compromises the church's loyalty to Jesus Christ above all or weakens the Christian's willingness to say "No!" to any power that seeks unqualified loyalty.

Drawing from the thought of sociologist and philosopher Alfred Schutz, liturgical theologian Mary McGann has argued that musical expressions in ritual events is an important way in which a community manifests and communicates itself as a social body. Individuals become a "we" as they join together in singing and "the musical process affect[s] the manner in which the community knows itself as a whole. For this reason, music in Christian ritual can have a powerful impact on how a community perceives itself as an ecclesial body."[2] Who are we as we gather in worship? When patriotic music is given a place in the worship of the church, this inevitably affects how the church knows itself and sees itself in the world.

---

1. Winship, "The Mission of Music in the Public School," 98.
2. McGann, *Exploring Music as Worship and Theology*, 24f.

Singing the Songs of Babylon

THE PLACE OF SINGING AND THE PROBLEM OF NATIONALISM

Diana Butler Bass describes the spiritual crisis and precipitating event that led her to resign from the staff of Christ Church in Alexandria, Virginia. For her the "final straw" was at a Sunday service following Independence Day. In lieu of a sermon there were patriotic readings. The church "sang the national anthem more vigorously than they ever sung any Christian hymn." She stood outside the sanctuary and listened. Upon completing the second verse, "Then conquer we must, when our cause is just. . . . And the star-spangled banner shall wave o'er the land of the free and the home of the brave," the minister pronounced, "Go in peace to love and serve the Lord!" "Apparently, no one noticed the irony," Bass observed, "as they jubilantly shouted back: 'Thanks be to God!'"[3] It is not only in that particular congregation that the irony goes unnoticed but in tens of thousands of others as well.

"Christians have always been a singing people," observed Marianne Micks.[4] At the very heart of the Bible is the Psalms, a collection of works created to be sung to celebrate the character and mighty deeds of God. The greatest events in the drama of salvation have evoked song. The exodus crossing of the sea moved Miriam to sing, and the birth of Jesus caused Mary to break out in song as well. Singing, Scripture tells us, is a crucial expression of worship; not only for humans but for angels as well. From the prophet Isaiah in the temple to the shepherds in the fields outside Bethlehem to John at Patmos, witnesses have described angelic voices singing praise to God as the one worthy of all honor and glory. "On earth as it is in heaven," the people of God have put words to music in response to the wonder and works of God. As hearts have been filled with godly joy, lips have erupted in song. The canticles in Luke's gospel and the bits and pieces of hymns in Paul's epistles show it is natural for Christians to join faith to song.

In singing "psalms, hymns and spiritual songs" (Eph 5:19) we rehearse the story of God's interaction with God's people. We cannot give thanks with genuineness unless we are reminded of the gracious deeds of God. It is the distinctive story of the creative, inviting, forgiving, guiding, judging, nurturing God to which Scripture bears witness that is to be expressed as

---

3. Bass, *Broken We Kneel*, 112f.
4. Micks, *The Future Present*, 62.

the congregation sings in worship. It is therefore imperative that great care is taken when making music selections, distinguishing those "which most faithfully name or address the God of Jesus Christ and those hymns which in one way or another diminish the gospel."[5]

Singing the faith proclaims the Christian truth through music. It is a proclamation of the gospel as surely as is a preached sermon. The sung word is more readily received—at least in some hearts—than is the spoken word. People have been touched deeply and enduringly through song. Beloved hymns are long remembered while the words of sermons—except the pulpit humor—are for the most part quickly forgotten. Consequently, what is sung in worship is serious business. Convictions are formed and character shaped by the words that are sung by the gathered church. For this reason Geoffrey Wainwright could write, "At its most characteristic, the Christian hymn may perhaps be considered a singing confession of faith."[6] If what is sung by the church is not rooted in the revelation of God in Christ, the power to misshape convictions and character will be at play as the congregation sings.

AFFECTION AND CONNECTION

It is beyond question that music touches us as the most persuasive presentation of ideas could never do. While the mind is capable of analyzing music, nevertheless music has the capacity to bypass the mind and to penetrate the soul. It evokes feelings and when it is combined with lyrics, it carries the message of the words much deeper than the words alone could ever reach. Even when the words are only half remembered, music adds power and meaning beyond any purely cognitive content.

Songs we know and love often serve as anchors for memories. They keep us connected to times gone by and the feelings that accompanied them. Of course it is not only music that does this. I recall years ago when I first visited a woman who was nearly 100 years old. She was seated in an overstuffed chair beside which was a stack of books. "Nothing I love better than a hot romance story!" she declared. "It makes me feel young again." Music often does something very similar. Hearing songs we heard when we were younger links us emotionally to the experiences we recall from those times and they can make us "feel young again."

5. Cooper, *Being Subject to One Another as We Sing*, 11.
6. Wainwright, *Doxology*, 183.

Often as we think back on important episodes in our lives—especially during the years of early adulthood—many of us can imagine a soundtrack in the background. That soundtrack reinforces and enriches our memories. As we listen, our hearts and minds are reconnected to affections and past experiences that we don't necessarily have at the forefront of our lives on a daily basis. It should be no surprise that singing is "the most genuinely popular element in Christian worship."[7]

We find this evocative power of music when couples speak warmly of "our song." They are talking about music that renews both emotion and memory that they share. "Our song" is the one that reminds the couple of the best of times. It is the soundtrack that goes along with the story of their budding love and deepening commitment to each other. Warm, fond memories and feelings are ignited. "Our song" is one that is filled with meaning that gets reawakened each time the piece is played. Hearing it can help provide a bit of refreshment to a relationship that may have grown stale from routine.

Patriotic songs have a similar role. They are most often learned when we are quite young. It was in the early elementary school years that many of us were taught "My Country 'Tis of Thee," "America the Beautiful," and the National Anthem. These songs accompanied the lessons of an idealized country and the air-brushed stories of near perfect founding fathers. Innocence and uncritical trust, uncomplicated by thoughts of slavery, the genocide of Native Americans, harsh child labor, inequality for women, unjust wars, or a host of other concerns were conveyed to us as we sang in our classrooms. The patriotic songs served as uplifting background music for what is presented as simpler, more pure times.

Just as "our song" arouses emotions and reinforces a couple's love, so, too, patriotic music awakens feelings and loyalty for the country. The attachment to and identification with America is deepened as words of the nation's virtues and history are put to music. Affections that began to be formed before we could possibly understand the lyrics are fostered anew as we hear the songs and give voice to the words. Patriotic music serves to help nurture us to be loyal citizens of a particular nation.

Music has connective power. It can renew the bond we have with others who share our affections and story. This can occur in numerous different ways. For instance, music connects people of the same generation. Big Band music fosters an emotional link between members of a generation

---

7. Ibid., 200

older than my own. Classic rock and soul music does the same thing for those of my own generation. I trust that alternative rock and hip-hop music will do the same for the generation younger than my own. While we may love and appreciate the music of other generations, it does not connect us emotionally with our own generational peers. It doesn't remind us of a shared history with its particular joys and challenges.

As we listen to the popular music of other generations, we listen as outsiders. We may very well appreciate the qualities of the music and the poetry of the lyrics. Still the emotional connection and shared history eludes us. The music does not join us to those of the generation from which the music came as it joins them to one another. In fact, instead of unifying us with others, some songs may make us more conscious of what separates us and underlines the differences between "us" and "them." The songs that best join us across generations are the songs that have been taught to the young from generation to generation. Patriotic music certainly serves this purpose.

Benedict Anderson, in his study of nationalism, notes that language, particularly singing, not only connects us emotionally to people who are our contemporaries but to the dead as well. He points to the singing of national anthems in many countries. The words may not be profound nor the music sublime. Still an experience is created, "an experience of simultaneity," as the people join their voices. "At precisely such moments, people wholly unknown to each other utter the same verses to the same melody . . . . How selfless this unisonance feels!" The very exercise of singing is an occasion "for the echoed physical realization of the imagined community." This singing joins us to others, many of whom we don't know, many of whom are not even physically present, some of whom are now dead, but at some time and place had sung the same words to the same melody. A connection is made. A unity is expressed and reinforced. A shared love and loyalty is voiced, a love and loyalty to a nation.[8]

The important question is whether songs that serve these ends should be used in church. Do they genuinely contribute to the purpose for which the church gathers as church in worship?

---

8. Anderson, *Imagined Communities*, 145.

SINGING FOR THE WRONG ENDS

Music in church has long been an occasion for controversy. Many centuries ago Augustine was suspicious of the emotional power of music. He issued strong warnings against its capacity to seduce the heart and distract the mind from the rightful object of faith. Conflicts exist between those who hold that hymns should present doctrinal convictions in a somewhat systematic manner and those who cherish hymns that express their experiences of faith and redemption in a more subjective and narrative way. More recently disputes have flared over contemporary Christian praise music and lyrics that some claim are trite and theologically shallow. Yet regardless of the differences, most who are concerned with the worship of the church agree that songs and hymns should express the faith that unites them. The question is, "Do patriotic hymns or songs serve this end?"

I am convinced they don't. Instead they serve a purpose, not only different from the purpose of the worshiping church, but directly at odds with it. The affections and memories that are evoked and the unity that is expressed as the congregation sings patriotic songs, especially in a superpower nation, pertains to Babylon, that archetype of human power and glory and source of meaning, security, and identity, and not to God and purpose of the church.

The purpose for which we sing in worship is *not* to meet our self-determined "needs," emotional, aesthetic, or otherwise. We sing to serve the ends God has for us as a people who have been called and given a distinctive identity and purpose. Consequently, we read in Scripture that we are to "be filled with the Spirit, as you sing psalms and hymns and spiritual songs among yourselves, singing and making melody to the Lord in your hearts, giving thanks to God the Father at all times and for everything in the name of the Lord Jesus Christ, being subject to one another out of reverence for Christ" (Eph 5:18–21). The rightful function of singing in worship has nothing to do with any identity or attachments that have not been given to all others who know God through Christ.

In our singing we give thanks. But *for what* do we give thanks? If the Psalms are to be any precedent for us, above all we give thanks to God for *who* God is and *what* God has done in creation and for the work of salvation. We give thanks for the wondrous acts of God. We do not—in contrast to some presidential proclamations for Thanksgiving Day—"thank God for the greatness of the American people." Any thanks that is an expression of corporate self-aggrandizement gives no honor to God. Rather, it worships and serves "the creature rather than the creator, who is blessed forever! Amen" (Rom 1:25).

The shape of worship in America has often been dictated by a pragmatism that focuses on drawing and keeping a crowd. To this end an emphasis in many churches has been upon meeting the perceived needs of current and potential adherents. While there has been a pronounced increase in their attitude—particularly in larger churches—during the past thirty-plus years, it is by no means entirely new. Liturgical historian James White writes of the approach of revivalist Charles Finney: "If something produces results, i.e., converts them, keep it. If it fails, discard it. This allows for plenty of experimentation, but unsuccessful ties are quickly eliminated. So pragmatism became the essential criterion in worship."[9]

It is not only in churches that design their worship services to be "seeker friendly" or contemporary that this is found. The worship practices in churches that are considered traditional in worship—admittedly, a broad category—are often just as pragmatic and instrumentalist as those that attempt to be in tune with current sensibilities. Evidence of this is seen in the long-standing inclusion of patriotic pieces in church hymnals. Among the 300 hymns most frequently printed in Protestant hymnals published between 1737 and 1960 are several such hymns.[10] "My Country 'Tis of Thee" tied for the forty-second place. "America," though not written until 1904, was tied for the forty-eighth place.

Several hymns that use martial language and that have frequently been included in worship services on national holidays also made the list. These include "Onward Christian Soldiers," "Soldiers of Christ Arise," and "Faith of Our Fathers," the national hymn. We would be mistaken if we were to imagine this is a strictly Protestant phenomenon. A study of the frequency of hymns in Roman Catholic hymnals also found patriotic hymns among the most frequently included. "My Country 'Tis of Thee," "O Beautiful for Spacious Skies," and "Faith of Our Fathers" were all higher on the list than in Protestant hymnals.[11]

The predictable presence of patriotic songs in worship suggests that there is a widespread and long-standing commitment in American churches to using liturgy for nationalistic ends. As one insightful commentator on

---

9. "The Americanization of Christian Worship or New Lebanon to Nashville," cited in Johnson, *The Conviction of Things Not Seen*, 60.

10. Marini, "American Protestant Hymns Project," 251ff.

11. Piscitelli, "Hymns in Roman Catholic Hymnals," 269ff.

worship in the United States has written, "Rather than the liturgy constituting and forming Christians, met in worship by a God whose 'ways are not our ways' re-presented in the sacraments, liturgy is often warped to simply express and celebrate 'our ways.'"[12] Consequently, the power of worship to shape and strengthen Christians as a peculiar people gets undercut. All too frequently worshipers fail to see how the songs and rituals of the nation don't compliment but compromise devotion to the God revealed in Christ. Americanized spirituality replaces distinctly Christian spirituality.

Patriotic songs convey a story, sanction a set of values, and elevate an object of attachment that is not intrinsic to the Christian faith. Yet in the process of singing them the church is impacted. Again to cite Wainwright, "The memorability of hymns allows their substance to penetrate thought and life."[13] This is advantageous if the substance of the hymn is shaped by the biblical story and the gospel of Jesus Christ. However, it is detrimental if the substance carried in the song is not grounded in genuine Christian convictions. Patriotic music imprints in the consciousness of the congregations viewpoints and visions that are absent from—if not contrary to—the faith confessed throughout the centuries and throughout the world.

Given that singing hymns has a formative effect on worshipers, what is formed when the songs sung at civic events by people who are gathered as citizens of a particular nation are also sung at church? Ritual singing—as with all ritual behaviors—inclines us to some practices and against others, toward some beliefs and against others. Worship that calls the congregation to sing songs of the nation has a formative effect. That effect *is not* to shape wholehearted disciples of Jesus Christ. Rather it is to form the worshipers into devoted citizens who often end up being less inclined to challenge the priorities of the nation in the name of the God who transcends all nations than to promote the interests of the American nation. Patriotic worship forms worshipers to be people who believe America is particularly blessed by God and to see America as important to the purpose of God in ways no other nation can claim. Therefore, support for America is support for the purposes of God. Worship that serves such nationalistic ends is worship that has departed from its rightful, singular purpose of glorifying God.

---

12. Clapp, "On the Making of Kings and Christians," 121f.
13. Wainwright, *Doxology,* 200.

Bowing Toward Babylon

ARE PATRIOTIC "HYMNS" REALLY HYMNS?

Though patriotic songs are often included in American hymnals, are these songs really hymns? Many centuries ago Augustine addressed the definition of a hymn. He asked,

> Do you know what a hymn is? It is a song with praise of God. If you praise and not sing, you utter no hymn. If you sing and do not praise God, you do not utter a hymn. If you praise everything else which does not pertain to the praise of God, although you sing and praise, you utter no hymn. A hymn, then, contains these three things: song and praise and that of God.[14]

Theologian Geoffrey Wainwright helpfully elaborates on Augustine's definition of a hymn.[15] First, he notes that public praise of God is, likewise, witness before the world. This being the case, a hymn of witness is to be counted as praise. Though not always overtly "praise," words sung that express confession of sin, declaration of dedication, prayer for forgiveness, or a request for divine aid, guidance, presence, or rule are all doxologically motivated, and, so, can be regarded as hymns.

Second, God must be the object of praise but the manner of address must not necessarily be in the first person. It may be in the second or third person or more indirect. A hymn may be addressed to any one person of the Godhead or to the Trinity in whole. A song expressing praise but not to God fails to be a genuine hymn. Rather, it is an expression of idolatry.

Third, a hymn is praise that is sung. The lyrical and musical forms are diverse and varied. The balance between the word element and the musical element may vary, sometimes the word being predominant—in which the singing is little more than rhythmic speaking—and at other occasions the musical expression may be predominant. Still, regardless of the diversity of lyrical and musical forms, those things that are expressly of God must remain the focus. All else are what the Orthodox thinker Nicholas Lossky has called "idle words." These are the words that "draw attention to oneself instead of directing all attention to God." And "oneself" includes one's nation.[16]

Using this classical definition of a hymn, do patriotic songs stand up as hymns? While these pieces are sung and do offer praise of a sort, is that

---

14. Augustine, *Exposition on the Book of Psalms*, 677.
15. Wainwright, *Doxology*, 198ff.
16. Lossky, "Theology and Prayer," 30.

praise truly directed to God or is it focused elsewhere? Surely the word *God* is used in patriotic songs included in hymnals. But is God the real object of praise or does God play a secondary and supportive role? And is the God named in patriotic songs the God of biblical faith or a god of a decidedly different character? A brief look at a few of the songs should help to provide an answer. You will find that God is often an afterthought appended to the praise offered to the nation. God receives little more than an honorable mention in some of these pieces.

Mentioned earlier was "The Star Spangled Banner," written by Francis Scott Key in 1814 and proclaimed by Congress to be the nation anthem in 1931. Though it has not often appeared in hymnals, it has been sung during numerous services of worship. What Key saw of the attack on Fort McHenry inspired the words we find in the song. The lyrics speak of military conflict and the display of battle: "the rockets' red glare, the bombs bursting in air." An enemy is described in disparaging terms as a "haughty host" who has "foul footsteps" and threatens "lov'd homes." The words of the song speak of triumph "when freemen [Americans] shall stand."

Only in the fourth verse, one that is rarely sung, is God mentioned. The sole defining characteristic of this god is in a relationship to America: "Praise the Pow'r that hath made and preserv'd us as a nation!/Then conquer we must, when our cause is just,/And this be our motto: 'In God is our trust.'"

The real object of praise is found in the refrain: the "star-spangled banner" that symbolizes "the land of the free and the home of the brave." The flag of stars and stripes is celebrated as emblematic of the United States, as it is at least in aspiration. God by any definition has no more than a supporting role in the national anthem. The word *God* has ceremonial presence but is void of content. This song displays no quality whatsoever that would justify it being included in Christian worship.

"My Country 'Tis of Thee," also known as "America," was penned by Samuel Francis Smith in 1832. As mentioned earlier, this piece is among those most often included in American hymnals. As in the national anthem, God is not mentioned until the last verse. Here, too, God is placed in a secondary role as the "author of liberty," a liberty defined *not* by the liberating acts of God in the biblical story but by references to the American story. It is this America-centric freedom that is "holy light." Jesus as the "light of the world" (John 8:12) is nowhere to be found.

The content and tone of "My Country 'Tis of Thee" is positive. From the narrative of the first verse, which speaks of the American experience as the "land of pilgrim's pride," it moves on to express deep love for the qualities of the land: "rocks and rills," "woods and templed hills." The country is personified and addressed with expressions of warm affection and praise, as one would speak to one's beloved.

As moving as the song may be for Americans, the references to God in the fourth verse remain an afterthought, not praise of the sort found in a genuine Christian hymn. Throughout the lyrics the "thee" to whom the rich praise is addressed is not the creator God, not the God who sent Jesus into the world for the sake of all nations, but a particular creation: America.

Katharine Lee Bates, a professor of English at Wellesley College, wrote the words of "America the Beautiful" in 1893. Her verses were joined with Samuel Augustus Ward's musical piece "Materna" and first published together in 1910. Since that time it has appeared in more hymnals that any other patriotic song. The lyrics combine images of the loveliness of the land with phrases that evoke the American story of pilgrims facing challenges in the wilderness and heroic self-sacrifice in the "liberating strife" of war.

On the one hand, "America the Beautiful" affirms the virtues of the American character. On the other hand, the lyrics carry a prophetic, self-critical note, not generally found in patriotic pieces. Implicit in the words are an acknowledgment of national failings and shortcomings. In the second verse we find the words, "God mend thine every flaw." In a later verse we read, "America! America! God shed his grace on thee/Till selfish gain no longer stain/The banner of the free!" Clearly, a national stain brought about by a self-seeking acquisitiveness that disregards the needs of others is being confessed.

Yet despite the commendable qualities found in this song, it should not be regarded as a hymn worthy of inclusion in Christian worship. While God is mentioned in each verse and the need for God's aid is acknowledged, it is the distinctively American story that is celebrated in the lyrics, not the broader biblical story that rightly shapes the church. The song is not about God, nor is the adoration of beauty addressed to God. Rather the "Thee" being addressed is America personified, as is the case with the previous song. How could including such a song is Christian worship *not* be idolatrous since it is another than God who is addressed and praised?

Less likely to be found in hymnals or used in worship services is Irving Berlin's "God Bless America." Still, it is not altogether unusual for the song to be included in a service of worship on the Sunday nearest to a national holiday. I do recall some while after the 9/11 terrorist attacks a woman who was a member in the congregation I serve coming to me upset that I didn't include any patriotic music in the worship services in any of the weeks that followed the tragic event. Angrily, she declared, "If our country is attacked again and we don't have any patriotic music in worship, I will stand up and start singing 'God Bless America' from where I sit in my pew."

It certainly would not have been the worst piece of patriotic music she could have chosen. "God Bless America" has the virtue of being free from military imagery. Likewise, anything that smacks of jingoism is absent. Instead the song speaks to the simple natural affection people—the American people—have for their homeland. There is nothing in the lyrics that suggests ill will toward enemies or a desire to triumph over others. Mountains, prairies, and oceans are mentioned but nothing is said to glorify national character.

But there is also nothing in the lyrics of "God Bless America" that draws attention to the God of biblical faith. The only thing we might discern from the song is that God might be inclined to bless and guide America as "my home sweet home." Essentially, "God Bless America" is a prayer of sorts. But it is not a prayer of the church. It is a prayer not greatly different from the affectionate prayers many of us voice for our own individual families. Just as a prayer for my own family put to music would not be fitting for a service of worship, the same can be said for "God Bless America."

Despite its lack of jingoism and militarism, singing this song in worship serves a purpose at odds with a community not defined by any loyalty and source of unity other than those determined by faith alone. While singing "God Bless America" may reinforce solidarity among Americans and heighten affection for the country, it does nothing to express who we are as people of Christian faith. It does nothing to foster the unity of the church joined in offering praise to the God of Israel revealed in Christ. It does nothing to focus the attention of the worshiping community on the one truly worthy of honor and praise.

When the church is true to its nature and purpose it will have no place for the songs of Babylon. The church exists as a Christ-centered alternative to the world of conflicting nations, races, and tribes. This is especially true for the church that exists in a superpower nation accustomed to privileged status. Rather than helping elevate the nation by sitting it apart and drawing adoring attention to it, in the gathered church voices join to praise the one who tears down barriers between peoples and unites them as one God-glorifying body. The church gathers in worship to joyfully respond to the prophetic call, "Sing to the LORD a new song!" (Isaiah 42:10). To draw from Walter Brueggemann, "The community is invited to stop singing the old domesticated songs of the empire. There need be no more government slogans, no more subservience in singing of loyalties . . . . The very whisper of the phrase 'Yahweh reigns' is a destabilizing assertion. It is a dangerous whisper of an alternative governance . . . as yet without earthly embodiment."[17]

But in fact that embodiment finds itself foreshadowed in the church insofar as the church practices what it prays. In worship the church anticipates a new order in which people are not treated as commodities or function as hostile competitors but live as cherished members of one another, joined for service and praise. As Mary McGann suggests, "The fruit of this redemptive reordering of relationships within worship is the empowerment of participants for the work of reordering relationships within the larger social arena. Within the whole sphere of this community's worship, lived and experienced as 'realized eschatology,' particular moments of communal song gathers up the expectation of the community,"[18] as the church looks forward to the kingdom of God coming in all its fullness while displaying signs of the kingdom in its practices right now.

However, when worship serves to preserve the walls that separate peoples, sanctions the pride and privilege of the powerful, or in any way underwrites injustice then it does not imitate heaven. Rather heaven is misrepresented as a glorified reflection of the brokenness of earth that may be to the advantage of some worshipers but at the expense of other worshipers. This gives little glory to the God who loves all without distinction. Faithful worship keeps in view the divine promise of a "new heaven and a new earth" (Rev 21:1). Every song sung, every prayer uttered, every gift given, every gesture of praise, eating the bread and drinking the cup together is eschatological—that is, God intends it all to point toward culmination in the fullness of time. That is the end that faithful worship serves.

We gather to sing as a people of the kingdom of God and for that very reason we cannot sing the praise of nations. We come together to give honor where honor is most truly due and as we do so we reject every idolatrous appeal for our adoration. As Hebrew scripture scholar Patrick Miller

---

17. Brueggemann, *Israel's Praise*, 49, 58.
18. McGann, *Exploring Music as Worship and Theology*, 78f.

has written, "We sing the praise of the Lord our God. That is the reason for being, that is our most articulate act, that is our fullest emotion. In so doing, we find ourselves in the holy place making the largest claims about all other places, both the market and the political order. We do not sing their praises; we do not set our trust there." He continues, " All our praise finally subverts any possibility that we can have another God. The community that sings the praises of God can hardly give its ultimate allegiance to any human claim for power over us. We have entered another service."[19]

Individually we bring our national heritage with us into worship but we don't allow it to define us corporately as come together as worshipers. Likewise, we bring our personal histories with us and lay them before the throne of God, allowing the story of God in Christ—and no other—to transform how we see our stories and how we understand ourselves in the company of others as a community of faith. In a sensitive and touching way Nancy Bauer-King speaks to this experience.

> I had completed my first year as a pastor and was standing behind the pulpit singing no. 133 in the *United Methodist Hymnal*: "What a fellowship, what a joy divine, leaning on the everlasting arms." I knew the people well enough to have learned some of their personal histories. I knew them well enough to look out over the congregation as I sang.
>
> Ruth and Roger both lost spouses to cancer and then found each other. Bernice's first husband killed himself with a shotgun. Ben and Gloria buried a two year old child. Bob's wife and two grandchildren were killed in an accident with a semi. Jim's son was in prison. J. C. lost his arm in a mishap with a corn picker. Sandy recently joined a support group for incest survivors.
>
> Then it hit me: they were all singing. How could they sing? How could they experience such tragedies, yet come to worship every Sunday and sing?
>
> I realized that these people had stories to tell, and not just stories of tragedies. They had experiences of faith that transcended their suffering. They might never tell these stories, but by attending worship and singing they were witnessing to their faith in the Christian story of love that overcomes death . . . . To gather in worship

---

19. Miller, *The God You Have*, 62.

is to witness to the central story of our faith—and to count on the everlasting arms in our faith community.[20]

This is something that singing the songs of Babylon can never do.

20. Bauer-King, "Song," 24.

CHAPTER 8

Born into a Larger Family and Eating at a Bigger Table Than Babylon

Human existence is embodied existence. The centrality of the incarnation in the Christian faith highlights the conviction God comes to us embodied form. In the sacraments God continues to meet us in material embodiment. The sacraments mediate the presence and the grace of God. Through them God confronts and overturns our idolatries so that we might experience gracious divine mercy in the kingdom of God. "It is in baptism and Eucharist that we see most clearly the marks of God's kingdom in the world.... The sacraments enact the story of Jesus.... [It] is not simply one that is told; it must be enacted," wrote Stanley Hauerwas.[1]

Baptism and the Eucharist are the expressions of worship least marked by the subversive influence of nationalism. That is not to say the sacraments have never been pushed into the service of nationalistic ends. But these efforts have been less obvious and successful, at least in America. Baptism and Eucharist can enable us to resist the impulses of nationalism as they imprint identity and bear witness to the unity in Christ in a way that "mitigates, obviates, and qualifies any other allegiance or political enthusiasm... [and]testifies to justification, not by works or ideology or manifest destiny

---

1. Hauerwas, *The Peaceable Kingdom*, 108.

or righteous cause, but by faith alone."[2] Attention to the meaning of baptism and the Eucharist can help protect us against the idolatrous impulse to bow toward Babylon.

DEAD IN THE WATER

The story of Jesus is acted out and made visible in baptism. "The objective givenness of baptism lies in it being a representation of the redemptive act of God in Christ, whereby life from the dead became possible . . . ."[3] The practice of baptism points to the acts of God in Christ for the salvation of the world. Baptism points beyond the person being baptized and the place where the baptism occurs to a much greater event that happened on behalf of not a single people, but all nations. Baptism signifies the self-giving of God who became flesh and dwelled among us, serving faithfully, sacrificially dying at the hands religious authority and imperial power, and raised from the grave by the power of God. The story that forms the church is dramatically reenacted with each baptism.

The world is encircled and held by the wet embrace of water. Water covers the greatest—and increasing!—proportion of the earth's surface. Water is both common and precious. It is essential for life, yet it can be dangerous. Water can both kill and give life. This is true physically as well as spiritually. The water of baptism is intimately connected with repentance, *metanoia*, the inward reorientation that leads to a redirection of life (Acts 2:38). It is a turning point in which one changes allegiances, loves, and aspirations. Baptism expresses a change of both heart and behavior. Reality is no longer the same for us after we are baptized. The world after baptism is different from the world before baptism because we no longer have the same stake in the world and its nations.

Speaking of his own death, Jesus said, "I have a baptism with which to be baptized" (Luke 12:50). This association of baptism with death is picked up when Christian baptism is addressed in Scripture. As the Apostle Paul wrote, "Do you not know that all of us who have been baptized into Christ Jesus were baptized into his death? Therefore we have been buried with him by baptism into death, so that, just as Christ was raised from the dead

---

2. Bill Wylie-Kellermann, "The assault on baptism's politically transcendent citizenship," *The Witness*, March 2002. http://www.thewitness.org/archive/march2002/ednotes.html.

3. Beasley-Murray, *Baptism in the New Testament*, 271.

by the glory of the Father, so we too might walk in newness of life" (Rom 6:3–4). Baptism is both a tomb where we are laid and a womb from which we are born.

"To die in Christ is to put away our idolatrous tendency to invest the finite creation with infinite significant significance," writes Kendra G. Holtz and Matthew T. Mathews.[4] The old self has not only to do with the individual self with its personal sins but the self as defined by the misguided attachments and affections that lend support to corporate sins and help advance hostile divisions. The self rightly killed in baptism is the self whose loyalty to a portion of humanity leads to the destruction of other portions of humanity. But the sinful self to which we die is defined to a substantial degree by the objects of our desires and the recipients of our devotion.

It is in these things that we find meaning and worth. We elevate them. They attach us to them as sources of our pride. We derive our sense of identity from them. We serve and believe ourselves to be served by these objects, aims, and powers in which we idolatrously invest ourselves. In the end these attachments and affections are expressions of self-deification that in fact do not make us more but less than God intends us to be. As this misshapen self is put to death in baptism the nature of our relationship to God and others change. A transfer of loyalties and refashioning of identity takes place in baptism.

This killing and life-giving work of baptism unites us with Christ and initiates us into the community of disciples we call church. It is in baptism that our life in Christ begins in companionship with others of like faith. We are joined with them and together we live and serve as "the body of Christ" that is enlivened by the Holy Spirit (1 Cor 12:12–13). We take on a new identity by being "clothed with Christ" in baptism; former identities are no longer allowed to primarily define who we are (Gal 3:27–28). Citizenship in an earthy nation becomes secondary. We are given a new identity with new citizenship and new loyalties since God has "transferred us into the kingdom of his beloved Son" (Col 1:13).

Nineteenth-century church reformer Alexander Campbell struck a blow against the idea that citizenship and Christian life are intrinsically joined when wrote that "a Christian is not born where he lives; he is born from above . . . . Is not the bond of union . . . faith or the new birth?"[5] He understood this to take place in baptism where one is born into another

---

4. Hotz and Mathews, *Shaping the Christian Life*, 142.
5. Campbell, *Millennial Harbinger*, Vol. 19, 1848, 365.

realm not of this world and joined with others who share, not the same earthy citizenship, but a heavenly citizenship that alters how we relate to earth and its nations.

BAPTISM AND BARRIERS

As I write these words the rancorous 2016 presidential campaign is taking place. Much concern is being expressed by some candidates about foreign refugees, illegal immigrants, and border security. One leading candidate is advocating building a huge wall along the southern border. I find little in the Christian faith that would make Christians sympathetic to such an endeavor. Baptism transforms boundaries, leading us to identify not primarily with citizens who share national territory with us, but with the baptized who are citizens of the kingdom of God, most of whom are considered "outsiders" by those who share our nationality.

Baptism is both local and universal, boundaried and boundary-breaching, status-creating and status-shattering. It separates and connects. Baptism occurs in a place, a specific location, and initiates us into a community that is local. But baptism does not so root us to a place that it establishes a boundary that sets us at odds with other places and the people that inhabit them. While at points in the history of the church "baptism came to be seen as coextensive with local or national citizenship,"[6] baptism into Christ does not fence us in but leads to the practice of boundary crossing. As Lathrop writes, "The immersion itself has always been understood to be . . . identification with the crucified Christ and so identification, in him, both with the wretched outsiders and with his resurrection to new life, beyond all oppression. Baptism introduces us to an assembly, but this assembly is not simply local. Rather, it is an assembly of assemblies or one worldwide assembly of those who are made witnesses to God's salvation for all things."[7] Baptism is local but it liberates us from the tyranny of the local values and interests that too often get absolutized. In the place of these, wider reaching connections are created.

For those who are baptized all claims of loyalty are qualified and conditioned by the supreme allegiance owed to Christ and the church. The bonds of blood and place are rendered secondary by the overriding devotion expected of those who have been called into "a chosen race, a

---

6. Lathrop, *Holy Ground*, 108.
7. Ibid.

royal priesthood, a holy nation, God's own people, that you may declare the wondrous deeds of him who called you out of darkness into his marvelous light" (1 Pet 2:9). Baptism so fundamentally changes who we are and how we relate to the world around us that it can be said, "We are moved from one country to another."[8] Our country is church and church is never coterminous with the nation in which we reside. Consequently, our most important loyalties are not determined by the border found on any map.

In much of life, particularly when we are young, we are acted upon far more than being actors in the world. So it is in baptism where something is received, an action done to us and on our behalf. We are in the hands of others, the visible hands of the one administering the baptism and, above all, in the invisible hands of the God who purifies, renews, and incorporates us into the body of Christ. We are passive, even if consenting, recipients of grace. More specifically, we are dependent upon the goodness of God. It is the goodness of God that calls into question all the other supposed goods we excessively elevate and to which we idolatrously give our hearts.

As baptism displays our utter dependence upon God and reenacts the story of Jesus, it undercuts our delusions of merit and our postures of pride. We are awakened to the reality that we receive all things as gifts, not rewards we deserve because of our efforts. This is not to say that what we do is of no importance. However, in baptism we find significance, not in ourselves or in the objects of our affection and pride but in what God has done in Christ. As we remember our baptism we are faced with the truth that our meaning and purpose is not finally found in where we come from or what we accomplish or in anything that is an extension of ourselves but in the God who created and mercifully redeemed us through the one who lived, died, and was raised from the dead.

Because we require the hands of another to be baptized, we find ourselves faced with the truth that we cannot be who God intends us to be apart from others. From the beginning of our life in Christ we find that we need others to do and to become what God desires. Karl Barth wrote, "As one who seeks baptism he begins with the knowledge of Jesus Christ, who discloses himself to him, but who is not a private Saviour, but the Messiah of Israel and the King of His people . . . he cannot pretend to be a bold individualist who is left to arrange things with God for himself, and to enter and tread his way alone . . . . From the very outset he is directed

---

8. Willimon, *The Service of God*, 103.

to the community."⁹ We never stand merely as an individual before God but always in communion with other people of God who support, nurture and guide us. And it must be emphasized that this community is not the "imagined community" of nation but the church.

While baptism is a human action, it is a work of God. The one being baptized is not the primary actor and neither is the one doing the baptism. Rather the unseen God works to do what we are incapable of doing, making us new, forgiving us, transforming and making us part of the body of Christ. We cooperate with what God is doing but we don't control it. In conversion we don't simply change our mind; we are given a new mind, one that bears the imprint of Christ. Hence, when Paul wrote, "Do nothing from selfishness or conceit," he did not call only for external change. Instead he said, "Have this mind among yourselves which is your in Christ Jesus" (Phil 2:3–5). This "mind" given in baptism enables us to recognize as friends those we had seen enemies and to recognize those we had seen as other than ourselves as brothers and sisters.

The baptism that kills us is also our birth into a family of faith, a family that is distinctive from the family of our flesh and not a natural extension of ourselves but one given to us with our new birth. This is the family of which Jesus spoke when someone told him his mother and brothers had come to see him: "Who are my mother and my brothers? . . . Whoever does the will of God is my brother and sister and mother" (Mark 3:35–36). This family is a product of the Holy Spirit who moves in and among us to create a people who embody the will of God and bear witness to the truth of God.

Baptism involves identification with Christ that disaffects us from the objects of our idolatrous affections. Baptism detaches us from attachments that don't foster an expansive love of God and others but narrows our loyalties in service of the fragmentation of the world. In baptism we are raised with Christ to relate to God with thankful praise and engage with the world in a transformed way that furthers reconciliation and harmony where there is division and animosity. As we clothe ourselves in Christ in baptism, we put on his love, a love that breaches barriers build by suspicion, fear, and injustice. We act as instruments of healing, not harm.

We who are baptized into Christ are no longer who we were. We have been given a new story that tells us who we are. The story that determines our self-understanding is no longer the one given to us by families, or ethnic groups, or nations. We have been incorporated into Christ and his story

---

9. Barth, *Church Dogmatics*, vol. IV, 49.

becomes our story, reorienting us, shaping the way we see ourselves and the world, and determining the way we live in the world. Paul could write, "I have been crucified with Christ; and it is no longer I who live, but it is Christ who lives in me. And the life I now live in the flesh I live by faith in the Son of God, who loved me and gave himself for me" (Gal 2:19-20). The old self, the old identity has been displaced so that the new self in Christ can guide our steps.

The closing words of the Gospel of Matthew have Jesus instructing his followers to go to all nations to make disciples, baptizing them into the name of the Father and of the Son and of the Holy Spirit (Matt 28:18-19). The aim of Jesus was not to wash away the distinctive traits of diverse peoples. He did, however, intend to give them a message of good news that would draw them all into a loving relationship with God and each other. The people of the many nations are to be brought together by the teachings of Jesus. In the water of baptism they are given a common identity in Christ that transcends their often incompatible affections and limited, provincial loyalties. In baptism a new nation from the many nations is created and a unity across borders comes into being.

It is precisely because of the shared experience of having been baptized into Christ that the Apostle Paul could declare, "There is no longer Jew or Greek, there is no longer slave or free, there is no longer male and female; for all of you are one in Christ Jesus" (Gal 3:28). The question, "Who am I?" can no longer be answered first of all by saying, "I am an American." Now we confess that we are Christ's people and we have been made one with all others who have been baptized in his name. No, we have not been blended into a homogeneous unity that has destroyed all of value and beauty found in the variety of clans and nations. Rather, in Christ all cohere one to another and serve each other's interests in mutual appreciation.

Again, in baptism the "passions and desires" that are crucified (Gal 5:24) are not only the ones that dwell in our individual bodies but those that are part of the body politic. National pride, hostility toward national enemies, the propensity to be suspicious of outsiders, or inhospitable toward immigrants are also "passions and desires" that must be killed. So, too, must the predisposition to judge those who share our nationality—or race, class, or ethnic identity—as more worthy of positive regard, compassion, or aid than others be put to death. "You have stripped off the old self with its practices and have clothed yourselves with the new self, which is being renewed in knowledge according to the image of its creator" (Col

3:9–10). That "old self with its practices" includes the idolatrous glorification of those things that are extensions of the self, such as are found exercises and attitudes associated with nationalism. The remedy for these spiritual malformations is found in the God-given alternative "knowledge according to the image of its creator."

Just as the question, "Who am I?" cannot be answered in the same way as it was before baptism, so too, the question, "Who are we?" cannot be answered in the same way as we once answered it. Even among Christians who share our nationality, we are not first of all Americans. We are the body of Christ. As such we are joined by the power of the Holy Spirit to all others with whom we have faith in Christ in common and also have been baptized in his name regardless of where they come from or who they are. What we have in common with those who share our nationality—or any other trait or experience for that matter—must never take precedence over the unity we share in Christ and the responsibility of love towards others in him. We cannot strain "the unity of the Spirit in the bond of peace" (Eph 4:3) by celebrating American identity and heritage. Neither can we defend American interests or support wars fought by the nation while risking the lives of those who are united with us in Christ. The baptized come together in worship as a people who find unity in Christ and nothing else.

BEYOND THE BAPTIZED

While baptism separates us from every pride and excessive affection of clan, tribe, and nation, it does not isolate us from others or produce a community that is ingrown and self-preoccupied. In other words, baptism does not lead the church to be a "sect" in the pejorative sense in which the word is often used. As Louis-Marie Chauvet has observed, "The difference inscribed on the body of every person through Christian initiation is so important that, far from imprisoning one into a clan or cultural group, as some other rites of initiation do, it opens onto a universal: by their baptism, Christians do not become members of a ghetto, but sisters and brothers of all humans in Jesus Christ."[10] The very baptism that unites us with Christ also relativizes and conditions all other attachments while at the same time uniting us with all humanity loved by the Lord. For this reason, we not only cannot kill those who are one with us in Christ, but we cannot kill any others who loved by God.

10. Chauvet, *The Sacraments*, 111.

In baptism we look back to the acts of Jesus in his death and resurrection but we also look forward in hope of the kingdom of God. "[I]n baptism . . . we participate in the event whereby the Kingdom came! That means that the forward look in baptism is much more than a wistful longing for a place in the Kingdom that is to be; we have been united the Christ who brought the Kingdom in his death and resurrection and shall complete it in his Parousia . . . . Baptism is thus an entry into the eschatological order of the new creation."[11] The misguided passions, self-serving endeavors, hateful and deadly competitions that exist both in individuals and among nations are neither inevitable nor unalterable in the eyes of those who have been baptized into Christ.

The hope of the kingdom bestowed in baptism is not a sentiment to be locked in the hearts of those of us who have been baptized. Rather it is a hope demonstrated in public as the church actively anticipates the kingdom of God through such practices such as hospitable inclusion, generous compassion, gracious forgiveness, and nonviolent love. In keeping with such practices the baptized community rejects national pride and refuses to participate in hostile actions against other peoples, actions that are so often perpetrated in the name of national interest. The church is a proleptic people who live toward the promise of the kingdom of God, displaying the future in the prophetic practices of the present.

Nothing less can be expected of those who gather to worship the God who so loved the world and who came to us in Jesus Christ filled with grace and truth. With longing the faithful church looks forward to joining the voices of those of the angelic choir who sing, "Great and amazing are your deeds, Lord God the Almighty! Just and true are your ways, King of the nations! Lord, who will not fear and glorify your name? For you alone are holy. All nations will come and worship before you, for your judgments have been revealed" (Rev 15:3–4). The song in the hearts of the baptized makes a melody that crosses space and time and joins heaven and earth in the kingdom of God.

In a report titled "Baptism Creates International Incident," Episcopal priest Fr. David Roseberry tells of an experience he had while leading a tour in the Holy Land. He had about thirty people with him when the bus pulled up to a recently renovated site commemorating the place traditionally believed to be the location where the baptism of Jesus by John the Baptist

---

11. Beasley-Murray, *Baptism in the New Testament*, 292.

occurred. This was also supposedly the place where Joshua led the Israelites to cross the Jordan River to enter the promised land.

He led the group in what he called "a very Anglican-style service" of renewal of baptismal vows. The participants had water from the Jordan sprinkled on their heads as he called upon them to recall the promises they made or were made on their behalf years earlier: "Remember that you are baptized in the Name of the Father, Son, and Holy Spirit." He then anointed each head with oil and said, "Remember that you are sealed by the Holy Spirit in baptism and marked as Christ's own forever."

However, one man stood apart. At the end of the service he approached Fr. Roseberry and declared, "I want to be baptized; I have never been baptized and I want to be today." The priest was surprised but he asked the man if he could agree with the vows of a Christian. Would he renounce the world, the flesh, and the devil and place his faith in Jesus Christ as his Savior, promising to follow and obey him as Lord? The man emphatically replied, "Yes!"

Fr. Roseberry asked him to take off his shoes and sweatshirt as he removed his own shoes. The man said to him, "Why don't you just let me get in by myself? I don't want you to get wet." He explained to the man that baptism is not something that a person can do to him or herself. "I'm going in with you." The two of them entered the cold, murky water.

The priest proceeded, employing the appropriate formula for an Anglican baptismal liturgy in the name of the Father and the Son and the Holy Spirit. He was caught off-guard when the man went completely beneath the surface of the river, being fully immersed. The man then sprung up from the water and immediately sucked in a deep breath. Fr. Roseberry continued,

> The moment he came up, a group of nuns from Lebanon and Egypt who were standing on the opposite shore of the river . . . *in Jordan . . . another country . . . not 10 yards away* . . . began cheering and singing "Amazing Grace." We joined them in singing. We all realized that we were part of a spectacle we would never forget. Christians from around the world separated into two countries by a river, but joined together in Christ over that same river as one brother came into the fellowship of our common Lord who had been also baptized in that same river. One man went under the water of baptism and when he emerged, a cloud of witnesses from across the nations and over the world gave thanks to God.[12]

12. Roseberry, "Baptism Creates International Incident," *Anglican Pastor*, February 2,

Baptism always creates an "international incident" whether there are people from other nations visibly present or not. All who are baptized are joined with all others in Christ, without regard to national identity or nationalistic loyalties. It is, indeed, "amazing grace" that brings us together across borders. This is not a union of souls that has nothing to do with the loyalty we practice with our bodies. In baptism we are made one with all who share faith in Jesus Christ and this oneness supersedes the attachment created by citizenship. Allegiance to nation is transcended by the loyalty members of the body of Christ owe to one another—but not only to one another—and so Scripture admonishes us to "work for the good of all, and especially for those of the family of faith" (Gal 6:10).

Yes, baptism creates a people who have a special love and loyalty for one another. But unlike nationalism, this love and loyalty for some does not lead us to work for the good of some to the detriment of others, but rather contains an abiding commitment to "work for the good of all." Baptism joins us to Jesus Christ who joined himself with Jewish children and adults, Roman soldiers, Samaritan women, poor and rich, old and young, the ill and the healthy, the devout and the impious. Baptism makes us part of a distinctive faith community. However, because that community is defined by the story of Jesus, the one whose life embodied the kingdom of God, it can never be an exclusive club. It must be connected through loving service with the baptized as well as the unbaptized of every nation.

This seems unrealistic in the eyes of many in a world often torn with strife and bitter hostility. However, since baptism incorporates us into the story of Jesus and the community formed by that story we cannot do otherwise than to reach across the divides that plague humankind to practice kindness, encourage respect, and foster harmony with all people. Regardless of whether or not this behavior seems realistic in the turmoil and violence of this present world, those of us who belong to the baptized community of faith live toward the promised kingdom of God. For us the future is already present. We see a different reality. "If anyone is in Christ, there is a new creation: everything old has passed away; see, everything has become new! All this is from God, who reconciled us to himself through Christ, and has given us the ministry of reconciliation" (2 Cor 5:17–18).

The idolatrous devotion to the nation limits what we can see and determines what we perceive as reality. Seeing through the lens of American pride and so-called national interests leads to an inability to see wider

---

2016, http://anglicanpastor.com/baptism-creates-international-incident/.

concerns and the multitude of options that are not near at hand. What is thought of as "realistic" is often a product of an impoverished, nation-bound imagination. In the critically acclaimed movie *The Room* a five-year-old boy whose mother was a victim of kidnapping and rape never saw outside of the room where he was born. He was kept captive there with his mother. His entire world was limited to what he could experience within the walls of his small room. He could not even imagine there was a sprawling world beyond the walls that confined him. For him there was nothing outside the room. The walls set the limits of his imagination.

Nationalism builds walls around the imagination and makes holy possibilities seems impossible. Deeply engrained affections and precognitive dispositions coupled with ideological assumptions construct the way the world is imagined in America. Yet, the world is not simply a fixed fact, a settled object "out there." It is imaginatively constructed. Baptism challenges the legitimacy of those walls as we become one with the body of Christ that extends around the globe and endures throughout the centuries. The world is reconstituted as we re-present the story of Jesus in the language and rituals of worship. Our eyes are opened to see what we previously could not see. We see the now-but-not-yet kingdom of God and live toward its fulfilment as we practice what we pray, "Thy kingdom come, thy will be done on earth as it is in heaven."

LORD'S SUPPER: RIGHTLY REMEMBERING

We are born into the family of faith by baptism but then we reinforce our "family values" and faithful vision at the Table of the Lord. For most of my life I had never seen the Lord's Supper pressed into the service of nationalism. Though I had repeatedly seen most other expressions of worship subverted by American nationalism, the Eucharist was above it all. Then several years ago, after a national tragedy I heard that a Roman Catholic priest in Texas had draped the altar with the American flag. Sometime later I saw in a United Church of Christ two American flags placed upon the communion table. I strongly suspect these are not totally isolated incidences. Regardless of how rarely they occur, such nation-adoring demonstrations deeply offend against the meaning of the Table and twist the narrative from which the Eucharist comes to serve an idolatrous and destructively divisive end.

The Lord's Supper "allows us to learn, absorb, and extend the values of God's Kingdom."[13] Using the Table to draw attention to Babylon's vision and values perverts the purpose of Communion, distracts from the praise due to God alone, and undercuts the unity of the church. A mockery is made of the Eucharist whenever any trace of nationalism is allowed a place at the Table. The Lord's Table can never be an American Table. Rather, as expressed in *Baptism, Eucharist, and Ministry*: "The Eucharistic celebration demands reconciliation and sharing among all those regarded as brothers and sisters in the one family of God and is a constant challenge in the search for appropriate relationships in social, economic, and political life."[14]

The Eucharist is a thanksgiving meal in which the church remembers whose and who it is. We give thanks for what God has done in Jesus Christ to teach, to heal, to befriend the outcasts and sinners, enduring rejection by the authorities, abuse, and death. We give thanks that through Christ we have been included by the grace of God and the Lord's Table is a symbol of our inclusion. We have been welcome to come and share in the meal despite our sin and brokenness. At the Table our attention is refocused and our lives are reoriented by what God has done in Jesus Christ, not on what we have done or who we are apart from our relationship with Christ. We re-present the story of Jesus as we participate in the bread and cup of communion. As we do so our affections for the One who loved us and our acknowledgement of who we are as his beloved are enhanced and deepened.

The external forms of the sacraments would be worthless without the interior action of the Holy Spirit working in and through them to strengthen, lead, and bestow love upon us. The Lord invites us to the Table and brings us near to be nourished and blessed. Together with other people of faith we share the joy of being in his presence. Holy Communion takes us to the night of the betrayal of the Lord when he gathered with his apostles and told them to remember him. We are incorporated into the story of Christ as we eat the bread and drink from the cup in his name, celebrating his body and blood. We remember him and in so doing we remember who we have been called to be. The Lord's Supper, like baptism, conveys and reinforces the identity of the church and shapes the church's imagination as it is grounded in the narrative of faith.

The remembering that takes place in Holy Communion is not an exercise in nostalgia. It is a living memory in the real presence of Christ. We

13. Wainwright, *Worship With One Accord*, 210f.
14. *Baptism, Eucharist and Ministry*, 14.

don't come to the Lord's Table just remembering a historical event of the distant past or to reaffirm a doctrine. We come to participate in the life of Jesus Christ. We come to be near him as a person who has made himself mystically present through the bread and the cup. We come to the brokenness of Christ so that our brokenness might be made whole as we share the table with others of like faith. We remember in a manner that gives us a new perspective and opens our eyes so that we can see the world and the events in it in light of the determination of God in Christ to love regardless of the consequences. We never come alone—this is not a Table for private devotion—but along with others in all their diversity, all who are beloved by God with whom we are part of the family of faith. "Our table fellowship reminds us that we are created in God's image to be sons and daughters of God, brothers and sisters to one another in Christ and temples of the Holy Spirit . . . . We have personal dignity. We are called to participate in community to seek the common good."[15]

We come to the Table to redemptively remember. Among many peoples and nations throughout the world old grudges too frequently are remembered in order to foster present hostilities. Old injuries and injustices are kept alive to feed resentment that can justify violence against the descendants of those who were perpetrators. But when we come to the Table of the Lord and we remember Christ rejected, abused, and tortured to death, our memory is not put into the service of violence and hostility. We don't remember so we might more intensely despise those who killed our Lord. What we remember above all is the suffering, nonviolent love that Jesus practiced among both friends and enemies. We remember the horrible abuse he was willing to endure in order to extend the embrace of truth and love across walls that had been built by hate. As we take the bread and the cup of communion and remember the holy victim we do so not with thoughts of reprisal, but with a commitment to follow Jesus as agents of reconciliation.

When the Apostle Paul issued the warning about "discerning the body" (1 Cor 11:29), he was not calling people to approach the Table while meditating upon the mangled body of Christ on the cross. Rather he wrote to the troubled and divided ancient congregation to condemn the practice of the wealthier members who excluded poorer members from sharing in the communal meal of the church. In their actions the wealthier ones disrespected the body of Christ which is the church by marginalizing those

---

15. Andrews, "The Lord's Table, the World's Hunger," 69.

who were less prosperous. The abundance of possessions rather than the abundance of divine grace became the qualification for full welcome.

The rich were so mindful of their social status they were forgetful of the lowly earthly status of the one they encountered in the bread and cup of communion. This led them to forget that all people of whatever status are to be indiscriminately welcomed into the fellowship and worship of the church. The practice of those who were more affluent so compromised the integrity of the worship life of the congregation that the apostle told them, "When you come together, it is not really to eat the Lord's Supper" (v. 20). Their behavior disfigured the meaning of the meal beyond recognition. Because they brought the injustice of the world, the very injustice that led to the crucifixion of Christ, into the worship of the church, Paul declared they "will be answerable for the body and blood of the Lord" (v. 27).

We come to the Table as equals. None has a right to be present due to superior accomplishment, exemplary morals, or superior faith. We come to the Table of the Lord as sinners without any qualifying virtue or entitling characteristic except the invitation of grace. We come as people who are needy and hungry. It is only by the merciful invitation of the Lord that we have a share of the bread and the cup. Our wealth, race, gender, or nationality give us no special access to the Table. Because we have been welcomed by the Lord without a qualifying trait we must welcome others in the same way, disregarding the barriers and borders that shut some out while privileging others. We come to the Table remembering that we are one with all others who have been invited.

To rightfully remember at the Table of the Lord we cannot forget our own complicity in various forms of injustice in the world. We do not come to the Table innocent of the injuries inflicted upon others for our gain. Most of us are beneficiaries of injustices done to those who are weak. We have gained from the exploitation of others with every purchase we make that is a product of cheap labor. The self-serving attitudes, values, and passions that send countless poor and powerless people to crosses of deprivation in our own time are not dissimilar to the attitudes, values, and passions that sent Jesus to the cross. We deceive ourselves if we imagine our affluence has not been purchased by blood, specifically blood shed by American imperialistic endeavors that have secured access to natural resources and cheap labor. As we approach the widely spread wounded hands of Christ to receive the bread and cup of communion we need to remember the wounding we have had a part in doing, both near and far.

In Communion we encounter the one who came in the world to stand with those who suffer and to reach out to those who were rejected. He was, as I heard someone say, "captivated by the crushed." He came close to share their misery. We cannot rightly remember at the Table unless we remember the broken and marginalized ones he loved and remember those who share their condition in our own time. Truly, "gratitude for holy food and the salvation it brings is fully expressed only when we remember that unleavened bread was first eaten by slaves on the run and the cup of some drink is a cup of suffering."[16] At the Table we rightly remember Christ crucified only if we remember to "discern the body" of the wounded near and far.

CHRISTIAN UNITY AND THE EUCHARISTIC IMAGINATION

I have the privilege of serving a congregation that is multiracial, multicultural, and multinational. When I stand at the Communion Table I look at the diverse people who have gathered in worship. First-generation immigrants—occasionally some who are undocumented—from over fifteen nations from North America, South America, the Caribbean, Asia, and Europe come to join hearts and voices in praise and to share in the bread and cup of the Eucharist. Despite all the differences, the people are one by faith in Jesus Christ, made one by the unifying power of the Holy Spirit. The suspicion and hostility that is seen in much of the world is absent. We are brothers and sisters. In such a church it is easy to remember that when we gather at the Table of the Lord it is not only with those under this particular roof or in the American nation that we commune but with all everywhere who eat the bread and drink from the cup in the name of Jesus.

As we come to the Table our imagination is cultivated by the performance of the Jesus story, a story that includes all who have faith in the one who welcomes us to share the bread and cup in his name. We see ourselves as members of a community that extends spatially and temporally far beyond here and now. The barriers of space and time collapse. The Eucharist is celebrated locally but it ties us to other worshipers near and far, past and present. The local church gathers at the Table as an expression of the whole church, not just a piece of the church universal. "Each Eucharist performed in the local community makes present not part of Christ but the whole Christ, and the eschatological unity of all in Christ . . . . The Eucharistic

16. Ibid., 71f.

breakdown of divisions . . . is a fundamental disfigurement of the imagination of citizenship in the territorial state."[17] When we gather at the Table we are never communing only with other Americans. We are joined with brothers and sisters everywhere in the presence of the Lord and we look forward to the time when our oneness will be fully manifested.

Occasionally Eucharistic integrity and so-called national interests come into direct conflict. The unity of the church called for at the Table butts up against hardening national borders. Support for one cannot be given without offending against the aims of the other. One occasion for this confrontation happened at Friendship Park, a plaza atop a bluff just south of San Diego. For decades this was a meeting place where residents of San Diego and people living in Tijuana could meet at the border fence to visit, sometimes passing small gifts or items of food back and forth.

Some Christians from both sides of the fence would also gather at the park each Sunday afternoon for Communion. The elements were distributed through the border fence as the worshipers acknowledged that they were one people in Jesus Christ. But after the terrorist attacks of September 11, 2001 many politicians became anxious about border security. The Department of Homeland Security took control of the Border Patrol and began construction in the area to make the border far less permeable.

When Friendship Park was first built there was no fence at all between the United States and Mexico but only a single low-hanging chain. People moved freely from one side to the other without threat. In the 1970s a simple chain link fence was erected. It allowed clear views between the countries and did not hinder transnational gathering. People could visit through the fence, kiss through the fence, grieve and cry together with fingers entangled through the fence. But the additional precautions and barriers would greatly hinder all of those interactions.

Likewise, the enhanced security was bound to interfere with the activity of the ecumenical group that gathered there to sing, pray, and commune. The worshipers were told by the Border Patrol agents that they could not pass anything through the fence or it would be considered a customs violation. Initially those who led this service complied with the restrictions. But later they decided that in clear conscience they could not obey. The nation's attempt to exclude could not be allowed to triumph over the church's mandate to invite and offer welcome at the Table.

---

17. Cavanaugh, *Theopolitical Imagination*, 50–51.

An American minister was on one side of the fence while a minister from Tijuana was on the other side as people from both nations gathered to worship. The Rev. John Fanestil wrote, "People formed into lines, one in each country, and came forward silently to receive communion. People were given the choice of receiving the elements from either celebrant, the people on the US side having been forewarned that the act of taking a small piece of bread to the fence might be considered by some an act of civil disobedience.... One by one my friends on the US side... approached the serving station and reached out their hands to receive the body of Christ through the fence."[18] Civil disobedience became an inevitable consequence of giving the unity of the Table priority over the security concerns of the nation.

Because of idolatrous devotion to America the supposed welfare of the nation is given priority over the faithfulness of the church or the interests of other nations. It is an empty and deceptive gratification that finds joy, not in the thriving of all, but the unhindered advance of national interests and security without regard to the needs and desires of other peoples. The sharing of bread and cup in the Lord's Supper stand at odds with the "sweet intoxicant of 'power over' that swells the patriot heart" when the interests of others is subverted for the gain on one's own nation. As Holtz and Mathews have written, "The grace of the Lord's Supper, as it restores and renews our sense of direction and delight, call us to remember the resurrection of Jesus Christ as God's 'no' to human violence, and it calls us in hope toward the ever-expansive love of the kingdom of God that liberates us from enslavement to the false god of the nation."[19] When we participate in Communion rightfully remembering, faithfully discerning, and with loving attentiveness our imagination will be transformed. We will begin to see possibilities that those who are America citizens first of all will not be able to entertain.

We need not seek to make the Lord's Table political. Rather we must stop spiritualizing the Table in such a way that its politics are stripped away. The Eucharist entails an alternative social order that is expansive in its welcome thereby overcoming the exclusion that is at work at other tables that are accessed only by those with special characteristics, characteristics that separate peoples, elevating some over others based on their station, race, ethnic identity, gender, or nationality. What we do at the Lord's Table changes how we approach every other table and affects how we welcome

---

18. Fanestil, "Border Crossing," 25.
19. Hotz and Mathews, *Shaping the Christian Life*, 152.

others who are often marginalized or excluded. Barriers and boundaries are overcome as we come together with all others who have been invited by the Lord. Even the barrier of death is transcended at the Table.

For those who share the bread and cup of Communion death itself cannot sever us from those who are one with us in Christ. Margaret Scott tells a story of an elderly woman who, after Salvadorian Bishop Oscar Romero was shot down while celebrating the Mass, went to his tomb. There she knelt down and began to quietly talk to the martyr: "*¿Amorcito, por qué te dejaste matar?*" (My dearest, why did you let them kill you?) From within her heart the answer was gently given: "*Es que Vos nos querías.*" (It was because you loved us.) As we partake of the Lord's Supper we commune, not only with those who are with us locally and not only those who are currently alive but with all others in every place and time who have been touched by Christ's love and who have extended Christlike love to others, even to the point of death.

THE LORD'S TABLE AND THE MESSIANIC BANQUET

When we come before the Lord at the Table we remember, not only the story of Jesus' past deeds, but the promise he made to eat again with his disciples in the kingdom of God (Luke 14:15; 22:16; 22:30). Paradoxically, we remember the future. We come to the Table in anticipation of the fulfilment of the promise of our Lord. As we eat and drink we practice for life in the new world that is coming when the will of God is "done on earth as it is in heaven." The passionate longing for the heavenly to be made real is manifested at Communion where no one who has heard the Lord's invitation is excluded. All who desire to come near to Jesus are welcome at the Table. By offering this expansive and indiscriminate invitation in the name of Jesus the kingdom of God is foreshadowed in the practice of the church.

As we partake in communion and find joy in the radiance of Christ who desires the flourishing of all who are made in God's image, we are reminded of the eschatological banquet where there is no place for the distorted narrowness of nationalistic religion. The experience of welcome that we and others who different from ourselves equally receive as we come into the presence of the Lord at the Table strikes a blow against the idolatry of nationalism. The self-glorifying impulses of nationalism and the deluded pride of place that leads to the exclusion or marginalization of "outsiders" is revealed for the ugly thing it is as Christ graciously welcomes all without preference for any nation.

We ready ourselves for the future God has promised as we eat and drink at a Table that is open to all. Because we are no more qualified to be at the Table than those who come from any of the other nation, even those nations hostile to our own, as we eat and drink we are being prepared to welcome them, not only at the Table but even as we step away from it. By eating and drinking together we begin imagining the possibilities of a more harmonious and beneficent world. Our Eucharistic practice prepares us for the world God intends and makes that world present through our corporate life. At the Table we participate in an eschatological meal anticipating the Messianic banquet. In this ritual we are shaped into a peaceable people, something we can never be as nationalists.

Though we continue living in a world where fear, suspicion, and competing interests put peoples at odds with one another, we come to the Table to rightly remember the future and to renew our hope in the promise of our Lord who said he would eat again with his followers in the kingdom of God. Rather than sanctioning the animosity and exclusion that is expressed in numberless ways in the name of security or defending freedom or protecting democracy, we affirm the promise of Jesus: "People will come from east and west and north and south, and will take their places at the feast in the kingdom of God" (Luke 13:29). We prepare for the future by attentively coming to the Table in the present where the arms of Jesus are opened wide. As William T. Cavanaugh has written, "In the Eucharist the church is always called to become what it eschatologically is . . . Christians are called to conform their practice to the Eucharistic imagination . . . a vision of what is really real, the Kingdom of God, as it disrupts the imagination of violence."[20]

It is within space and time that the church "mystically" becomes at the Lord's Table what it truly is. If the true church is only something unseen, this leaves the church without a social witness and undercuts any tangible hope it offers to a divided and damaged world. But in fact the church gathers at the Table and in the name of Jesus extends a welcome—without regard to national identity and loyalty—to people of every race and place. The church gathers to celebrate the sacrificial love of God in Christ for the whole world. In this practice the invisible and mysterious action of God becomes visible in the life of the church on the historical stage of this

---

20. Cavanaugh, *Torture and Eucharist*, 206.

present world. In this practice the church anticipates and prepares for the time when "the kingdom of the world has become the kingdom of our Lord and of his Messiah" (Rev 11:15).

It is certainly true, as Cavanaugh says, that "The Eucharist has lost much of its eschatological import precisely where the church has come to feel at home in the world, forfeiting its sense of the transitory nature of the Christian sojourn among the earthly kingdoms."[21] When the pride, security, and sense of meaning had by Christians in America is derived from the nation there is little likelihood that there will be much of a "longing for a better country" (Heb 11:16). Where this longing is absent, so, too, is missing the divinely subversive imagination which moves people of faith to develop affections unfettered by the love of the nation and to develop practices of gracious service that challenge narrow loyalties to things American. Concrete manifestations of the kingdom of God in the life of the church end up being stifled.

It is for this reason that the bread and cup of Communion must be partaken, not only as a memorial to Jesus' life, death, and resurrection, but also as a taste of the promised future. As the Apostle Paul wrote, "For as often as you eat this bread and drink the cup, you proclaim the Lord's death *until he comes*" (1 Cor 11:26). At the Table the church of the present draws its life from both from past and future. Memory and hope converge as the church lives as the body of Christ between the time of the earthly life of Jesus and the return of Lord. Because it is a distinctive hope and memory that gives the church its shape, the members of the church will be committed to the gracious and embracing kingdom of God practices that seem out of place in the fractured world but are perfectly suitable for the realm that is yet to come. To be people of faith is to live in that tension.

The Eucharist demands that worshipers accept and extend a welcome that overcomes the alienation that separate peoples. The Eucharist requires radical sharing in a selfish and acquisitive world in which competition for food and resources leads to destructive competition. The Eucharist requires an equal welcome be given to all without reserving a privileged place for people more like ourselves in race, or strength, or wealth, or intelligence, or language, or nationality. The Eucharist allows no place for the sort of suspicions that justify preparations to do violence to people some national leaders perceive as threats. Instead we come to the Table and engage in a celebration of peace. As we gather together to share the Lord's Supper we

---

21. Ibid., 225.

perform the kingdom of God, proclaiming and putting into practice in the present a world that is yet to come.

The more we become the body of Christ at the Table the less at home we will be in America. Rather than exalting in the history, prestige, and military prowess of the nation, we will remember the broken and bloody one vindicated by the power of God in the resurrection whom we encounter in the bread and cup. Rather than brandishing the stars and stripes and blustering about "The Power of Pride," as we find on bumper stickers and billboards, we remember, "God chose what is low and despised in the world, things that are not to reduce things that are" (1 Cor 1:28). If we come to the Table rightly remembering, faithfully discerning the body, and in anticipation of the kingdom of God, American Christian nationalism will be given no place in the life of the church.

Those of us living in America who are devoted to the one who came in vulnerability to practice selfless service and demonstrate nonviolent love reside in the mightiest nation the world has ever known, the Babylon of our time. But if we are faithfully shaped by the story of Jesus we will resist the temptation to bow toward Babylon. As we worship in a manner that represents Jesus in a way uncontaminated by nationalism we will be formed into a people who are made one in Christ along with other people of faith in every nation. As a people defined by Jesus Christ we will not find our meaning in America and we will refuse to be enlisted in violent endeavors that insure American dominance at the expense of others. Instead, we will gather in worship to rehearse for life in the kingdom of God and then go into the world to reach across every wall of hostility with the determination to do good to all for whom Christ died.

Bibliography

Anderson, Benedict. *Imagined Communities: Reflections on the Origin and Spread of Nationalism*. London: Verso, 1983, 1991.

Anderson, Branden P. *Chosen Nation: Scripture, Theopolitics, and the Project of National Identity*. Eugene, OR: Cascade, 2012.

Andrews, David. "The Lord's Table, the World's Hunger: Liturgy, Justice, and Rural Life." In *Liturgy and Justice: To Worship God in Spirit and Truth*, edited by Anne Y. Koester, 63–73. Collegeville, MN: Liturgical, 2002.

Augustine. *Exposition on the Book of Psalms*. *The Nicene and Post Nicene Fathers*. First series, vol. 7. Edited by Phillip Schaff and A. Cleveland Coxe. Grand Rapids: Eerdmans, 1974.

Bader-Saye, Scott. "Figuring Time: Providence and Politics." In *Liturgy, Time, and the Politics of Redemption*, edited by Randi Rashkover and C. C. Pecknold, 91–111. Grand Rapids: Eerdmans, 2006.

Balch, George T. *A Patriotic Primer for the Little Children*. Indianapolis: William B. Burford, 1895.

Baptism, Eucharist and Ministry. Geneva: World Council of Churches, 1982.

Barth, Karl. *Church Dogmatics*, vol. IV. Translated by G. W. Bromiley. Edinburgh: T&T Clark, 1969.

Bass, Diana Butler. *Broken We Kneel*. San Francisco: John Wiley & Sons, 2004.

Bauer-King, Nancy. "Song." *The Christian Century*, October 28, 2015, 22–26.

Beasley-Murray, G. R. *Baptism in the New Testament*. Grand Rapids: Eerdmans, 1965.

Beaune, Colette. *The Birth of an Ideology—Myths and Symbols of Nations in Late-Medieval France*. Berkeley, CA: University of California Press, 1991.

Bellah, Robert. *Broken Covenant: American Civil Religion in a Time of Trial*. New York: Seabury, 1975.

———. "Civil Religion in America." In *American Civil Religion*, edited by Russell E. Richey and Donald G. Jones, 21–44. New York: Harper & Row, 1974.

Bellamy, Francis. "Americanism in the Public Schools." National Education Association, *Journal of Proceedings and Address: Session of the Year 1892 Held at Saratoga Springs, New York*. New York: National Education Association, 1893.

———. "A New Plan for Counter-Attack on the Nation's Internal Foes," Bellamy Papers, May 1923.

Bibliography

———. "The Newest Movement. What Mr. Bellamy is Doing. A Systematic Effort to Intensify and Elevate the Teaching of Americanism in the Public Schools." Bellamy Papers, 1892.

———. "The Spirit of Americanism—Perils from Immigration—Liberty, Equality, and Fraternity in Relation to the New American Idea." *Portland Daily Press*, January 13, 1893.

Bellware, Daniel, and Richard Gardiner. *The Genesis of the Memorial Day Holiday in America*. Columbus, GA: Columbus State University, 2014.

Bentham, Flip. "I Am Not Ashamed of the American Flag." Dallas: Operation Save America, n.d.

Berrigan, Daniel. *The Nightmare of God*. Portland, OR: Sunburst, 1983.

Boime, Albert. *The Unveiling of the National Icons: A Plea for Patriotic Iconoclasm in a Nationalist Era*. New York: Cambridge University Press, 1997.

Bordelon, Marvin. "Thanksgiving Day." *Worship* 36.10 (November 1962) 655-57.

Brown, George Pliny, ed. *The Public School Journal*, XIII.1 (September 1892).

Brueggemann, Walter. *Israel's Praise: Doxology Against Idolatry and Ideology*. Philadelphia: Fortress, 1988.

———. *Theology of the Old Testament: Testimony, Dispute, Advocacy*. Minneapolis: Augsburg Fortress, 1997.

Brunner, Emil. *The Divine Imperative*. Philadelphia: Westminster, 1947.

Budde, Michael L. *The Borders of Baptism: Identities, Allegiances, and the Church*. Eugene, OR: Cascade, 2011.

Buechner, Frederick. *The Sacred Journey: A Memoir of Early Days*. New York: Harper, 1991.

Burrell, Brian. *The Words We Live By: The Creeds, Mottoes, and Pledges that have Shaped America*. New York: Free Press, 1997.

Byars, Ronald P. "Creeds and Prayers-Ecclesiology." In *A More Profound Alleluia: Theology and Worship in Harmony*, edited by Leanne Van Dyk, 83–108. Grand Rapids: Eerdmans, 2005.

Campbell, Alexander. *Millennial Harbinger*. Vol. 19, 1848.

Canipe, Lee. "The Pledge of Allegiance in Cold War America." *Journal of Church and State*, 45.2 (Spring 2003) 205–323.

Cavanaugh, William T. *Theopolitical Imagination*. New York: T&T Clark, 2002.

———. *Torture and Eucharist: Theology, Politics, and the Body of Christ*. Malden, MA: Blackwell, 1998.

Chauvet, Louis-Marie. *The Sacraments: The Word of God at the Mercy of the Body*. Collegeville, MN: Liturgical, 2001.

Clapp, Rodney. "On the Making of Kings and Christians." In *The Conviction of Things Not Seen: Worship and Ministry in the 21st Century*, edited by Todd E. Johnson, 109–22. Grand Rapids: Brazos, 2002.

Clark, Charles Sidney. "Honors to the Flag in Camp and Armory." *St. Nicholas* 24 (1897) 760–62.

Cochrane, Arthur C. *The Mystery of Peace*. Elgin, IL: Brethren, 1986.

Collins, Herbert Ridgeway. *Threads of History: Americana Recorded on Cloth 1775 to the Present*. Washington, DC: Smithsonian Institution, 1979.

Cooper, Randy. *Being Subject to One Another as We Sing*. The Ekklesia Project, pamphlet #IV. Eugene, OR: Wipf and Stock, 2004.

Craddock, Fred. *Craddock Stories*. St. Louis: Chalice, 2001.

Bibliography

Cushing, John. "A Discourse Delivered at Ashburnham, July 4, 1796." In *Nationalism and Religion in America: Concepts of American Identity and Mission*, edited by Winthrop S. Hudson, 17–19. New York: Harper & Row, 1970.

Davis, Derek H. "The Pledge of Allegiance and American Value." *Journal of Church and State*, 46.2 (Spring 2004) 657–68.

Dreier, Peter, and Dick Flacks. "Patriotism's Secret History." *Nation* (June 3, 2002) 39–42.

Duck, Ruth C. *Worship for the Whole People of God: Vital Worship for the 21st Century*. Louisville: Westminster John Knox, 2013.

Editorial. *Illustrated American* 22/23 (August 28, 2897) 258.

Ellis, Richard J. *To the Flag: The Unlikely History of the Pledge of Allegiance*. Lawrence, KS: University Press of Kansas, 2004.

Ellul, Jacques. "Modern Idolatry." In *The Lion Handbook of Christian Belief*, 253–55. Tring, Hertfordshire: Lion, 1982.

Eslinger, Richard L. "Civil Religion and the Year of Grace." *Worship*, 584 (July 1984) 372–83.

Etzioni, Amitai. "Holidays and Rituals: Neglected Seedbeds of Virtue." In *We Are What We Celebrate: Understanding Holidays and Rituals*, edited by Amitai Etzioni and Jared Bloom, 1–40. New York: New York University Press, 2004.

Evans, Donald. *Struggle and Fulfilment: The Inner Dynamics of Religion and Morality*. Philadelphia: Fortress, 1981.

Fanestil, John. "Border Crossing." *The Christian Century* (October 7, 2008) 22–25.

Gladden, Washington. "The Nation and the Kingdom." In *God's New Israel*, edited by Conrad Cherry, 255–70. Englewood Cliffs, NJ: Prentice-Hall, 1971.

Goldstein, Robert Justin. *Saving Old Glory: The History of the American Flag Desecration Controversy*. Boulder, CO: Westview, 1995.

Guenter, Scot M. *The American Flag, 1777–1924: Cultural Shifts from Creation to Codification*. Cranbury, NJ: Associated University Presses, 1990.

Guthrie, William Norman. *The Religion of Old Glory*. New York: George H. Doran, 1918.

Harrelson, Walter J. *The Ten Commandments and Human Rights*. Macon, GA: Mercer University Press, 1997.

Hauerwas, Stanley. *The Peaceable Kingdom: A Primer in Christian Ethics*. Notre Dame, IN: University of Notre Dame Press, 1983.

———. *War and the American Difference: Theological Reflections on Violence and National Identity*. Grand Rapids: Baker Academic, 2011.

Hayes, Carlton J. H. *Essays on Nationalism*. New York: MacMillan, 1928.

Hendel, Ronald S. "Social Origins of the Aniconic Tradition." *Catholic Biblical Quarterly*, 50 (1988) 365–82.

Heschel, Abraham Joshua. *I Asked for Wonder*. Edited by Samuel H. Dresner. New York: Crossroad, 1983.

Hobsbawm, Eric. *Nations and Nationalism Since 1780: Programme, Myth, Reality*. Cambridge: Cambridge University Press, 1990.

Hotz, Kendra G., and Matthew T. Mathews. *Shaping the Christian Life: Worship and Religious Affections*. Louisville: Westminster John Knox, 2006.

Hoover, A. J. *God, Germany and Britain in the Great War: A Study of Clerical Nationalism*. New York: Praeger, 1989.

Howard-Brook, Wes, and Anthony Gwyther. *Unveiling Empire: Reading Revelation Then and Now*. Maryknoll, NY: Orbis, 1999.

Bibliography

Hudson, Winthrop S. *Nationalism and Religion in America: Concepts of American Identity and Mission*. New York: Harper & Row, 1970.
Hughes, Richard. *Myths Americans Live By*. Champaign, IL: University of Illinois Press, 2004.
Hutchison, William R. and Hartmut Lehmann. *Many Are Chosen: Divine Election and Western Nationalism*. Minneapolis: Fortress, 1994.
Hutchison, William R. "Introduction." In *Many are Chosen: Divine Election and Western Nationalism*, edited by William R. Hutchison and Hartmut Lehmann, 1-25. Minneapolis: Fortress, 1994.
Johnson, Todd E. "Disconnected Rituals." In *The Conviction of Things Not Seen*, edited by Todd E. Johnson, 53-66. Grand Rapids: Brazos, 2002.
Johnson, Todd E., ed. *The Conviction of Things Not Seen*. Grand Rapids: Brazos, 2002.
Jones, Jeffrey Owen, and Peter Meyer. *The Pledge: A History of the Pledge of Allegiance*. New York: St. Martin's, 2010.
Kalb, Judith E. *Russia's Rome: Imperial Visions, Messianic Dreams, 1890-1940*. Madison, WI: University of Wisconsin Press, 2010.
Kavanagh, Aidan. *On Liturgical Theology*. New York: Pueblo, 1984.
Kellogg, Bob. Quoted in "Response Swift to Pledge Ruling." *Family News in Focus* (June 27, 2002).
Kraybill, J. Nelson. *Apocalypse and Allegiance: Worship, Politics and Devotion in the Book of Revelation*. Grand Rapids: Brazos, 2010.
Kselman, Thomas. "Religion and French Identity: The Origins of the *Union Sacree*." In *Many are Chosen: Divine Election and Western Nationalism*, edited by William R. Hutchison and Hartmut Lehmann, 57-79. Minneapolis: Fortress, 1994.
Lathrop, Gordon W. *Holy Ground: A Liturgical Cosmology*. Minneapolis: Fortress, 2009.
———. *Holy Things: A Liturgical Theology*. Minneapolis: Fortress, 1993.
Leepson, Marc. *Flag: An American Biography*. New York: St. Martin's, 2005.
Lehmann, Hartmut. "'God Our Old Ally': The Chosen People Theme in Late Nineteenth And Early Twentieth-Century German Nationalism." In *Many are Chosen: Divine Election and Western Nationalism*, edited by William R. Hutchison and Hartmut Lehmann, 85-107. Minneapolis: Fortress, 1994.
Leithart, Peter J. *Between Babel and Beast: America and Empires in Biblical Perspective*. Eugene, OR: Cascade, 2012.
Lieven, Anatol. *America Right or Wrong: An Anatomy of American Nationalism*. New York: Oxford University Press, 2004.
Longley, Clifford. *Chosen People: The Big Idea that Shapes England and America*. London: Hodder & Stoughton, 2003.
Lossky, Nicholas. "Theology and Prayer: An Orthodox Perspective." In *Ecumenical Theology in Worship, Doctrine and Life*, edited by David S. Cunningham et al., 24-32. New York: Oxford University Press, 1999.
Luther, Martin. "The Large Catechism." In *The Book of Concord*, edited by Theodore G. Tappert. Philadelphia: Fortress, 1959.
Marini, Stephen A. "American Protestant Hymns Project: A Ranked List of Most Frequently Printed Hymns, 1737—1960." In *Wonderful Words of Life: Hymns in American Protestant History and Theology*, edited by Richard J. Mouw and Mark A. Noll, 251-64. Grand Rapids: Eerdmans, 2004.
Marvin, Carolyn, and David W. Ingle. *Blood Sacrifice and the Nation: Totem Rituals and the American Flag*. New York: Cambridge University Press, 1999.

Bibliography

McGann, Mary E. *Exploring Music as Worship and Theology: Research in Liturgical Practice.* Collegeville, MN: Liturgical, 2002.

McKim, Robert, and Jeff McMahan. "Introduction." In *The Morality of Nationalism*, edited by Robert McKim and Jeff McMahan, 3–7. New York: Oxford University Press, 1997.

Melville, Herman. *White Jacket; or, The World in a Man-of-War.* Boston: St. Botolph Society, 1892.

Micks, Marianne. *The Future Present: The Phenomenon to Christian Worship.* New York: Seabury, 1970.

Miller, Patrick D. *The God You Have: Politics, Religion and the First Commandment.* Minneapolis: Augsburg Fortress, 2004.

———. *The Ten Commandments.* Louisville: Westminster John Knox, 2010.

Miscevre, Nerad. "Introduction: The (Im-)Morality of Nationalism." In *Nationalism and Ethnic Conflict: Philosophical Perspectives*, edited by Nerad Miscevic, 1–21. Peru, IL: Open Court, 2000.

Moltmann, Jurgen. *The Coming of God: Christian Eschatology.* Minneapolis: Augsburg, 2004.

Moore, Russell D. "Fly It Responsibly." *Christianity Today*, July-August 2012, 82–84.

Muir, Diana. "Proclaiming Thanksgiving Throughout the Land." In *We Are What We Celebrate: Understanding Holidays and Rituals*, edited by Amitai Etzioni and Jared Bloom, 194–212. New York: New York University Press, 2004.

Muller-Fahrenholz, Geiko. *America's Battle for God.* Grand Rapids: Eerdmans, 2006.

Nandy, Manish. "A Flag in the Church." *DisciplesWorld* (July-August, 2003) 44.

Niebuhr, H. Richard. *The Kingdom of God in America.* New York: Harper & Row, 1937.

O'Leary, Cecilia Elizabeth. *To Die For: The Paradox of American Patriotism.* Princeton, NJ: Princeton University Press, 1999.

Omar, Atalia, and Jason A. Springs. *Religious Nationalism.* Santa Barbara, CA: ABC-CLIO, 2013.

Parsons, Talcott. *Structure of Social Action.* Vol. 1. New York: Free Press, 1967.

Paterson-Smyth, J. *God and War: Some Lessons of the Present Crisis.* London: Hodder and Stoughton, 1905.

Piscitelli, Felicia. "Hymns in Roman Catholic Hymnals." In *Wonderful Words of Life: Hymns in American Protestant History and Theology*, edited by Richard J. Mouw and Mark A. Noll, 269–72. Grand Rapids: Eerdmans, 2004.

Pleck, Elizabeth H. "Who Are We and Where Do We Come From?" In *We Are What We Celebrate: Understanding Holidays and Rituals*, edited by Amitai Etzioni and Jared Bloom, 43–60. New York: New York University Press, 2004.

Rad, Gerhard von. *Deuteronomy.* Translated by Dorothea Barton. Philadelphia: Westminster, 1966.

Richard, Pablo, Barbara E. Campbell, and Bonnie Shepard. "Biblical Theology in Confrontation with Idols." In *The Idols of Death and the God of Life: A Theology*, 3–25. Maryknoll, NY: Orbis, 1983.

Richardson, Cyril, ed. "Letter to Diognetus." *Early Christian Fathers (Library of Christian Classics).* Philadelphia: Westminster, 1953.

Rodeheaver, Homer A. *A Patriotic Exercise for Juniors: Building of the Flag, or Liberty Triumphant.* Chicago: Rodeheaver Co., 1917.

Roland, Richard. "Yes, a Flag in the Church." *DisciplesWorld* (November 2003) 23.

Bibliography

Saliers, Donald. *Worship as Theology: Foretaste of Glory Divine*. Nashville: Abingdon, 1994.
Salmond, Alex. "Preface." In *National Days: Constructing and Mobilizing National Identity*, edited by David McCrone and Gayle McPherson, xiii–xv. New York: Palgrave Macmillan, 2009.
Smith, H. Augustine. *A Pageant of the Stars and Stripes*. Boston: American Institute of Religious Education, 1918.
Smith, James K. A. *Desiring the Kingdom: Worship, Worldview, and Cultural Formation*. Grand Rapids: Baker Academic, 2009.
Smith, Larry D. "We Pledge the Flag; We Say the Creed." *God's Revivalist and Bible Advocate* (November 2001) 26–27.
Snyder, Louis. *The Meaning of Nationalism*. Westport, CT: Greenwood, 1968.
Stevens, Leonard A. *Salute!: The Case of the Bible vs. the Flag*. New York: Coward, McCann and Geoghegan, 1977.
Stiles, Ezra. "The United States Elevated to Glory and Honor." In *God's New Israel: Religious Interpretations of American*, edited by Conrad Cherry, 82–92. Englewood Cliffs, NJ: Prentice Hall, 1971.
Stookey, Laurence Hull. *Calendar: Christ's Time in the Church*. Nashville: Abington, 1996.
Tacitus, *Agricola*. Translated by M. Hutton and R.M. Ogilvie. Cambridge, MA: Harvard University Press, 1970.
Taylor, Charles. *Modern Social Imaginaries*. Durham, NC: Duke University Press, 2004.
———. "Nationalism and Modernity." In *The Morality of Nationalism*, edited by Robert McKim and Jeff McMahan, 31–55. New York: Oxford University Press, 1997.
US President. *Public Papers of the Presidents of the United States* (Washington, DC: U.S. Government Printing Office, 1958).
Volf, Miroslav. *The End of Memory: Remembering in a Violent World*. Grand Rapids: Eerdmans, 2006.
———. *A Public Faith: How Followers of Christ Should Serve the Common Good*. Grand Rapids: Brazos, 2013.
Wainwright, Geoffrey. *Doxology: The Praise of God in Worship, Doctrine, and Life*. New York: Oxford University Press, 1980.
———. *Worship With One Accord: Where Liturgy and Ecumenism Embrace*. New York: Oxford University Press, 1997.
Wallace, David Foster. *Infinite Jest: A Novel*. Boston: Little, Brown and Company, 1996.
Walls, A. F. "Carrying the White Man's Burden: Some British Views of National Vocation in the Imperial Age." In *Many are Chosen: Divine Election and Western Nationalism*, edited by William R. Hutchison and Hartmut Lehmann, 29–50. Minneapolis: Fortress, 1994.
Wannenwetsch, Bernd. "The Desire of Desire: Commandment and Idolatry in Late Capitalist Societies." In *Idolatry: False Worship in the Bible, Early Judaism and Christianity*, edited by Stephen C. Barton, 315–30. London: T & T Clark, 2007.
Warner, W. Lloyd. *American Life: Dream and Reality*. Chicago: University of Chicago Press, 1962.
Weil, Simone. *The Simone Weil Reader*. Edited by George A. Panichas. New York: David McKay Co., 1977.
Welch, Michael. *Flag Burning: Moral Panic and the Criminalization of Protest*. New York: Walter de Gruyter, 2000.

Bibliography

West, James Lee. "A Native American's Reflection on Thanksgiving." *Andover Newton Quarterly*, 11.1 (September 1970) 12–16.

Willimon, William. *The Service of God: How Worship and Ethics are Related*. Nashville: Abingdon, 1983.

Wills, Anne Blue. "Pilgrims and Progress: How Magazines Made Thanksgiving." *Church History*, 72.1 (March 2003) 138–58.

Winship, A. E. "The Mission of Music in the Public School." In *Music Education: Source Readings from Ancient Greece to Today*, 2nd ed., edited by Michael L. Mark, 97–99. London: Routledge, 2002.

Zelinsky, Wilbur. *Nation Into State: the Shifting Foundations of American Nationalism*. Chapel Hill: University of North Carolina Press, 1988.

Index

Aaron, 22
Adams, Gridley, 117
affections, religious, 36–37
Agnus Dei symbol, 13–14
Alberty, Kent, 124
All Saints' Day, 74–75, 83–84
All Souls' Day, 74–75
America
    associated with biblical Israel, 52–53
    as chosen nation, 52–54
    military budget of, 61
    as new Babylon, 60–63
    as New Israel, 50
"America," 141–42
"America the Beautiful," 142
American Civil Liberties Union, 119, 120–21
American expansionism, 53
American flag. *See* national flag
American Legion, 99, 122
"The American Patriotic Salute," 112–13
Americanism, new, 116
Americanized god, 8–9
Anderson, Benedict, 136
Anderson, Branden P., 79–80
Augustine, 137, 140
Aylmer, John, 59

Babylon/Babylonians
    as gift to the world, 17
    as the Great Whore, 17–18
    idolatrous worship, 15
    Jeremiah's instruction to, 15–16
    living faithfully in, 15
    as a metaphor, 11–12, 16
    spiritual significance of, 14, 60
    sustained by idolatry, 17–18
Bader-Saye, Scott, 71–72
Balch, George T., 93, 112–13
baptism
    as birth into family of faith, 152
    clothed in Christ, 149
    creating a new nation, 153
    creating an international incident, 157
    creating commitment for the good of all, 157
    death associated with, 148–49
    for hope of kingdom of God, 155
    objective of, 148
    to resist nationalism impulses, 147
    transforming boundaries, 150–54
    as work of God, 152
"Baptism Creates International Incident" (Roseberry), 155–57
Barber, Hiram, Jr., 97
Barnette, West Virginia v., 122–23
Barth, Karl, 151–52
Bass, Diana Butler, 133
Bates, Katharine, 142
Bauer-King, Nancy, 145
Bellah, Robert, 9
Bellamy, Francis, 113–14, 117, 124
Benham, Flip, 105–6
Berlin, Irving, 142–43

177

Index

Berrigan, Daniel, 60
Berry, E. Y., 100
Bradford, William, 50, 85
Brown, W. P., 119–120
Brueggemann, Walter, 21, 44–45, 144
Brunner, Emil, 7
Budde, Michael L., 10–11, 83
Building of the Flag, or Liberty Triumphant (Rodeheaver), 94
Bush, George H.W., 101, 102
Bush, George W., 54

Caesar Augustus, 17, 29, 111
calendars, 68–69. *See also* church calendar
Campbell, Alexander, 149
Campolo, Tony, 61
Canipe, Lee, 126
capitalism, 116
Cavanaugh, William T., 10, 166, 167
ceremonial deism, 127
Charles I, King of England, 59
Chauvet, Louis-Marie, 154
chosen nations, 55–60
chosenness, 50, 54–55
Christian flag, 94. *See also* national flag
Christian unity, 162–65
Christian worship. *See* worship
church calendar
  All Saints' Day, 74–75, 83–84
  Easter, 73
  incarnational cycle, 74
  Ordinary Time, 74
  paschal cycle, 74
  Pentecost, 73–74
  sanctoral cycle, 74, 83–84
Church of England, 58–59
churches
  American flag placed in, 92–93
  as community of faith, 36
  conception of time, 71–75
  disciples Christians in Americanism, 12
  flag idolatry in, 104–9
  manifested in communities of faith, 63–64
  Memorial Day activities in, 82–83
  transcends boundaries, 10

civil disobedience, 163–64
civil religion, 8–9
Columbian Exposition, 113–14
Columbus Day, 114–15
community of faith, 34–36, 63–64, 73, 108, 132, 145, 157
Constantine, 55
Cotton, John, 51–52
Cox, Sullivan, 97
Craddock, Fred, 5
Crammer, Thomas, 58
Creator vs. creature, 39
Cushing, John, 52–53, 77

Daoud, Alex, 102
Daughters of the American Revolution (DAR), 92, 112
Davis, Derek H., 127
Decoration Day, 80
Dobson, James, 126
Docherty, George M., 125
Dostoyevsky, Fyodor, 57
Dr. Martin Luther King Jr. Day, 74

Easter, 73
ecumenical creeds, 127–130
Edward VI, King of England, 58–59
Eichman, U.S. v., 102
Eighth Day of the week, 72
Eisenhower, Dwight D., 124, 125
Elijah Voice Society, 119
Ellis, Richard, 113, 117
Ellul, Jacques, 24
England, as chosen nation, 58–60
Epistle of Barnabas, 72
eschatological gathering, 10, 144, 166–67
Eslinger, Richard L., 84
Etzioni, Amitai, 76
Eucharist
  Christian unity, 162–65
  eschatological import and, 166–67
  overcoming alienation that separate peoples, 167–68
  redemptively remembering at, 159–160
  remembering that takes place at, 165
  as thanksgiving meal, 159

Index

Evans, Daniel, 19
Exodus, 22–23

faith identity, 32
Fanestil, John, 164
Finney, Charles, 138
First Commandment, 19–20, 24
"First Thanksgiving" story, 84–86
flag. *See* national flag
Flag Code, 99
Flag Day, 100, 106, 122
Flag Protection Act of 1989, 101–2
Ford, Daniel, 115
Fourth of July, 77–80
France, as chosen nation, 57–58
Frankfurter, Felix, 121
Friendship Park, 163–64

Germany, as chosen nation, 57
Giuliani, Rudy, 19
Gobitis, Minersville School District v., 121
God
   expressing gratitude in worship, 87
   linking to country, 113
   name used in vain, 125–27
   of nationalism vs. one revealed in Jesus Christ, 126
   public praise of, 140
   as rightful object of worship, 66
   self-promotion vs. glorification of, 37–38
   special covenant with America, 79
   worthiness of, 41–42
"God Bless America," 142–43
golden calf, 22–23
Goldstein, Robert Justin, 101
governing authorities, submission to, 29–30
Grand Army of the Republic (GAR), 92
gratitude, 27–28
Gue, George, 93
Guenter, Scot, 113
Guthrie, William Norman, 95–96
Gwyther, Anthony, 17

Hale, Sarah Josepha, 86
Haley, James, 100–101

Halter v. Nebraska, 97–98
Harrelson, Walter, 22
Harrison, Benjamin, 114–15
Hart, Kenneth, 30
Hatch, Orrin, 102
Hauerwas, Stanley, 61, 127, 147
Henry VIII, King of England, 58
Heschel, Abraham Joshua, 43
holidays. *See* national holidays
Holtz, Kendra G., 33, 149, 164
Holy Communion, 158–162
Holy Roman Empire, 55–56
Howard-Brook, Wes, 17
human greatness, 37
humility, 27–28
Hutchison, William, 56–57
hymns
   definition of, 140
   as expression of idolatry, 140
   of witness, 140

"I Am Old Glory" (poem), 104–5
"I Am the American Flag" (poem), 104–5
identity
   in community, 36–37
   confusing, 33–36
   faith, 32
   national, 32
idolatrous worship, 15, 20
idolatry
   alongside God, 24
   American flag as, 104–9
   as communal commitment, 21
   forbidding images of, 20
   hymns and, 140
   of Israelites, 22–23
   linked with political power of rulers, 21–22
   recognizing, 19
   temptation in wilderness and, 24
   undermining human value, 20–21
   U.S. military, 61
Ignatius, 72
image of god, 37, 44
immigrants, 117
Imperium christianum, 55
Independence Day, 77–80

Index

Infinite Jest (Wallace), 129–130
Ingle, David W., 24, 105, 108

Jackson, Robert, 122–23
James I, King of England, 59
Jehovah's Witnesses, 119–122
Jeremiah, 15–16, 19, 20
Joan of Arc, 57–58
Johnson, Lyndon, 80
Johnson, Texas v., 101
Joshua, 20
Judah, 14

Kavanagh, Aidan, 129
Key, Francis Scott, 141
Knights of Columbus, 124

Ladies Memorial Association, 80
Lamb of God symbol, 13–14
Lathrop, Gordon, 66–67, 150
Leithart, Peter, 12, 33
life-or-death sacrifice, 25
liturgical calendar, 74–75
local worship, 63–67
Lord's Supper. *See* Eucharist
Lossky, Nicholas, 140
loyalty
    definition of, 46
    idolatry and, 21–22
    multiple claims of, 20
    to the nation, 47
    nation vs. God, 8
    through baptism, 150–51
Luther, Martin, 20–21

Marvin, Carolyn, 24, 105, 108
Mary, Queen of England, 59
Masciotra, David, 82–83
Massachusetts Bay Colony, 51, 89–90
Massasoit, 85
material intermediaries, 22
Mathews, Matthew T., 33, 36, 149, 164
McGann, Mary, 132, 144
McKim, Robert, 7–8
McMahan, Jeff, 7–8
The Meaning of Nationalism (Snyder), 6
Memorial Day, 80–84

"A Memorial Day Challenge" sermon, 82
Messianic banquet, 165–68
Methods for Teaching Patriotism in Public Schools (Balch), 93
Michelet, Jules, 58
Micks, Marianne, 72, 133
military, idolatrous adoration of, 61
Miller, Charles Kingsbury, 97
Miller, Patrick, 24, 144–45
Minersville School District v. Gobitis, 121
Moltmann, Jurgen, 56
Monotheism, 23
Moore, Russell D., 107–8
"The Moral Meanings of the World War" (sermon), 54
Moses, 20
Muir, Diana, 86
music. *See also* patriotic music; song/singing
    to bypass the mind and penetrate the soul, 134
    in church, controversy of, 137
    connective power of, 135–36
    expressions in ritual events, 132
    renews emotion and memory, 134–36
"My Country 'Tis of Thee," 141–42

National Day of Prayer, 88
national flag. *See also* Christian flag
    to advertise products, 96
    anti-desecration legislation, 97, 100
    associated with war, 106
    burning of, 100–103
    as Christian symbol, 105–6
    conveying inclusiveness, 107
    desecration of, 98, 100–103
    disloyalty act (Texas), 98
    displayed in other countries, 108–9, 112
    displaying, 91–92
    as essential symbol at worship, 88–89
    etiquette, 99
    of first European settlers in America, 89–90

Index

Flag Code, 99
  honoring, 112–13
  idolatry in churches, 104–9
  inculcating children into cult of, 112–13
  placed in churches, 92–93
  propagating war, 94
  protection laws, 97–98, 101–2
  religious meaning in, 90–91, 106–7
  sacredness of, 96–97
  schoolhouse flag movement, 112–15
  use of, 90
National Flag Conference, 115
national holidays
  celebrated in churches, 75–77
  Columbus Day, 114–15
  Dr. Martin Luther King Jr. Day, 74
  effectiveness of, 69–70
  Independence Day, 77–80
  Memorial Day, 80–84
  spirituality of, 76
  Thanksgiving Day, 84–87
national identity, 32
national loyalty, 47
national unity, 121
nationalism
  biblically justify, 28–30
  building walls around the imagination, 158
  definitions of, 7
  expressing in worship, 3–4
  life-or-death sacrifice and, 25
  liturgy of, 45–48
  loyalty and, 8
  loyalty claims, 7–9
  merging of religious faith and, 8
  as precedence over religion, 48
  religious, 7
  rituals, pressure to participate in, 123
  spirituality of, 76–77, 81
nation-state, 46–47
Nebraska, Halter v., 97–98
needs of the people, 30–31
new Americanism, 116
Nicholls, Carlton, 120
Niebuhr, H. R., 53

Omar, Atalia, 7

Ordinary Time, 74
Our Country's Flag (Gue), 93
Owsley, Alvin, 99

A Pageant of the Stars and Stripes (Smith), 94–95
pastoral care, 30–31
Paterson-Smyth, J., 59–60
patriotic music. *See also* music; song/singing
  "America," 141–42
  "America the Beautiful," 142
  for character formation, 132
  "God Bless America," 142–43
  as a hymn, 140–45
  "My Country 'Tis of Thee," 141–42
  not intrinsic to Christian faith, 139
  in public school, 132
  renews emotion and memory, 135
  "The Star Spangled Banner," 90, 141
patriotic worship, 26–27, 30
patriotism, 5–7
Patterson, Marvin, 82
Patti, Frank, 102
Patuxet tribe, 85
Paul, Apostle, 73, 148–49, 152, 153, 160–61
Paxton, John R., 92–93
Pentateuch, 58
Pentecost, 73–74
personal identity, 36
personal patriotism, 5–7
pilgrims, 50–51, 85
Pledge of Allegiance
  to advance Americanism, 118
  background of, 111–18
  on church websites, 110–11
  drafting of, 115
  immigrant assimilation through, 117
  insertion of "God" in, 124–27
  Jehovites and, 119
  meaning and motives, 116
  Mennonites and, 118–19
  for national unity, 121
  objections to, 118–19
  passion for, 118–124
  religiously based refusal of, 118–123
  revisions to, 124–27

Index

Pledge of Allegiance *(continued)*
   socialism and, 115–17
Plymouth Colony, 50–51
political idolatry, 19–25
Pollitt, Katha, 103
Powell, Gerland W., 99
Prager, Robert Paul, 98–99
"Prayer for Our Military—A Prayer for America" poster, 33–35
pride, 5, 15, 33, 35, 42, 61–62, 151
Protestant Reformation, 57
Puritans, 51–52, 59, 78–79
Puteoli, 18

Reagan, Ronald, 106
realized eschatology, 144
Rehnquist, William, 101
Rehoboam, 23
The Religion of Old Glory (Guthrie), 95–96
religious affections, 36–37
religious nationalism, 7
Religious Right, 54
Richard, Pablo, 21
ritual events, musical expressions in, 132
ritual signing, 139
Rodeheaver, Homer A., 94
Rogers, Adrian, 79
Roman classicism, 52
Roman Empire, 55–56
Rome, 16
Roosevelt, Franklin D., 99
Roseberry, David, 155–57
Russia, as chosen nation, 57
Rutherford, Joseph, 120

Sabbath, 72–73
sacraments
   baptism, 148–150
   definition of, 147
   Eucharist, 158–162
   imprint identity and bear witness to unity in Christ, 147–48
sacrifice and death, 25
Saliers, Don, 44, 66
Salmond, Alex, 69
Sanctoral Cycle, 74

schoolhouse flag movement, 112–15
Schutz, Alfred, 132
Second Commandment, 20, 22
the self, killed in baptism, 149
self-importance, 35
self-referential, 37
Service for God and Country (Powell), 99
Shirley, Jerry, 82
Smith, H. Augustine, 94–95
Smith, James K.A., 45
Smith, Samuel Francis, 141–42
Snyder, Louis, 6
"So Much to Remember" sermon, 82
social citizenry, 113–14
social imaginaries, 45
socialism, 115–17
"A Song of Peace" (hymn), 6
song/singing. *See also* music
   to give thanks, 137–38
   proclaiming Christian truth through, 133–34
   as rehearsal of God's interaction with God's people, 133–34
   to serve ends God has for us, 137
Spanish-American War, 94
spiritual location, 49
spirituality, expressed in nationalist holidays, 76–77, 81
Springs, Jason A., 7
Squanto, 85
St Nicholas (children's magazine), 112
"The Star Spangled Banner," 90, 141
Starr, E. V., 98
Starr, Kenneth, 101
Stevens, Leonard A., 123
Stiles, Ezra, 53
Stowe, Harriet Beecher, 91
Stuttgart Confession of Guilt, 57
Suetonius, 18
Sundays, as the Lord's Day, 72–73

Tacitus, 17
Taylor, Charles, 45
Texas v. Johnson, 101
Thanksgiving Day, 84–87
theological integrity, 31
Tooley, Michael, 108

Index

transcendence of God, 22–23, 126
transcendence of religious faith, 125
transformation, 43–44, 163–64
translatio imperii, 56
Tremain, Russell, 119
Truman, Harry, 100
Tyler, Scott, 102
Tyndale, William, 58

United States. *See* America
United States Flag Association, 118
unity, Christian, 9–11, 162–65
universal loyalty, 7
Upham, James, 115
U.S. Ninth Circuit Court of Appeals, 126
U.S. Supreme Court, 97–98, 101, 102, 121, 127
U.S. v. Eichman, 102

Vischer, Lukas, 33
visible material intermediaries, 22
Volf, Miroslav, 63, 83
Von Rad, Gerhard, 19–20

Wainwright, Geoffrey, 128, 134, 140
Wallace, David Foster, 129–130
Wampanoag tribe, 85
Ward, Samuel Augustus, 142
Warner, W. Lloyd, 76, 80
Washington, George, 86
Washington Gladden, 53
Washington High School, 123–24
Watkinson, W. L., 59
Weil, Simone, 24
West, James Lee, 85–86
West Virginia v. Barnette, 122–23
Whitten, David, 81–82
Wills, Anne Blue, 85, 86
Wilson, Woodrow, 98, 100
Winship, A. E., 132
Winthrop, John, 51
Women's Relief Corps, 80

worship
  accommodation and, 64
  as act of pastoral care, 30
  acts of, 35–36, 40
  adoration in, 33
  affections to form temperament, 36–37
  biblically justify nationalism in, 28–30
  confessing creeds in, 129
  creative freedom in, 65
  cultural forms used in, 64–66
  definition of, 25, 41
  forms character, 36
  gratitude expressed to God in, 87
  to honor one nation and its flag, 2
  local, 63–67
  as meaningful for us, 42–43
  national flag as essential symbol at, 88–89
  nationalism expressed in, 3–4, 26, 38
  nationalistic holidays celebrated in, 70, 75–77
  needs of the people and, 30–31
  patriotic, 26–27
  patriotic songs in, 138–39
  purpose of, 41
  removing flag at, 88
  to resist seductive lure of America, 62
  serving our purpose, 42–43
  shaped around story of Jesus, 42–43
  shapes heart of church, 40
  subverting transformative effects of, 65
  as transformative, 43–44
  worthiness of God in, 41–42

Yahwehist idolatry, 21, 23
The Youth's Companion (magazine), 113–14

Zelinsky, Wilbur, 89

www.ingramcontent.com/pod-product-compliance
Lightning Source LLC
Chambersburg PA
CBHW031433150426
43191CB00006B/489